Professionals Commend
Serafina Corsello, MD

❧

"...I have read over one hundred books on female health issues and have found *The Ageless Woman* to be the most readable and comprehensive...."

— From the Foreword by Jeffrey Bland, PhD
President, Institute for Functional Medicine

"Given the many options to cure ailments, a physician needs to be familiar with all the approaches. Dr. Corsello has the knowledge and sensitivity to match the cure with the patient's specific needs. I first benefited from this approach as her patient and have since enthusiastically supported her work. As a reproductive endocrinologist and an Indian trained in Ayurvedic medicine, I appreciate her understanding and skill at combining ancient knowledge with the latest medical tools. Her patients are very fortunate.

— Satty Gill Keswani, MD, FACOG

"As a physician, it was uniquely refreshing for me to find a practitioner who is comfortable with alternative remedies without having forfeited a facile working knowledge of advanced biochemistry and pharmaceutical mechanisms. ... I have never met a MD with such a superb balance of the two, which she uses with remarkable effectiveness and powerful insight."

— Danielle J. Kenny, MD

"Dr. Serafina Corsello is one of the few rejuvenating therapies experts in the United States. *The Ageless Woman* is essential reading for every woman interested in maintaining optimal health into their 50s, 60s, 70s and beyond."

— Carolyn DeMarco, MD
Author *Take Charge of Your Body*

"Having been involved in the field of nutrition for more than half a century, I have never met anyone who could match Dr. Corsello's genius for understanding human biochemistry – a gift that she skillfully uses in helping the most sick and debilitated get well."

— Betty Kamen, PhD
Nutritionist and Author

Patients Praise
Serafina Corsello, MD

"This enigmatic and energetic woman is such a powerful life force. She changed my health and my life. I went to her feeling 20 years older than I am and under her care I feel 20 years younger than I am."

— Terri Schug

"As I was approaching menopause, I didn't want to go the conventional route, where Premarin and Provera become the 'magical cure' for every woman. I wanted to find a doctor who was in sync with my natural, health-promoting lifestyle. That doctor is Serafina Corsello. Natural hormone replacement therapy has restored my old – now younger self. I'm feeling better than ever – energetic, healthy and happy."

— Rachelle Weisberger

"I brought my 7-year-old daughter, diagnosed with severe rheumatoid arthritis, to Dr. Corsello in 1997, after having exhausted the most renowned hospitals and doctors in the Northeast. They put my daughter on high doses of steroids and told me that she would be dead or severely crippled within 10 years. As a RN, I knew the long-term devastation those medications would have on Meggie.

"From the moment Meggie and I walked into Dr. Corsello's office we were given hope, although we were told to expect a battle. Now 2½ years later, Meggie, who has not taken any conventional medications in 20 months, runs, gets all 'A's' in school, fights with her brother and has recently taken to stuffing her undershirt with tissues for 'boobs' – a normal, healthy 10-year old. Meggie wants to take over Dr. Corsello's practice after she becomes a doctor.

"'You know, Mom, I mean only after Dr. Corsello gets real old – not sick – but maybe wants to grow a big organic garden!'"

— Camille Harlow

"Dr. Corsello has a special gift. She is not only a formidable healer, she is also a wonderful teacher – and that is a blessed thing."

— Susan Merians

"My twin sister and I are lawyers/actresses, former teachers and interior designers, who have finally found the fuel for our *joie de vivre*. After 4 months in the hands of Dr. Corsello, the problems I have suffered with for 20 years – digestive disturbances, yeast, diarrhea, fatigue and flu-like symptoms are gone. I am the person I was 20 years ago, rejuvenated – and more excited, more powerful than ever – thanks to the highest level of holistic medicine practiced by Dr. Corsello."

— Roni Pall

"I have been all over looking for a doctor who could give me total care and a feeling of security. After only 2 months on Dr. Corsello's program, I feel wonderful. Her concern for body, mind and spirit leaves nothing neglected. I am so grateful for her tender, loving care."

— Connie Silveri

The
AGELESS
WOMAN

Serafina Corsello, MD

CCI

The purpose of this book is educational and by no means should be considered an alternative to appropriate medical care. Although the author made her best effort to ensure that the information presented in this book is accurate, there is a constant flow of new research, and it is possible that some of the data presented here may be invalidated. The author and publisher expressly disclaim responsibility for any adverse effects arising from the use or application of the information contained in this book.

Cover Art:	Monica Miller Kinderhook, NY
Cover Design:	Ed Atkeson/Berg Design Albany, NY
Text Design & Illustrations:	Gail Hada-Insley Design Rancho Palos Verdes, CA
Author Photograph:	Christophe Von Hohenburg New York, NY
Writer:	Sherry Kahn Los Angeles, CA
Copyeditor:	Gita Brenner/Professional Papers Associates New York, NY

Corsello Communications, Inc.
200 W. 57th Street
New York, NY 10019
Website: http//www.corsello.com

Printed in the United States of America.

ISBN 0-9672219-0-0

This book is dedicated to my daughter,
Paola.

Acknowledgements

Back in March 1998, which now seems like eons ago, I was approached by one of my listeners as I left the podium, after lecturing on women's health issues at a large integrative medicine conference in Los Angeles.

She said, "I have been sent by a New York literary agent, who knows many of your patients, and she wants to know why you don't have a book about all the innovative things you do."

My answer was, "I have not yet found someone who can express my concepts in a readable yet harmonic way."

She looked at me and said, "I might be that someone."

Then and there began the alliance that has made this book possible.

Sherry Kahn has been able, through a very laborious process, to make my holographic, convoluted, interactive concepts more linear and accessible, without losing "the music." As the great yogi teachers say, "The master comes when the student is ready." I know it was God's will that Sherry and I would get together. She has been able to translate nearly 40 years of clinical experience into reader-friendly language. I am very grateful to her for her "labor of love," and I commend her fantastic skills, intelligence, sensitivity, and above all, her ability to grab the fire and turn it into a sphere of love.

I am very grateful to painter Monica Miller, who brilliantly translated my vision of *The Ageless Woman* into a most magnificent painting, from which the cover art was photographed. Ed Atkeson very skillfully designed the book cover to support Monica's art, while Gail Hada-Insley gracefully carried my vision into the text design. I also appreciate Gita Brenner's painstaking copyediting.

My thanks also goes to my wonderful staff, all of those present and past, who have assisted me in making my vision of "good medicine" a reality. In particular, I thank Jennifer

Heuman, Catherine Kelly and Hal Hance. Jennifer, who has been associated with me for many years, continues to have the patience of an angel in translating my scribble into typed prose. She has put in many, many hours in the doing and re-doing of this book. Catherine Kelly, whose devotion and indefatigability is a great gift to me, has carefully overseen the organizational details of this involved process. And Hal Hance has attended to whatever else I needed done on this project, with good grace and good humor.

I am also very appreciative of the efforts of Eleanor Barrager of HealthComm International, Inc. and Genesis Center for Integrative Medicine, who put her technical eye to the manuscript and very willingly provided needed research articles. Barbara Schiltz, currently a staff member of HealthComm International, Inc., was also very generous in supplying research materials. Our association and bond goes way back to the time when she was head nurse in my Manhattan Center. Nutritionist and author Betty Kamen is the epitome of *The Ageless Woman*, and I am very grateful for her long-term and bountiful support. And my thanks also goes to George Klabin of Klabin Marketing, who has generously supported me with invaluable technical advice.

Of course, my patients have taught me much of what I know. They have encouraged me with their wonderful support and their desire to see my precepts in print. Their love and devotion have given me the stamina to put in the long hours that my clinical practice requires, yet devote any free moment and all my weekends to this wonderful endeavor.

I hope the collective efforts of all these people make the presentation of my clinical experience a worthwhile voyage, which will enrich the souls, hearts and minds of my readers.

Contents

*The Graying of America *What is Aging?
*We're Getting Older Sooner *The Dynamics of
Health and Wellness *Premature Aging Unrecognized
*Aging Theories *Cellular Changes *Under the
Microscope *Free Radicals Cause Disease *New
Understandings About Aging *Longevity *The Choice

*Multiple Factors *The Best Approach *Genes and
Reserves Play Their Part *Aging Versus Rejuvenating

*A New Paradigm *What Genes Do *Lifestyle
Influences Genetic Expression *Genetic Glitches
*Organ Reserves and Aging *Maintaining Cellular
Energy *Maximize Your Heritage

*Balance is Key *Mind-Immunity Connection
*Psychological Wellness *Spiritual Wellness
*Nature *Music *Meditation *Prayer *The Power of
the Positive *Affirmations *Mental Exercise *People
Need People *Happiness *Humor

*Lifestyle Makes a Difference *Stress *Diet General
Nutrition Guidelines *Dysglycemia *The Diet Theory
Maze *Nutritional Supplements *Exercise

Foreword

The Ageless Woman is the book that many of us have been waiting for, written by the author we thought was best for the assignment. I have had the privilege of knowing Serafina Corsello, MD for the past 20 years. She is a high energy, life-long learner who blends extraordinary clinical skills with a probing mind looking for new answers to the health challenges that her patients bring to her. Her busy New York medical practices have provided her with a "laboratory" to evaluate the value of conventional and integrated/functional medical therapies with her diverse patient population. She has developed a truly unique and successful approach to female health problems as a consequence of these experiences and the intellectual rigor that she has employed in making her assessments of what works and what doesn't.

In *The Ageless Woman,* she describes her own journey in evolving her medical practice through the experiences that she has had with thousands of patients. As the president of the Institute for Functional Medicine I am proud that she calls herself an integrative/functional medicine practitioner. Functional medicine has been said by some to be plain old "good medicine." It is using the right tools at the right times for specific patients to improve their overall function. Functional medicine doesn't just treat symptoms, but rather helps improve overall function, and in so doing, prevents later stage, more serious illness.

Dr. Corsello is an expert in knowing how, when and why to use various integrated therapies to improve the health and quality of life of her patients. As such, she is one of the leaders in both integrated and functional medicine. As has been said by some about present day medicine, "If all you have is a hammer, then everything is a nail." As an expert in functional/integrative medicine, Dr. Corsello has more tools in her toolkit and therefore is able to tailor the therapy to meet the needs of the individual patient. This concept is beautifully described in *The Ageless Woman* using numerous case histories, the medical/scientific literature and simple summary action points as teaching tools.

I have read over one hundred books on female health issues, and I found *The Ageless Woman* to be the most readable and comprehensive. I was very pleased to see that Dr. Corsello discusses the mind/body issues in health and healing in a style that blends Western reductionistic methods with Eastern intuitive and vitalistic concepts. This helps set the tone of the book as balanced and providing a "whole person" reading experience.

I particularly found the chapters on female hormones, menopause and maintaining energy balance after age 40 to be of great insight and clinical wisdom. There is significant "genius" in this book that comes from decades of dedication as a doctor and observing patterns in patients, which results in new therapeutic insights.

I thank Dr. Corsello for her contribution in helping to make complex concepts understandable and for providing sensible approaches to the achievement of healthy aging. I know that *The Ageless Woman* will be of tremendous value not only for the women who follow its suggestions, but also for men, who can implement many of the recommendations that are applicable to us all.

Jeffrey Bland, PhD
President, Institute of Functional Medicine

Prologue
∾

In the last 35 years, a plethora of terms, all trying to describe the complex array of nonconventional medical interventions, has flooded the collective consciousness here and abroad. Let me shed some light on this most interesting phenomenon: the attempt to put a recognizable label on a most revolutionary paradigm shift.

Conventional medicine, also known as *allopathic medicine*, began in the 1930s to effectively suppress all other forms of medical practices, such as homeopathy and other naturopathic interventions that prestigious European physicians had brought to this country at the turn of the century. Conventional medicine's main tools include drugs, surgery, and invasive high-tech diagnostic tests and therapies. I call this form of medical practice *mainstream medicine*, as it is still the most prevalent model.

Holistic medicine, a term that has been around since the early '60s, describes a paradigm that has turned out to be a harbinger of the revolution that has brought us to our current state of medical awareness. It is a term that took issue sociologically and politically with the Cartesian view of conventional medicine that separated the body from the mind. The term holistic medicine has, over the last few decades, come to describe any medical intervention that takes into account our wholeness – body, mind and spirit – and it has been more loosely used to describe any intervention that isn't mainstream.

The term *alternative medicine* emerged in the early '70s to define a group of nonconventional approaches that include homeopathy, nutritional medicine, acupuncture, massage therapy, energy balancing – and any other tools not in the domain of mainstream medicine. The practice of alternative medicine is not limited to physicians, as some modalities, such as massage and energy therapies, do not require medical licensure. Around the same time, in England, conventional physicians began to include homeopathy and other forms of alternative therapies in their practices. The term *complementary medicine* was coined there (by Prince Charles, I am told) to describe the practice of "complementing" conventional medicine with alternative approaches.

In the '90s, another descriptive term has emerged – *integrative medicine*. I personally like this term because it more closely fits my conceptual model of medicine and doesn't make a value judgement about one system of practice being superior or inferior to another. An integrative physician chooses from a vast array of medical options, which meet the needs of individual patients. These options include phytotherapy (herbal medicine) from China, India and our own Native Americans, homeopathy, energy balancing, nutritional medicine (including intramuscular injection and intravenous infusion of large quantities of antioxidants and other nutrients), chelation therapy and behavioral medicine (biofeedback, meditation, etc.). Appropriate modalities are selected and combined, utilizing the knowledge accumulated from conventional medical training and years of clinical practice. This is the type of medical practice futurist Alvin Toffler described many years ago in his visionary *Third Wave*.[1] What is so exciting about practicing integrative healthcare today is that a knowledgeable physician can select the best of all medicines from all traditions – natural and conventional – to provide the best possible care.

Let me now introduce the most recent addition to the "new medicine" vocabulary: functional medicine. This term describes a practice of medicine based on the study of cellular and organ functions. The emphasis is on diagnostically spotting early preclinical changes and reversing these malfunctions before they progress to a disease state. The leading expert and proponent of *functional medicine* is biochemist Dr. Jeffrey Bland, president of the Institute for Functional Medicine, and CEO and director of research of HealthComm International, Inc., located near Seattle, Washington.[2] He has been teaching this exciting new approach to many integrative healthcare practitioners, both in the United States and abroad.

I am an integrative healthcare physician who practices functional medicine. Subtle functional disturbances can be easily corrected in the early stages; but, if left untreated, they can lead to permanent damage. While severe deficiencies manifest themselves in visible disease processes, *insufficiencies* can only be identified by functional medicine diagnostic means, which currently are not widely accepted and are rarely reimbursable by insurance companies. In functional medicine, we can, for instance, detect early defects in vitamin B_1, often seen in alcoholics, by measuring transketolase, an enzyme that is vitamin B_1 dependent. Early intervention with vitamin B_1 injections can preclude the nerve damage that is one of the serious consequences of this disease. Pernicious anemia, a vitamin B_{12} deficiency that can cause permanent damage of the spinal cord, can be diagnosed by measuring the level of methylmalonic acid. Medical researchers have reported post mortem findings of unsuspected vitamin B_{12} deficiency in the choroid plexuses (the spongy part of the brain) of Alzheimer's patients. Injection of large doses of vitamin B_{12} (2,000 – 5,000 micrograms) weekly, as part of a comprehensive approach, can alleviate or prevent the disease.

Unfortunately, new medical findings typically don't enter mainstream consciousness until 30 years after their discovery. Integrative healthcare practitioners, such as myself, have made it our business to incorporate the most *avant-garde* research in the medical literature into our clinical practices. Many diagnostic tests, such as darkfield microscopy, and analysis of organic mineral, amino acid and essential fatty acid (EFA) levels, are well-researched tools, which can greatly assist in early diagnosis of impending disease and in pointing the way to proper interventions. My hope is that many more physicians will utilize these tests and that insurers, recognizing their value, will begin to make them reimbursable.

One of the other major tenets of functional medicine is

that each individual is biochemically unique. Because of my clinical verification of this tenet, I have found it most difficult to write the prescriptive part of this book regarding nutritional supplements. Many parameters enter into proper supplementation. For example, we classify some amino acids as nonessential – meaning our bodies can make them from other amino acids. Some people, however, have glitches in their metabolic make-ups that impair their bodies' ability to make some of these amino acids. For them, these so-called nonessential amino acids are "conditionally essential." This means these individuals need nutritional supplements of specific amino acids and other nutrients to compensate for the defective transformation process. The amount of nutrients an individual requires also varies, depending on such factors as size, body type, health status and the severity of metabolic glitches. A 95-pound young woman with marginal metabolic defects has far different requirements than a 200-pound middle-age man with a number of health problems, caused by a poor lifestyle or inborn cellular abnormalities. Finally, to achieve the most benefit from supplementation, it is necessary to know which specific state or states of imbalance are being addressed.

In response to many requests, I have included some general recommendations about supplements, based on my clinical experience with thousands of patients. *I advise you, however, to check with a knowledgeable integrative healthcare practitioner about implementing any of my recommendations (about supplements and others), particularly if you currently have a serious medical problem or are taking prescription medications.*

The Ageless Woman is not so much prescriptive as it is educational and, hopefully, inspirational. To illustrate the power of my approach, I have included descriptions of some of the exciting transformations my patients have undergone. Their names and some of the details have been changed to protect their privacy. I hope you enjoy reading this book as much as I enjoyed writing it!

*I*ntroduction

One of the magnificent gifts of maturity is perspective. You gain a bird's eye view of significant events and of the people who have shaped your life and brought you to the present moment.

As a young girl growing up in Italy, I was in love with music. I was blessed with a quality of voice, a dramatic sensibility and a disciplined nature – the gifts of every operatic singer. Opera was my family's passion, and I felt it was my destiny. I was about to immerse myself with great joy in the long hours of study and practice that such a career requires when something unexpected befell me.

My wondrous world appeared to collapse around me when I was hospitalized with typhoid fever and death hovered in the wings. I was only 14. But – as I have learned over the years – even in the depth of darkness, there is always a glimmer of light. For me, this light came in the form of a young and compassionate physician.

One afternoon, after I had already spent more than a month struggling to regain my health, a young, handsome man in a white coat walked into my hospital room. He sat on my bed, took my hand and gently said to me, "Little girl, I'm going to warn you about something that can be potentially dangerous for you, but if you know what to do, there will be no problem."

I was hardly a "little girl," but I then realized that my sunken eyes in an emaciated body and my long braids did, indeed, make me look like an 8-year-old. His warm manner (and good looks) were compelling, and I became very eager to know what he had to tell me. He proceeded to explain, in simple terms, what happens to the intestine during the healing phase of typhoid fever.

"Where you had all those ulcers in your 'fighting intestine,' there are now scabs. If a scab is sitting on an intestinal blood vessel, you might bleed to death when it falls off. When you feel the pain, scream. We'll all be there in a few seconds to save you," he assured me, smiling.

I spent the remaining days of my hospitalization waiting for the pain that never came, hoping to see my "white knight" rushing to rescue me. In my adolescent fantasies, the handsome, medical resident was always the first one to reach my bed.

That young man changed my life forever. Not only was he instrumental in my recovery, he also inspired me to pursue a different calling. Motivated by his example, I decided that I was going to be a physician, and that, like him, I would make the same effort to educate and support my patients.

I followed my new calling, attended and completed medical school in Rome, and subsequently moved to New York. Knowing even then that there was far more involved in the practice of medicine than simply trying to eliminate symptoms or fix diseased organs, I decided to pursue my residency training in psychiatry.

Fully engaged in my career as a practicing psychiatrist, my life took another sudden turn in 1972, when a patch of ice propelled the car I was driving into the path of an oncoming car. Seconds before I lost consciousness, I heard a terrifying cracking sound in my neck, as my head smashed against the car's ceiling. Eight days later, with a diagnosis of a broken cervical vertebra, I was finally able to stand on my feet. But I had a long way to go. My doctors insisted that surgery was the only option for insuring the healing of my neck. Intuitively, however, I knew there were other truths. That intuition led me to a chiropractor and to a local spa where I could learn yoga.

The spa became my healing sanctuary. Every Monday morning, before I began my workweek, I did yoga with a wise and compassionate teacher, who tailored the exercises to facilitate the healing of my neck. A sauna and a session with a masseuse followed. The masseuse – a stunning South African, with a voice that could span four octaves, and sensitive, energy-emitting hands – was another beacon of light, pointing me in a direction I had not yet explored. She suggested that taking some specific nutritional supplements might speed my recovery. With her recommended list in hand, I went home and dug into my biochemistry books. The calcium and magnesium she had recommended, I learned, nourished the bones. The tryptophan would become the calming neurotransmitter, serotonin. To my great surprise, everything she said was well documented in my biochemistry books.

A further turning point was my own menopause, which became yet another teacher for me. When the conventional approach of an estrogen patch led to an ominous growth in my breast, I again found myself looking for other options. This included not only natural supplements but also a comprehensive change in my lifestyle.

Every encounter with disease became my teacher, but the first and most powerful teacher of all was my grandmother, Filippa. She introduced me to my two major passions – music and medicine. During those dark years of the Second World War, when all family physicians were ministering to dying soldiers, my grandmother became a highly respected lay healer, working in synchrony with the laws of nature to cure all types of disorders. She inspired me as a young girl and to this day sustains me in my life and in my work.

My first entrée into natural medicine, as a physician, occurred more than 25 years ago, while I was still practicing psychiatry. One of my patients came into my office with her face twisted into a horrific grimace, a symptom of what was considered an incurable neurological disease. In fact, as it soon became apparent, this frightening condition had been caused by the psychiatric medications I had unwittingly prescribed for her. And so, she became the first patient I treated with nutritional supplements to detoxify the effects of poisonous medications.

My grandmother's example, my own experiences and those of my patients have reinforced my faith in and respect for the natural laws of healing. My primary approach is to restore the body's inborn healing forces through the use of nutrients, homeopathy, behavioral medicine and any other natural therapy that facilitates the process. Instead of treating a disease, I treat the whole person – body, chemistry and spirit.

During the course of my practice, I have observed that when a patient's innate harmony is restored, there is a concomitant increase in vitality – one of the major landmarks of youthfulness. My patients often tell me that they never knew they could feel and look so good. Thus, I have gradually come to realize that what I practice, in essence, is *anti-aging medicine*. And, in my opinion, we no longer have an option. Our society is getting older at a younger and younger age. The cancer wards are no longer populated only by crippled old people but by a growing number of young mothers and fathers, and their offspring. Autoimmune diseases that used to occur only in middle and late age are now afflicting young children. My youngest patient is 29-months-old. She has rheumatoid arthritis, which was first diagnosed when she was 17-months-old. In contrast, I see myself and my long-term patients getting younger and younger. People often find it difficult to place me in a specific chronological frame of reference and have often commented that I am ageless.

The Ageless Woman is designed to provide you with an understanding of what aging really is, the multiple insidious forces that age us, and what you can do yourself to slow the process. Some of the strategies I will share with you are ancient – a few possibly as old as time itself. Others are derived from the exciting, new frontiers of physiology, biochemistry and genetics. Synergistically combined, they offer an unsurpassed path to wellness and longevity.

Much of what you will find in *The Ageless Woman*, with the exception of some specific hormonal prescriptions, is also applicable to men. I encourage you to share this book with the men in your life. As you become younger and more vital, you will want your male companions to be able to keep up with you! Faust's dream of eternal youth is within everyone's reach, and you don't need to sell your soul to the devil. All you need is knowledge and motivation.

This is not a quick-and-easy-fix book. It is not about simply replacing pharmaceuticals with natural remedies. It is about making comprehensive and integrated changes that will, over time, restore your organs to optimal functionality and your entire body to a youthful vitality. If you are in poor health currently, remember that it took you some time to reach that state. You will need time, discipline and faith to heal and rebuild. If you are basically in good health, this book will give you the tools to sustain your health and youthfulness.

I bring to you in *The Ageless Woman* almost 40 years of experience as a physician, more than 25 of which have been spent practicing and continually learning the art and science of holistic medicine. I have treated thousands of patients with conditions ranging from mild imbalances to serious, life-threatening diseases. When I see the spark of wellness infusing my patients' bodies – when I see the light return to the eyes of depleted and depressed patients – it is celestial music to my ears and unrepressed joy to my heart.

In Latin, *docere*, from which the word "doctor" derives, means to teach. I am, first and foremost, a teacher. I teach my patients how to regain and maintain their health. I invite you now to follow me into my virtual classroom – and to become a member of my therapeutic extended family. Let me guide you along your personal path to wellness and longevity. Let me take you into the realm of *The Ageless Woman*.

The
AGELESS
WOMAN

1 *The Ticking Clock*

*We can't stop the clock from ticking,
but we can change its chime.*

The Graying of America

 *M*ore and more of us are moving into our "mature years" each day. The 76 million members of the baby boom generation are turning 50 at the rate of one every 10 seconds. About 6,000 people each day celebrate their 65th birthday. Today, nearly 3.5 million Americans are over 65, and a full 20% of the population will fall within that age group by 2030.

Seeing the potential for billion dollar revenues in those numbers, pharmaceutical companies have jumped with both feet into the development and marketing of drugs aimed at the symptoms of aging – weight gain, incontinence, memory loss, sunspots, balding and impotence, among others. More than 90 pharmaceutical companies are feverishly researching anti-aging medicines, with nearly 200 currently under development.

The anti-impotence drug Viagra accounted for 94% of all new prescriptions dispensed in the United States within the first three weeks of its release. Just a few weeks later, we heard of the first heart-related deaths associated with taking the drug. In their rush to profit, the pharmaceutical industry minimized the importance of some basic physiological facts and ignored its responsibility to educate physicians. Viagra is just one example of what, unfortunately, has become commonplace in mainstream medicine when a treatment focuses on symptoms and profit rather than on the actual causes of disease. The causes of aging, which is where I and other holistically-oriented healthcare practitioners concentrate our attention, are complex and – at the same time – are responsive to natural methods of intervention. In *The Ageless Woman*, I will take a close look at the multiple forces that cause aging and present strategies that you can implement yourself to restore balance and maintain wellness. However, before sharing the drama with you (the performers, the script, the music), let me first set the stage with some understanding of what this phenomenon we call "aging" is all about.

What Is Aging?

The calendar announces that it's the anniversary of our birth and we realize that we are a year older chronologically. *Chronological aging* occurs at a constant and uniform rate. If you and your neighbor turned 50 last month, you are the same age chronologically and will continue to be the same chronological age throughout your lives.

Biological aging is an entirely different story. Even though you and your neighbor are both 50 chronologically, biologically you may be 40 and your neighbor 65. Biological aging is the sum of all the physiological changes that occur over time. As our tissues sustain more and more injury, our body organs start to deteriorate and our system functions begin to decline. Leading medical researchers are now defining aging as a chronic, progressive, hereditary disease that eventually affects everyone.[1, 2] The rate at which biological aging occurs varies from person to person, and, as you will learn, there is much you can do to slow the process.

My primary motivation for writing this book is my concern

that so many people are unnecessarily far older biologically than they are chronologically. Consequently, they suffer with a myriad of diseases and often are unable to fully engage in life. Such a situation also imposes a burden on society because medical technology is now capable of keeping people alive far beyond their ability to function independently. Families are going bankrupt financially and emotionally as they attempt to maintain the care of their ailing loved ones. We must, at the very least, match biological age with chronological age. Ideally, we can turn the biological clock way back, and live full and productive lives into our 100th year and beyond.

We're Getting Older Sooner

Diseases of old age – immune deficiency, autoimmune disorders, cancer, nervous system deterioration, cardiovascular disease and diminished capacity to handle stress – are striking people at a much earlier stage of life. For example, the American Parkinson Disease Association recently reported an alarming increase of the disease in people in their 30s and 40s. Actor Michael J. Fox's recent disclosure underscores this dismaying fact. These diseases of adaptation used to occur in much older people, when various body systems became weary after a long lifetime of use.

Not only are we seeing diseases of old age in younger and younger adults, we are seeing them in very young children. My 29-month old patient with rheumatoid arthritis began aging in the womb. Why? Her mother suffered from poorly controlled gestational diabetes – an imbalance in the body's sugar-regulating mechanism. This hormonally-triggered disease in the mother's body impaired the baby's immune defenses, which, in turn, led to the arthritis, an autoimmune disease.

The encouraging news, in the midst of this frightening trend, is that debilitating diseases, such as this child's arthritis and any degenerative disease you may be experiencing, can be halted and reversed by restoring proper balance among the body's neurologic, hormone and immune systems.

The Dynamics of Health and Wellness

Before we go further, I need to share my concept of holistic health so you can understand my approach to healing and anti-aging medicine. To me, health is the ultimate equilibrium of opposing forces, which can occur only when the body's energy fields, biochemical forces and physical structures are in equilibrium with each other. To visually imagine it, I conjure up an image from my classical training – Sandro Botticelli's painting, *Springtime,* in which three lovely maidens join hands together in a harmonious and intertwined dance of life.

The dance could not exist without the simultaneous engagement of all three. Similarly, health can only exist if the three templates – energy, chemistry and the physical body – are in harmony with each other. Health – which I also call wellness – is the unison and perfect balance of the three templates, interdependent and interactive with each other.

All the templates are connected, yet each still maintains its individual identity. The energetic template includes the spiritual, emotional and mental aspects of our inner life. The second – the chemical template – encompasses all the complex and magnificent biochemical reactions that occur in the interactions between the mind and the body. The third template – the physical – manifests the comfort or discomfort of the other two templates in the physical body.

The Three Templates

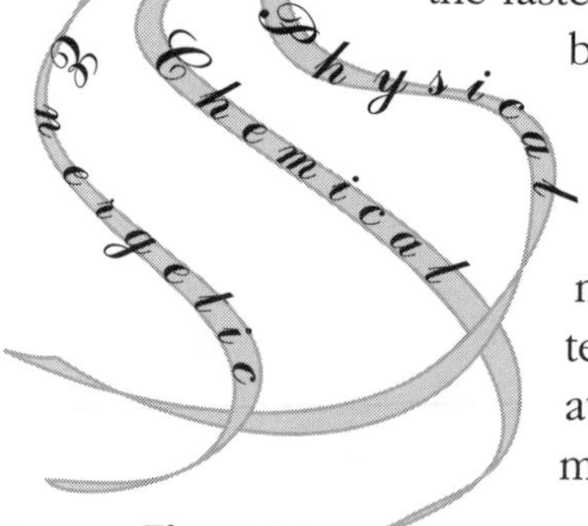

The energetic template vibrates at the fastest rate. Usually, it is physically visible only to clairvoyants. The chemical template vibrates at a slower frequency and is denser. It can be measured by the tools of modern medicine, such as blood tests. Biochemical reactions also create an energy field, such as the one measured by electrocardiograms

Figure 1-1

(EKGs) and electroencephalograms (EEGs). The physical template is the densest of the three. It is here that the imbalances of the three templates manifest themselves as physical disease.

Wellness exists when each template is in a state of internal balance and each one is dynamically in harmony with the other two ("dynamic equilibrium"). For example, we are surrounded by electromagnetic energy fields that negatively affect the energetic template. We can maintain equilibrium in this template, however, by counterbalancing the negative fields with positive ones – through such practices as meditation and positive thinking, and by using energetic healing tools (crystals, magnets, etc.). When the negative forces overwhelm the positive ones, we experience an imbalance in the energetic template, which subsequently impacts the chemical and physical templates.

The equilibrium in the chemical template can be disrupted by the inevitable chemical toxicity to which we are all exposed. These negative factors can be counterbalanced by good nutrition, adequate antioxidants and appropriate dietary supplements. The same dynamic holds true for the physical template. For example, jogging inevitably creates micro-injuries to the muscle fibers. Flexibility exercises and appropriate nutrients can counterbalance the damage.

Wellness exists as long as there is a dynamic equilibrium within each template and among all three of them. Imbalance within one template ultimately spills over into the other two. Let's look at a person who appears to have a healthy lifestyle. She has a nutritious diet, takes appropriate supplements and exercises properly. She, however, is still carrying the burden of resentment from her unhappy childhood. One day, while jogging, this seemingly "perfectly-tuned" woman tears the ligaments in her ankle. In spite of her heroic efforts – adequate protein, anti-inflammatory supplements, chiropractic adjustments, healing oils, etc. – her injury does not heal. The hidden resentment created an imbalance in the energetic template that prevented healing on the chemical and physical levels.

During the '60s and '70s, I saw many patients who had adopted a so-called natural lifestyle, which included a vegetarian diet. In spite of this, they were not well. In many cases, their diets were not providing adequate protein and important nutrients, such as zinc, carnitine and vitamin B_{12} found mostly in animal foods. Imbalance on the chemical level affected both the physical and energetic templates, resulting in fatigue, an inability to stay focused and a whole host of other problems.

Premature Aging Unrecognized

Practitioners of mainstream medicine often fail to recognize the imbalances in the energetic and chemical templates before they express themselves with clear-cut signs and symptoms in the physical one. Many of us have either known or heard of someone who died suddenly soon after being proclaimed "perfectly healthy." If you look at health within the context of the three templates, you can begin to understand what probably happened. The physician, unable to detect early and subtler signs of imbalance, focused primarily on the physical template during the exam – and perhaps on a portion of the chemical one.

However, even if the chemical template had been comprehensively examined, the physician may have missed some important warning signs. "Normal" reference ranges on laboratory tests are based on the screening of a sick population and the law of averages. As long as a lab value is within the reference range, most physicians ignore it. I recently saw a patient who had undergone a quadruple coronary artery bypass (CABG) 2 years previously, and whose triglycerides had tripled within the past 3 months. His internist told him that he was fine because even though the value was on the high end of the range, it was still "normal." To me, this dramatic increase was a red flag that required further investigation.

Complex interactions among body chemistries and pathways

that lead from one physiological process to another are frequently not fully understood because of the mechanistic medical training of physicians. Most physicians are still unaware that a combination of low cholesterol and low uric acid is an indicator of dangerous cellular pathology that can lead to such serious outcomes as sudden cardiac arrest. I have been attentive to these findings for years. I am particularly concerned with low cholesterol, as an adequate amount is a prerequisite for the production of hormones – fundamental regulators of all body functions. Everyday, patients arrive on my doorstep with conditions that have become serious because subtle signs of cellular and organ malfunction were overlooked.

The mainstream medical model is limited by an incomplete understanding of the true nature of health. To make things even worse, in this era of "quick fix medicine," physicians are forced to limit the amount of time they spend with patients and the number of diagnostic tests they can order. A recent study published in the *New England Journal of Medicine* highlights this point.[3] The Canadian study found that older patients with a chronic disease are undertreated for seemingly unrelated disorders, even when the treatment of those disorders would be uncomplicated. Dr. Robert Steinbrook, a deputy editor of the journal, noted in an accompanying editorial that managed care pressures are a major contributing factor to such inadequacies in care in the United States.[4]

Another, and equally frightening, reason why premature aging is not detected is the increasing specialization in medicine. Medicine has become fragmented into specialties, which have then been divided even further into subspecialties. An ideal symphony is not just dependent on the proper sound of the violin, but on how it resonates with the piano, the bassoon, and all the other instruments playing the orchestral piece. Medicine today has lost this symphonic interplay. I often see patients, who having consulted a variety of specialists and subspecialists, are still sick because none of the consulted doctors was able to understand the overall picture.

Aging Theories

Many scientists have proposed theories about why we age, and new ones are being developed all the time. I will briefly describe the more significant ones, starting with the Free Radical Theory of Aging, which I believe is the unifying theory underlying all others.

Dr. Denham Harman, Professor of Biochemistry at the University of Nebraska College of Medicine and founder of the American Aging Association, developed the Free Radical Theory of Aging in 1954. He recognized that the human machine burned oxygen imperfectly and that the byproducts of this process (free radicals) accelerated cellular aging.[5] Since that time, several other major aging theories have been advanced. But when you examine them, they all lead back to uncontrolled free radical activity (oxidative stress) as the ultimate cause of aging.

The idea, popularized by respected UCLA gerontologist Dr. Roy Walford, of calorie restriction as an anti-aging strategy, is based on reducing cellular "wear and tear."[6*] The food we eat requires metabolic processing, which produces free radicals. When it is loaded with toxins, free radical production is even greater. By decreasing our intake and processing of food, we decrease free radical damage.

Proponents of the Neuroendocrine Theory of Aging, developed by noted Russian gerontologist Dr. Vladimir Dilman,[7] hold that degenerative changes are the result of a breakdown in the feedback loops among the hormones produced by various glands and the brain. It is my opinion that when these feedback mechanisms don't function properly, uncontrolled free radical damage also occurs.

The Glycosylation Theory, also advanced by Dr. Dilman, is one of the more recent aging theories. It is based on the fact that excessive circulating glucose in the blood "coagulates" vital cellular proteins, most noticeably in red blood cells and immune system cells. When the cells become glycosylated, they are unable to carry out their designated functions and become overwhelmed by free radicals.

Cell biologist Dr. Leonard Hayflick, who has researched and lectured on the subject of biological aging for more than 30 years, proposes that our cells can only divide 50 times before their final demise.[8] If all cells have the capacity to divide only 50 times, and cells divide when the mother-line of cells has been damaged by excessive free radicals, slowing oxidative stress will postpone cell death and the consequent need for cell division. This, in turn, will lengthen the lifespan of cell lines and extend the chronological survival of the entire body. This theory of aging explains why people who are in the "fast lane" get sick earlier and die sooner, unless they take very good care of themselves.

Dr. Alan Goldstein, chairman of the biochemistry department at George Washington University, proposes that the thymus is the immune system's master gland and that its shrinkage weakens the system and hastens aging. The thymus releases several hormones that regulate many immune functions, including the production of cells that scavenge free radicals. As these same hormones interact with the entire neuroendocrine system, scientists suspect that the thymus may actually be the pacemaker of the aging process.

The Telomere Theory of Aging, developed by Geron Corporation genetic engineers, is the latest addition to the list. Telomeres are like caps on the ends of our chromosomes, which function to maintain the integrity of our genetic material. Each time a cell divides, the telomeres are shortened. When the telomeres are reduced to a critical length, the cell ages and subsequently dies. I suspect that protecting our tissues from oxidative stress will allow the telomeres to last longer.

Cellular Changes

Aging begins at a cellular level – the primordial unit of human life. Loss of elasticity is one of the first biomarkers of aging. Tissue pliability is lost when many cells in a given tissue "wrinkle" or lose moisture. Another cause of cellular loss of elasticity is inflammation, which can cause very resilient tissues, such as muscle fibers, to become rigid.

Pick up the skin from the top of your hand with your thumb and forefinger. If it is supple, it will fall right back into its original position. If it doesn't, your skin is showing some signs of aging. Multiply this by the millions of cells that comprise your internal organs, and you begin to get a sense of what aging looks like on the cellular level.

Under the Microscope

Let's look at the cells a little closer – at the many chemical changes that accelerate their aging process. All theories about the biology of aging ultimately focus on the cellular biochemical changes that result from oxidative stress – the imbalance between free radicals and the neutralizing antioxidants within each cell.

You have observed oxidation many times in your daily life, probably without being aware of it. When a cut piece of fruit turns brown or butter becomes rancid after being left out of the refrigerator for a while, that's oxidation. Oxidation is simply the process of oxygen combining with another molecule and robbing that substance of electrons.

Oxidation in the body begins with breathing. When we breathe, we transfer oxygen from the air to our blood, where it is used for many metabolic functions. Oxygen molecules, however, are unstable and highly reactive. If they lose an electron during the process of "cellular combustion," they become free radicals.

Free radicals are like pirates stealing electrons from other substances. Because they are incomplete, each free radical molecule goes ferociously in search of an electron to make itself whole again. The original molecules, once they find their missing electrons, become stable, but now the substances from which they robbed these electrons turn into incomplete molecules. These molecules, now free radicals, attack still other substances, setting off other damaging chain reactions. Thousands of these reactions can occur in just seconds.

Not only do we produce free radicals internally by the natural act of producing energy for our vital functions, but we are also surrounded by free radical-activating (oxidative) substances in our environment. Air pollution, cigarette smoke, some medications, ultraviolet light and pesticides all create free radicals. Some of our experiences, such as trauma, infections, consuming alcohol, negative thinking – and even strenuous exercise – also are sources of free radicals. Untempered by sufficient antioxidants, free radicals can wreak havoc with our bodies' natural balance and hasten the aging process.

Free Radicals Cause Disease

When a molecule is robbed of an electron, the molecule is altered and may no longer function appropriately. For example, if the molecule is part of the cell's protective membrane, it may be less selective in allowing nutrients into or out of the cell. Or it might disable the cell's ability to accept hormones, such as estrogen or insulin. Imagine what can happen when millions of molecules in a cell membrane are changed in this fashion. Free radical production is a self-propagating phenomenon that, if not stopped, will ultimately damage all body systems.

When free radical damage takes place in the structure of vital enzymes (proteins that regulate chemical reactions) or in the DNA (the nucleic acid that is the blueprint of our genetic code), serious diseases may be the result. Uncontrolled free radical damage (oxidative stress) has been linked with at least 50 diseases, including cancer, heart disease, diabetes, arthritis and other autoimmune disorders, macular degeneration, cataracts, Parkinson's disease – and, of course, all processes of aging. As more people experience excessive oxidative stress at younger and younger ages, the diseases of "old age" appear earlier and earlier.

New Understandings about Aging

The prevailing view that chronological aging is synonymous with degeneration and loss of function is being replaced by one that is far more optimistic. According to this newer body of opinion, you can extend the length of your life and postpone the age at which disability occurs by engaging in health-promoting behaviors. The results are functional independence and vigor in your later years, and many more years in which to enjoy a productive and fulfilling life. When it comes your time to pass from one reality into another, the disease or disability that usually accompanies this transition becomes compressed into a very short period. This idea is known as "the rectangularization of the health curve."

This concept is not just fanciful thinking. In a recent article in the *New England Journal of Medicine*, researchers scientifically validated this view with their report of the results of a 32-year longitudinal study of more than 1,700 university alumni.[9] The authors concluded that, "Not only do persons with better health habits survive longer, but in such persons, disability is postponed and compressed into fewer years at the end of life." The MacArthur Foundation Study longevity researchers[10] and clinicians like myself witness such reality on a daily basis.

Longevity

At the turn of the century, average life expectancy was 47 years. According to the Centers for Disease Control (CDC), it increased to 76.1 years in 1996. The World Health Organization (WHO) predicts that the average person in the United States will live more than 80 years by 2025. The MacArthur Foundation Study researchers, who studied more than 1,000 high-functioning older adults over a 10-year period, are making even bolder predictions. They expect centenarians to be common in the 21st century. Today, there are already 61,000 in the United States, and they predict there will be more than 600,000 centenarians by 2050. This increase in our average lifespan is directly related to gains made in prevention, and the sophisticated diagnosis and treatment of our three most prevalent killers – heart disease, cancer and stroke. Longevity that is sustained only by high-tech medical procedures or by excessive (and often toxic) medications, however, is not an attractive option. A far better approach, I believe, is to use natural tools to assist us in adding years to our lives and life to our years.

The Choice

Age we must, but how we age is up to us. I hope this book will inspire you to choose the path that leads to a long and healthy life.

I invite you now to join me on two journeys. Let's go first to the local assisted living facility. We walk in from the busy street and notice a dramatic shift in the noise level. There sit 30 people – mostly older women – staring into space. The silence is deafening. As you look closer, you notice that a couple of them are trying to connect to you with their eyes. One is mumbling to herself, and another, with great effort, hoists herself up from her chair to her walker and slowly shuffles across the carpeted room. This is the reality we all fear.

On the other side of town, an entirely different script awaits us at a yoga studio. Class has already begun. We tiptoe in and stand against the back wall and quietly watch. Here, again, the room is filled mostly with women – some younger than you, some older. And then you notice the teacher. She is twisting, bending and flexing with the grace of a dancer. Her voice is a soothing melody, guiding the students to breathe slowly and relax into the stretches.

You notice a news clipping about her on the bulletin board. You learn that the teacher is 75-years-young. She began practicing yoga at the age of 50, after having raised four children. Her classes are always filled to capacity. This is a true story and the reality to which we all should aspire.

I just presented you with two options of what your older

years could look like – the more frequent picture of decay and disability, and the alternative of health and vitality. The choice is yours.

2 *Overloading Our System*

There comes a point where the seesaw tips.

Multiple Factors

*W*hen we are balanced on all levels, we are able to maintain a state of equilibrium in the midst of constantly changing internal and external environments. Conversely, when we become overloaded with injurious stressors, the harmony among the three templates – energetic, chemical and physical – becomes disrupted and we become more susceptible to disease. These harmful factors arise from many sources. Stress is the most damaging of all, as it simultaneously has an impact on all three templates. Other causes include toxic substances, repeated infections, allergies, poor nutrition, inadequate sleep and a host of additional factors concomitant with the busy lives we all lead.

Each factor on its own has a negative impact on our equilibrium; combined, these noxious factors are interactive, synergistic and cumulative. They add up geometrically rather than arithmetically, with complex and unfavorable effects. First, subtle manifestations of disease, such as aches, malaise or fatigue, may occur. Later, the consequences can be accelerated aging and serious degenerative diseases. I call this model of disease and aging *The Loading Theory*. It has been the basis of my clinical practice for nearly three decades and is the underlying foundation of this book.

The Loading Theory

Figure 2-1

Conventional Western medicine still looks at the last drop in the bucket of years of harmful events as the sole cause of any health crisis. This linear, simplistic approach is responsible for many diagnostic and therapeutic failures. Recently, support for the multifactorial disease concept is beginning to appear in medical journals.[1] It is my hope that the Loading Theory approach to evaluating disease becomes widespread among practicing physicians because we will then all enjoy better outcomes and fewer therapeutic failures.

Let's see how this translates into everyday reality by looking at what's been going on with Jessica. Jessica is a young woman with a highly stressful and sedentary job, who also goes to school at night. She is a wife and mother of two young children. She was used to doing it all and never tiring. During the course of the last 6 or 7 years, she has slipped into some very bad habits, including not exercising and eating junk food on the run. She felt invincible – as if the rules of healthful living didn't apply to her.

One morning, Jessica found herself unable to lift her head

from her pillow. The evening before, after a hectic day at work, she had rushed to a dinner party, where she ate and drank more than usual. To her, this was just another typical day, but by the end of the evening she was sniffing and achy. By morning, it had turned into a healing crisis that has the ominous name of chronic fatigue immune dysfunction syndrome (CFIDS). Jessica had used all her body's reserves down to the last drop. The virus was the incidental factor that precipitated the crisis, but her condition was the cumulative result of her lifestyle and her attitude of invincibility.

The Best Approach

The best approach to health, vitality and longevity is to avoid or minimize exposure to factors that are injurious to our bodies. As you learned in Chapter 1, all types of stressors generate free radicals, which damage our tissues and accelerate the aging process.

Although an ounce of prevention is worth a pound of cure, it is never too late to undo cellular damage and rejuvenate the whole body. The results of recent research prove that the adoption of health-promoting habits can decelerate the aging process and reverse degenerative disease, no matter how old you are.[2, 3] I have treated thousands of patients in their 40s, 50s, 60s and 70s, who were far older biologically than their chronological age. Invariably, these patients felt better and looked younger once the disease process that brought them to our Centers was controlled and reversed.

Genes and Reserves Play Their Part

The organ or system that becomes your Achilles heel is usually related to your genetic predisposition. The severity of the illness, however, is related to how strong your reserves are and how many factors are involved in creating the condition. Since the Loading Theory is alien to the Western linear concept of medicine and since most of you have been imbued with this approach, let's look at a few more examples that illustrate the validity of this paradigm.

Have you ever watched the progression of the seasonal office cold? Some people don't get sick at all, some have minor symptoms, while others may get very ill. One of them may even progress into pneumonia. That person who became very ill was most likely depleted of immunological reserves and may also have had an inherent weakness of the lungs.

Traditional Chinese medicine (TCM) has understood and used this concept for thousands of years. It uses acupuncture needles to stimulate the energy pathways (meridians) that are associated with specific body organs. Herbs are often added to the treatment plan to assist in building organ vitality. Restoring the balance of the energetic and chemical templates with these therapeutic interventions mitigates inherent organ weaknesses. The body is gradually brought to a state where it is more able to resist disease.

You may have heard media accounts about the death, at age 65, of Shari Lewis, the beloved puppeteer. She was diagnosed with uterine cancer and two months later died of pneumonia after receiving chemotherapy. This is another example of how two powerful stressors, chemotherapy followed by the pneumonia bacteria, irreversibly tipped the balance of a weakened immune system, which had been very gradually depleted over the years.

Another example of the interaction of stressors and organ reserve involves a young opera singer, Anna, whom I recently met. Unlike the opera singers of previous generations who carried substantial weight, many of today's singers are forced to respond to the aesthetic expectations of their audiences. They exercise strenuously and maintain a low-fat diet, which leads to an attractive, lean physique. Although aesthetically pleasing, this type of body may not be able to withstand the challenging training and even more demanding performances of an operatic career.

Inappropriate dieting and lifestyle practices can lead to a lean body with poor glycogen stores – the carbohydrate reserves that the body transforms into glucose (blood sugar) for fuel. Many young singers, like Anna, do not have sufficient glycogen to sustain themselves during an arduous 3- or 4-hour performance. Such a performance is a physical and emotional marathon that promotes a constant outpouring of the stress hormones, adrenaline and cortisol. When glycogen reserves are not available, the cortisol will promote transformation of amino acids into the glucose the body needs for fuel. This is a laborious and tortuous process, which takes place mostly at the expense of muscles, and does not always proceed fast enough. As a result, Anna had often been exhausted by the middle of a performance and, at times, when on tour, had been forced to cancel.

The constant stress had also resulted in a suppression of Anna's immune system and, consequently, repeated upper respiratory infections. The prolonged interaction of stress, low glycogen reserves and immune suppression inevitably led to successive treatment with conventional antibiotics. These man-made antibiotics not only kill the invading bacteria but also the intestine's protective bacteria. An intestine depleted of protective bacteria becomes inflamed and eventually depleted of its natural immune defenses. Thus, the cycle of exhaustion and infection, if not interrupted, can lead to major health crises.

Aging versus Rejuvenating

As you have seen, the causes of disease are multifactorial and interactive. Reversal of disease and the rejuvenation of damaged systems requires multiple, synergistic interventions commensurate with the many factors that went into the disease process. Many stressors – some obvious and others insidious – have the potential for aging us, particularly when they pile up on each other. On the other hand, there is much we can do to keep ourselves well and young. When combined, these synergistic strategies are a powerful force that counteract the stressors that debilitate and age us.

My overall approach to anti-aging medicine is to "unload

the burden" layer by layer, return every cell to a healthy balance and revitalize all the organs. When the mission is accomplished, people feel better than ever because all of their organs' functions have been raised to a more efficient level. With good health habits and a balanced lifestyle, this optimal state of vitality and youthfulness can be sustained for many, many years.

What you see in Figures 2-2 and 2-3 are two diagrams of a 7-petaled flower. In the first diagram, the flower depicts the aging forces; the other shows the rejuvenating ones. The aging forces cause the wilting of our symbolic flower, while the rejuvenating ones call forth its blossoming. Allow me to guide you as we tiptoe inside each petal. Together let's open the door of awareness to undo what damages us and potentiate what allows us to blossom into ageless, harmonious, wondrous beings.

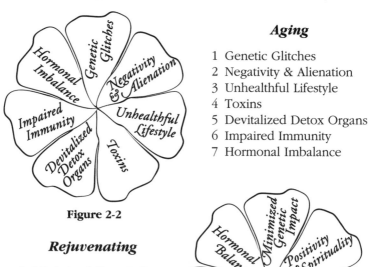

Figure 2-2

Aging

1 Genetic Glitches
2 Negativity & Alienation
3 Unhealthful Lifestyle
4 Toxins
5 Devitalized Detox Organs
6 Impaired Immunity
7 Hormonal Imbalance

Rejuvenating

1 Minimized Genetic Impact
2 Positivity & Spirituality
3 Healthful Lifestyle
4 Minimized Toxins
5 Vitalized Detox Organs
6 Enhanced Immunity
7 Balanced Hormones

Figure 2-3

3 Express the Best

Genes are our blueprint, not our destiny.

A New Paradigm

*D*o you remember being taught in school that genetics was destiny? You inherited half of your gene pool from your mother and her ancestors and half from your father's side. If you had healthy ancestors, you were lucky. If you had ancestors with variable health, your personal health status was determined by how the potential gene pool mixed when you were conceived. It was basically a genetic lottery, and there was nothing you could do to change your lot in life. The belief was that genes determined the expression of diseases of aging. If your parents and their ancestors all died of heart disease at an early age, that was your fate too.

A radically different paradigm is now unfolding. Our genetic template, researchers reveal, is a blueprint. It represents the potentiality for genetically-linked disease to be expressed – not the inevitability. The heart disease of your ancestors simply alerts you to the fact that you have an increased risk for acquiring the disease if the biochemical processes that lead to the disease are not appropriately controlled.

Scientists have now discovered that lifestyle choices have a far greater impact than our genes on our ability to be well now and in the future. We actually have two types of genes – *constitutional* and *inducible*. One-quarter of our genes are constitutional and unresponsive to modifying influences. The remaining three-quarters are inducible. They do respond to lifestyle and environmental factors. After age 40, approximately 75% of our genetic expression is modifiable by factors which are largely under our control.[1] By that age, severe familial illnesses, such as Huntington's chorea, have taken the lives of those unfortunately afflicted.

What Genes Do

Genes are an instructional manual for the development and functioning of all organs and systems in our bodies. Every cell contains 50,000 different genes within its nucleus, but not all genes are active in all cells. According to the specialized nature of the cell, some genes are active while others remain idle. For example, the genes that are put to work in muscle cells are not the same as those that are active in nerve cells. Genes have many different jobs. One of the most important is directing the manufacture of enzymes – proteins that facilitate a wide variety of metabolic processes.

Lifestyle Influences Genetic Expression

Our lifestyle influences how genes express themselves. For example, it is well established that there is an association between a high intake of cruciferous vegetables, such as brussel sprouts, cabbage, kale, etc., and a decreased risk of carcinogen-induced cancer. When we look at what is going on at the molecular level, we find that cruciferous vegetables increase the production of the enzyme glutathione S-transferase in both the intestine and the disease-fighting immune cells. This enzyme is a powerful endogenous antioxidant, which combats free radical damage propagated by toxic substances and cellular stress. Eating lots of these vegetables optimizes genetic expression of the protective enzyme.

Other lifestyle choices, such as smoking, may prevent the expression of our genetic best. Researchers recently found that postmenopausal women who are smokers have a much higher risk for breast cancer than do their nonsmoking peers, regardless of other lifestyle factors. Smoking encourages the expression of a particular enzyme that leads to poor detoxification of the deleterious chemicals contained in cigarettes.[2]

Genetic Glitches

Each one of us is unique biochemically (and in many other ways!). Sometimes that uniqueness includes genes that have glitches that prevent them from performing optimally. Scientists are now discovering, for example, that many adverse reactions to prescribed drugs may be related to variable genetic expression of specific enzymes.[3]

Like cholesterol, the amino acid homocysteine is a useful participant in biochemical reactions when it is present in normal levels. However, when its levels are too high or if it is not metabolized correctly, it can cause serious damage to the lining of blood vessels. In a number of recent studies, scientists have found that elevated homocysteine levels are associated with an increased risk for heart disease.[4, 5] Researchers have discovered that 10% of individuals carry a gene that inhibits the proper metabolism of homocysteine.[6] This metabolic glitch is easily remedied by large amounts of vitamins B_6, B_{12} and folic acid. Scientists estimate that we would see a 20% decrease in heart attacks, a 40% decrease in strokes and a 60% decrease in peripheral blood clots if everyone supplemented their diet with these common B-vitamins.[7]

Two devastating neurological diseases are associated with suboptimal genetic performance. People who develop Parkinson's disease and Alzheimer's disease often have liver enzymes that have an impaired ability to detoxify certain chemicals. This metabolic glitch, like the one for homocysteine, can be remedied by adding specific nutrients to the diet. Glutathione, sulfates, N-acetyl-cysteine, glycine, vitamin B5, vitamin C and molybendum all play a role in helping the liver enzymes do a better job.[8, 9, 10]

We now know that many people have genetic characteristics that are expressed in different ways as a consequence of nutritional exposure. Hundreds of nutritional substances that influence genetic expression have already been identified. Many age-related health disorders associated with altered gene expression can be modified by nutritional interventions, including heart disease, autoimmune and neurological diseases, diabetes, and certain forms of cancer.

Organ Reserves and Aging

The human body, a most remarkable creation, is designed with multiple and complex metabolic pathways that produce energy and provide the necessary reserves to defend against a myriad of stressors. When we are young we typically have far more energy reserve than we need to maintain basic functions. Over time, through the wear and tear of daily living, our organ reserves become depleted and some of the metabolic pathways that support organ function are significantly reduced. When physiological resiliency is hampered, we find ourselves less able to adapt to the impact of stressors. For example, as we get older we may find that we are more susceptible to becoming sick during the cold and flu season. Slowing the biological aging process requires the preservation of multiple biochemical pathways that produce cellular energy and the maintenance of the gene pool's ability to correctly translate metabolic messages. Living in a way that takes care of our organs will allow our organs to take care of us.

Maintaining Cellular Energy

To keep our organ reserves strong, we need to protect the energy factories of our cells – the mitochondria. These tiny organelles live in the cellular material that surrounds the cell's nucleus and have the very important job of turning food into energy. Like the nucleus, they contain genetic material (DNA) that activates and instructs enzymes. The DNA in the mitochondria, however, is 2,000 times more susceptible to oxidative damage than nuclear DNA.[11]

Oxidative damage to mitochondrial DNA has been found to be associated with increased Alzheimer's disease[12] as well as other conditions. You may have heard about Greg LeMonde, the world famous bicyclist, who suddenly became exhausted and unable to compete. The source of his problem turned out to be induced mitochondrial myopathy (malfunction of the muscles due to mitochondrial damage). His mitochondria were unable to produce energy at the levels required by the muscles of an elite athlete. Such a result was probably due to the cumulative effect of environmental pollutants and strenuous muscle work without adequate antioxidant protection. The mitochondria were damaged and were consequently unable to produce the required energy.

Cellular energy can be compared to monetary funds. Let us assume that you were born with genetic machinery that has few metabolic glitches. It's like being born an heiress to a large fortune. You now have two choices. You can squander the money and go bankrupt at a tender age, or you can be prudent and remain rich. Most of us, however, are born into more modest circumstances, with genetic machines that have their share of glitches. Despite our initial limited resources, with hard work, we might be able to bring ourselves up to the same energetic level as the heiress. All of us can live long and healthy lives. Conversely, not maximizing what you have been blessed with can have dire consequences. To my great despair, some of my dearest friends, endowed with phenomenal genes, abused themselves to the point where they no longer share my plane of reality. They were like heiresses with holes in their hands.

Even if we have already created some damage, hopefully

we can acquire wisdom in time to replenish a dwindling "energy account." This, of course, takes longer and requires more effort than being wise earlier. I love to assist young people on the verge of energetic bankruptcy, who come to our Centers with symptoms of chronic fatigue, asthma, severe allergies and other debilitating symptoms. I teach them how to restore their energy accounts with lifestyle modifications, clean and balanced foods, ample nutritional supplements, and a completely new view of life.

Like any wise investment strategy in which you put your money into a variety of financial instruments, I advise my patients to employ a variety of healing strategies to enrich all of the body's energy systems. If one system fails, an over-abundant reserve in another might be able to compensate while the overall energy machinery is being overhauled. If you have taken all the steps necessary to heal and bring your intestine and liver up to maximum efficiency, these two systems will bail you out in times of immunological crisis. If you have learned to handle your stress by practicing your favorite relaxation technique, you will be far more prepared to handle any crisis. Exposure to multiple infective and toxic agents, like instability in the monetary market, is not always under our control. Therefore, it is wise to take charge of those factors that are within our dominion. By sustaining strong reserves, we can survive many unforeseen crises and live long, productive and healthy lives.

Maximize Your Heritage

In 1990, the Human Genome Project was initiated to unravel our genetic code and find ways to prevent disease. Thus far, about half of the 50,000 genes have been carefully scrutinized, and valuable information is being produced about which genes are involved in which diseases. As we begin to learn more about genes and their associated metabolic pathways, we will be able to identify and correct specific genetic glitches early in life and even in the womb.

Although more exciting discoveries will be unfolding in the future, there are many things we can do today to assure a long and healthy life.

Know your family history and compensate for it.

∼

Knowing your family history allows you to become aware of your individual risk factors. This knowledge is a tool that can assist you in making beneficial lifestyle adjustments that are supportive of your particular genetic blueprint. If you come from a family with a history of Alzheimer's disease, it would be wise to avoid toxic chemicals and to take actions to maintain a healthy liver. If a propensity for heart disease is in your lineage, taking vitamin B supplements and exercising are good ways to minimize your risk. The turnaround of my patient, Jeff, provides a good illustration of how lifestyle changes can counteract genetic risk factors.

Jeff's Transformation

Jeff, a 45 year-old businessman who I have know for more than 20 years, came to our Center after being diagnosed with possible hardening of the arteries (atherosclerosis). High cholesterol was common on both sides of his family, and his father had suffered several heart attacks. Physical and lab exams revealed that Jeff, too, had elevated levels of cholesterol and triglycerides, as well as allergies.

Jeff's diet was centered around carbohydrates, and he seldom exercised. I suspected that the basis for the familial elevated blood fats (hyperlipidemia) was a faulty carbohydrate metabolism. I, therefore, recommended that he decrease the carbohydrates, increase low fat protein and vegetables, and add essential fatty acids (EFAs), as well as vitamin B complex and extra vitamin B_6, B_{12} and folic acid. I also recommended that he start a routine exercise program. A year later, as a byproduct of this heart-saving program, his allergy symptoms were gone, his energy level was up and all his lab tests became normal. Jeff, a man I adore, looks and feels 10 years younger.

Whatever your personal situation and genetic history, you have control over many of the factors that age you and cumulatively weaken your protective defenses. In this book, you will find many other tools that you can utilize to optimize your genetic potential and maximize your lifespan.

4 *Stay Uplifted & Connected*

Harmony heals.

Balance Is Key

*A*s I have previously said, the energetic template is the governing force of our entire body. Imbalance in any aspect of our inner workings, first and foremost, affects the energetic template and accelerates the aging process. The mental, emotional, spiritual and physical facets of our physiology work in unison and affect each other. People who are harmonious in the energetic template are healthier people. When they become ill, they recover more quickly. Inner balance is a powerful attribute, memorialized by poets and philosophers since the beginning of time.

Mind-Immunity Connection

Our minds talk to our cells and our cells talk to our minds – all the time. This constant chat can make or break our resistance. Researchers in psychoneuroimmunology (PNI), now a well-respected branch of medicine, have produced voluminous data validating this relationship. Our hormone and immune systems, which maintain our health and well-being, are directly influenced by our mental and emotional states. Each attitude, thought and feeling sets in motion chemical messengers from the nervous system (neurotransmitters) that also affect the activity of the immune cells. Synthesis of opiate-like endorphins, which are capable of reducing pain and enhancing pleasure, is activated by positive states of mind. Negative expressions, such as anger, fear and helplessness, depress endorphin production, and stimulate the production of cortisol and other stress-related hormones. Thus, the reason depressed people have poor immunity is because the infection-fighting cells (lymphocytes) and the brain cells respond to the same neurotransmitters. When the chemicals are low in the brain (depression), they are also low in the lymphocytes (suppressed immunity). Our immune system "knows" how we think and feel, and takes action in direct response to the information it receives. Let's take a look at how the mind-immunity interaction played out in my patient, Eileen.

Eileen's Transformation

Eileen is a 17-year-old who, two years earlier, had contracted a common flu from which she never recovered. Visits to more than a dozen of the best infection specialists resulted in a diagnosis of chronic fatigue immune dysfunction syndrome (CFIDS) and an even grimmer prognosis. From a high-performing student, Eileen became a totally dysfunctional bedridden, depressed person, who went from one sore throat to another, perpetually suffering with muscle aches, low grade fevers and an inability to stand up. When her parents brought her to us as their last resort, Eileen was completely demoralized. Whether the dysfunction in the neurotransmitters was one of the major forces in her immune collapse or whether the immune collapse had caused her depression, it mattered not. Something had to be done to uplift the energetic template and restore her immune system.

Eileen, however, was most resistant and refused to have anything to do with a "shrink." Unbeknown to her, I planted some values in her belief system that became the stimuli for her recovery. We patiently peeled the immunosuppression layers, which were the result of years of allergies, repeated infections and an overuse of antibiotics, while we waited for a change of attitude. After 7 months, we were able to reintegrate her into school, and her health had improved to the point where she was almost able to live a normal life. She then underwent minor surgery, and she fell apart once again – back to bed and back to bouts of fever.

This time, I was able to convince Eileen to let us help her emotionally and reduce the chronic underlying malaise that had made her immune system so sensitive to any minor stimulus. She understood this intellectually, but it took a while to overcome her emotional resistance. Within 3 months of beginning supportive individual and family therapy, she was able to leave the house, no longer besieged by daily fevers. This past summer, Eileen was a healthy teenager backpacking through Europe.

Psychological Wellness

Psychological wellness is the capacity to adapt emotionally to the events of life. Some emotional traumas, of course, are of such a magnitude that they are capable of breaking anyone's psychological strength. However, if you are routinely able to pick yourself up, brush yourself off and get back in the saddle, you are psychologically healthy.

Emotional wellness is the result of a balanced psychological infrastructure, which is also very much dependent upon biochemical equilibrium, as Peter's case will illustrate. Some unfortunate people are born with an inherent psychological vulnerability and can easily become dysfunctional from relatively minor traumas. Nevertheless, I am a firm believer that both inborn and acquired biochemical disequilibrium can be corrected by a loving and supportive healer, coupled with target nutrients and proper diet. Cooperation and support in the patient's immediate environment is also necessary. Time and again, I have witnessed the emotional transformation that is a natural consequence of such interventions.

Peter's Transformation

Peter was a scrawny, young man, besieged by anxiety, anger and irritability, and was visibly malnourished as a result of chronic diarrhea. Peter had been prescribed many anti-anxiety drugs over the previous years, but they had made him worse. So he came to us with a clear mandate: "no medications." His anxiety was so severe that he was incapable of following our nutritionist's recommendations.

We realized we needed to lift Peter out of his demoralized and nutrient-starved state as quickly as possible. I convinced him to take concentrated digestive enzymes and to let me give him vitamin B shots twice a week to nourish his depleted nervous system. Four weeks later, he was able to maintain food in his intestines at least for a few hours, and he was visibly calmer. This was a turning point in his journey back to wellness. Sixteen months later, Peter has emerged as an emotionally-balanced, energetic, muscular and optimistic young man. He is very grateful to our senior nutritionist Colette Iannuzzi-Heimowitz, MS, who stayed at his side during the difficult, early stages of his recovery.

Spiritual Wellness

People who have faith in a grander scheme of life, whatever their belief system, are more centered. As a result, they are more capable of accessing correct information and of maintaining emotional equilibrium than atheists or agnostics. The results of many studies indicate that people who have a sense of connectedness with some form of spiritual belief and with other people are healthier than those who don't.[1, 2, 3] An affiliation with religious organizations provides this benefit for many. Individuals, who have become disillusioned with organized religion, need to find a solution that achieves the same results.

One of my colleagues recently shared with me how she had felt very connected to God as a child when she attended church services on a regular basis. As an adolescent, like so many of us, she became disenchanted with the church's organizational structure and with attitudes that contradicted the spiritual teachings of Christ. She withdrew not only from church services but also from her spiritual connection. Recently, she found herself drawn to sitting in a neighborhood church sanctuary when no one was there. Each time she sat down, she found herself sobbing. She came to realize that what was missing in her life was not the church service but the spiritual connection she had abandoned so many years earlier. She now prays daily and practices individual meditation to reestablish the spiritual connection that sustained her as a child.

Often, illness unexpectedly provides a spiritual opening. Many patients who come to our Centers for nutritional counseling have found or rediscovered a sense of inner peace and balance they didn't think possible.

Marriane's Transformation

Marriane, a 47-year-old Catholic, Italian immigrant, had come to the United States as a young woman. She married an abusive man who took out his frustration on her. Busy raising her children, she accepted her situation as some sort of punishment for sins she thought she must have unknowingly committed. She came to our Center with recurrent viral hepatitis, angina pain, exhaustion and severe menopausal symptoms. During our initial visit, she admitted that she had lost her faith in God, although she had been very religious as a young girl. A spark of life came to her as she recalled how much she had enjoyed saying the rosary every evening with her loving grandmother.

Knowing that prayer is a potent healing force, I suggested that she return to saying her nightly rosary and imagine her grandmother there with her. I knew this would make the biochemical interventions we were initiating work faster. Marriane also began seeing our counselor to learn how to regain her self-esteem and deal with her abusive husband. She did everything I advised her to do.

Her reinstituted prayer routine gave her the courage to stand her ground with her husband even before her body completely regained its balance. A year later, she manages her chronic hepatitis with occasional visits. She has recaptured the beauty and vitality of her younger years, and has gained a new confidence. She is now an inspiration to women in situations similar to hers.

Nature

The unfathomable beauty of a mountain peak, a sunset, a star-filled night sky, or the seemingly endlessness of the ocean can humble and elevate us at the same time. Contemplating the motion of the waves or gazing upward at a forest of trees tends to minimize whatever concerns or worries we may be carrying and reminds us that we are part of a grander scheme. This grander scheme includes the physical dimension. The air near beaches, mountains, waterfalls and forests are filled with negative ions. These charged molecules increase our capacity to absorb and utilize oxygen, which is why we feel so energized and refreshed in such natural wonderlands.

Make some time for nature in your life. If you can't get out of the city, take a walk in your local park. It can create the same feeling, if you allow it – especially if you let your bare feet touch the earth or hug a tree! Put plants and miniature waterfalls in your home and office. Buy yourself flowers. Continually remind yourself of the wonders of the natural world and let your heart be filled with joy.

Commune with nature.

Music

The Greek legend of Orpheus, who with the music of his lyre was able to convince the god of the underworld to release his beloved Eurydice, reminds us that music has the power to "soothe the beast." Refined music tames those lower instincts that prevent us from being in harmony with the greater wholeness. Music, created by the great classical composers, is not merely pleasure for our ears, but is also a link with our higher-selves – the ultimate source of true healing.

Don G. Campbell's account of his own miraculous self-directed cure in *The Mozart Effect*[4] is a powerful demonstration of this truth. In his compelling book, Campbell, a classically-trained musician and psycho-acoustic expert, documents classical music's ability not only to enhance health, but to increase mental and creative abilities as well. It has inspired many educators to implement or strengthen music programs. The governor of Georgia became so convinced of the importance of early classical music input that he has proposed allocating state funds to provide a classical CD or tape for each newborn being sent home from the hospital.

Although classical music can elevate us, not all of its offerings are relaxing. Smetana's *The Moldau*, for instance, can get my adrenaline soaring. To produce a soothing, healing effect, music must balance both hemispheres of the brain and evoke alpha brainwaves. Alpha brainwaves (7 to 14 cycles per second), produced during meditation and other relaxed states, are slower than the beta brainwaves (14 to 22 cycles per second), produced during ordinary waking consciousness. Some Mozart and Bach pieces, for example, create such effects, as does medieval chant music. Contemporary offerings by music pioneer Steven Halpern[5] and some other New Age composers can also move us into a state of deep relaxation.

At the other end of the spectrum is the disturbing effect of discordant sounds, such as hard rock music, on living organisms. Some years ago, Peter Tompkins and Christopher Bird recounted in *The Secret Life of Plants*[6] the results of music experiments conducted on plants: plants exposed to classical music thrived, whereas those placed in a rock music environment withered or died.

I am so interested in learning more about the powerful role of sounds on health that we recently performed our own small, simple experiment to explore this relationship. One

Listen to elevating and relaxing music.

∾

group of patients listened to the relaxing New Age sounds of Steven Halpern; the other group was exposed to the discordant sounds generated by a leaf blower. Ten minutes later, we looked at the patients' blood samples under the microscope and found that the blood cells of those patients exposed to the leaf blower clumped together, limiting the cells' capacity to utilize oxygen and nutrients. The blood cells of the patients exposed to Halpern's music showed healthy streaming activity.

A number of studies have provided evidence of the beneficial effect of music therapy in clinical settings. One researcher played taped relaxing, classical music to critically ill patients hospitalized in intensive care units (ICUs).[7] Following the intervention, the patients' blood pressure was significantly reduced, and anxiety, depression and pain were diminished. Relaxing music has also been found to successfully ameliorate chemotherapy-induced vomiting and nausea in cancer patients.[8] Other studies have shown that relaxing music decreases the level of cortisol, one of the major stress hormones secreted by the adrenal glands.[9, 10]

Music therapy is gaining acceptance as a viable method for treating many age-related conditions. Researchers, who conducted a landmark study at the Veterans Affairs Medical Center in Topeka, Kansas, found that people institutionalized with severe dementia exhibited improved learning and enhanced performance of certain practiced activities when they participated in rhythm-based activities.[11] In 1992, the federal government amended the Older Americans Act to recognize music therapy, and Medicare began reimbursing some specific applications. Rhythm for Life, an organization sparked by the government's interest in the field, is a unique coalition of music therapists, and music merchants and manufacturers, including internationally known REMO drums. The organization's mission is to promote rhythm-based therapy and to expand drumming experience, in general.[12]

Listen to good music regularly – both pieces that relax you, and those that remind you of the power and glory of the universe. It nourishes body, mind and spirit.

Meditation

All religions include some form of meditation, but we need not participate in organized religion to meditate or receive its benefits. Meditation, like communing with nature and listening to fine music, is another way to establish rapport with that something that is far greater than our individual selves. Meditation is a state of relaxed but alert silence in which we are unified with all that is. With continued practice, it allows us to experience that state of consciousness in our everyday lives. Over time, we become more relaxed and less reactive to external stressors. *There are very few things that can slow down the aging process more than a calm inner self.*

The regular practice of meditation has many physiological benefits. Since the 1970s, hundreds of studies have been published in professional journals, documenting meditation's ability to calm the nervous system, increase resistance to stress,[13] improve immunity[14, 15] and relieve pain.[16, 17] In addition to wonderful physiological benefits, meditation provides many psychological ones as well. Meditators are typically happier, more optimistic and less anxious and hostile than their nonmeditating peers. They experience joy more frequently, develop deeper personal relationships and depend less on external circumstances for happiness.[18, 19]

Perhaps the most exciting research findings of all are those that document the beneficial impact of meditation on biological aging. Using near vision, hearing threshold and blood pressure as biomarkers of aging, researchers found that each of these functions improved with the long-term practice of meditation and were dose-related. Individuals who had been meditating fewer than 5 years were on the average 5 years biologically younger than their nonmeditating peers. Those who had practiced meditation for more than 5 years were on the average 12 years younger biologically. The results were consistent for both younger and older subjects, and were dramatic indicators of the power of meditation to slow the aging process.[20]

Other researchers, who used disease, hospitalization and physician visits as longevity markers, reported similarly significant results. Meditators had 50% fewer physician visits and hospitalizations, 80% less heart disease and 50% less cancer than nonmeditators. And the greatest difference between the two groups was found in individuals aged 65 years and older.[21]

Dehydroepiandrosterone (DHEA) is a very important adrenal hormone associated with youthfulness (see Chapter 12). In a recent study, researchers compared the DHEA levels of meditators and nonmeditators. They found that the meditators' DHEA levels were equivalent to those of individuals 5 to 10 years younger, with the largest difference occurring in those over age 45. These results were independent of other contributing factors, such as exercise, diet, weight and alcohol consumption.[22]

Consistent meditation brings a sense of peace that allows us to move through our everyday lives less reactive to stress. With fewer stress reactions, our adrenal glands stay younger, longer and our bodies retain higher levels of DHEA. Good DHEA levels are associated with decreased death from all diseases. Thus, we have the potential to live longer and better by just being still (in an altered state of consciousness)!

Meditation Techniques

Some meditation techniques involve sitting still while others incorporate movement into the practice (e.g., *hatha yoga* and *tai chi*). No technique is any better or more powerful than another. What will be most effective for you is the one that you can commit yourself to on a daily basis. As researchers have shown, the effects are cumulative, so consistency of practice is important. Regardless of how different the techniques may appear on the surface, they all have the *Meditate.* same endpoint. Each provides you with an approach to entering that place at the center of life that is pure awareness, infinite creativity and the source of rejuvenation.

Classes, books and other instructional materials are available on specific meditation techniques. To get you started, I present one sitting technique. Begin with 5 minutes and over time increase it to 40 minutes a day – 20 minutes in the morning and 20 minutes in the evening (40 minutes was the amount of time shown by researchers to have an impact on biological aging). Make meditation a new habit. Be consistent and patient. You will experience results.

Focus Meditation[23]

Find a quiet environment where you will not be disturbed.

1. Sit in a comfortable position with your back straight but relaxed.
2. Close your eyes.
3. Breathe from your abdomen, allowing the air to move in and out through your nose. Make sure you are not holding your breath between the inhalation and exhalation.
4. Allow yourself to become comfortable with your own natural breathing rhythm.
5. Move your full attention to the flow of your breath, thinking "in" as you inhale and "out" as you exhale. If you prefer, think "new" on the inhale and "old" on the exhale.
6. Continue focusing on the movement of your breath in and out.
7. If your mind should be distracted by thoughts, feelings or body sensations, gently bring it back to the flow of your breath.
8. When you have sat as long as you are able to, gently open your eyes and allow yourself to move slowly into wakeful consciousness.

Prayer

Prayer is as old as time and its power is legendary. Only recently have we begun to seek scientific explanations and verifications of its effects on healing. The proof is now in. Dr. Larry Dossey, a respected colleague,[24] has been a pioneer in showing that prayer has a positive effect on health. Prayer has been documented as being "good medicine" in more than 130 research studies.[25]

One of the findings of these studies is that prayer is effective regardless of the religious affiliation of the person praying. Religion is a set of beliefs that comprise a doctrine of how the universe operates and typically incorporates rituals, such as prayer, to support its worldview. In contrast, spiritual refers to those aspects of nature that are unseen and nonphysical. *It is this connection with the power of the unseen that is the basis of effective prayer.* Prayer is another way, like communing with nature, listening to great music, and meditation, of connecting with that which is larger than the individual self.

Pray.

As the researchers have shown, prayer has no boundaries. It works locally and at a distance. It works for you individually, and it works for others when you pray for them. It works aloud and in silence. It works as well with words as with images. There is no "right" way to pray, but here are some tips, gleaned from experienced prayer therapists, which may be helpful to you.

Prayer Tips

1. Before you pray, become still, let go of your worldly concerns and bring all your energy into the present moment.
2. Connect so deeply that you feel completely one with both the universe (God/Spirit) and the person or situation upon which you are focusing your prayer.
3. Be absolutely convinced – have unwavering faith – that your prayers are being answered.

4. Think, speak or see the positive outcome in present time. If using language, frame the prayer affirmatively. For example, "I am in perfect health now." or "Jim has peace of mind and clarity regarding his next career step now." If visualizing, see the desired results in as much detail as possible.

5. Specify the "what" (e.g., health, prosperity, happiness, resolution of conflict, etc.) but let the universe figure out the details – the "how" and the "when."

6. Express your gratitude to the universe. Give thanks to the unseen, which works in the most creative and often unimaginable ways.

7. Release the prayer and allow the universe to do its highest good. Amen literally means, "so be it."

The Power of the Positive

Researchers no longer doubt that positive thoughts and attitudes promote wellness, whereas negative ones lead to disease. This has been known and practiced by civilizations since the beginning of time. That we have a choice in how we think about things and view our world is also ancient wisdom. William Shakespeare's Hamlet tells us in the play with the same name that, "There is nothing either good or bad, but thinking makes it so." Thoughts, beliefs and attitudes can be changed, regardless of upbringing, traumatic life events, societal beliefs or current environment. Positive thoughts, attitudes and beliefs are essential to maintaining and sustaining the harmony of the energetic template.

Affirmations

To affirm means to assert to be true or to state positively. Using affirmations is a lot like reprogramming your computer. You simply insert the new program over the old one. For example, you may be overweight and have the attitude that you will always be this way because you believe it is a family trait. By clinging to the thought, "I will always be overweight," you are keeping yourself from changing. Attention goes to where thought is. By changing the thought to "I am thin and energetic, and I love how my body looks," you are changing the focal point of your attention. By focusing on the new positive image you allow the old one to wither away from lack of attention.

Affirmations bring the future into the present through the intention of your thought. The words you choose to use in your affirmations are very powerful, so take care in selecting them. The words "I am" make a claim about your very being. Saying "I am fat" will keep you so. Saying "I am thin and energetic" will help move you into that new reality.

Because the old patterns you are now changing may be deeply ingrained, you will need to repeat your new beliefs until your computer brain really "gets" the new program. Write your affirmation down on note cards. Place the note cards where you will see them constantly – on your mirrors, closet doors, on your nightstand, etc. Carry one with you, and look at it often throughout the day and before you go to sleep at night. The more senses you involve in the process, the better. In addition to looking at your written affirmation, repeat it aloud if your lifestyle permits. Otherwise, repeat it silently with your eyes closed and your attention completely focused on the thought. Feel and visualize it as you say it. The more you involve yourself with your affirmation, the more real it will be for you.

Reprogram yourself at least 30 times a day, combining looking at, saying, thinking, feeling and visualizing your affirmation. Continue with the affirmation process until you feel the new beliefs take root and your environment reflects those changes back to you. Thoughts create a mental atmosphere that is magnetic to those of a like nature. *As your thoughts change, what you attract also changes.*

Affirm the positive.

∼

Mental Exercise

Besides thinking positively, your mind needs to be active to maintain its youthfulness. The mind, like the body's muscles, grows weaker if it is not exercised. *An active brain is a younger brain.*

If you are undergoing a major change in your lifestyle, such as leaving your job to raise a family or retiring, you need to make sure that you maintain sufficient mental stimulation to keep your mind alert and interested. Learning a new language, joining a book club or challenging yourself with crosswords or other types of puzzles are just a few ways of doing so. Researchers are finding that an active and engaged mind is one of the characteristics of those who live long and productive lives.[26]

Stay mentally active.

〜

People Need People

Recent research has documented the relationship between social ties and health and longevity. An article recently published in the *Journal of the American Medical Association* reported that loners were four times as likely as those with an active network of social support to succumb to a cold.[27] Psychologist Dr. Joan Borysenko, has noted that people who have a sense of connnectedness have twice the level of immune cell activity as do people who feel lonely.[28] The MacArthur Foundation Study researchers found that frequency of emotional support is a powerful predictor of both maintained and enhanced health in older adults.[29] Even staying connected with others through holiday greeting cards has been shown to boost the receivers' self-esteem and feelings of belonging.[30]

Stay connected with people.

〜

The old adage is true: people need people. Friends, family, work colleagues and members of social groups are essential to our well-being and longevity. Stay involved with people in whatever way, shape or form feels right for you.

In addition to engaging in recreational activities, you might consider volunteering. Helping others can also help you. In a national survey of individuals who volunteered to help others, researchers found that 95% reported that helping on a regular basis gave them an immediate "feel-good" sensation and continuing feelings of calmness and self-worth.[31] In the Cornell Retirement and Well-Being Study, similar results were reported: one-fourth of newly retired people volunteer, and increased energy, self-esteem and personal satisfaction are the rewards of engaging in such activities.[32]

Volunteering, besides keeping you involved with other people, gets you out of yourself and your self-limited concerns. It allows you to give something back to life. It is a great antidote to exaggerated fears, depression and other negative states that are more likely to occur when you spend too much time alone and dwelling on the past.

If for some reason you find yourself unable to interact with people on a frequent basis, don't accept isolation. If you can't find people to come to you, get a pet. Inpatients receiving canine visitors at the UCLA Medical Center reported improved emotional states, and elevated blood pressures decreased. Some retirement facilities have added pet residents for these same reasons.

Happiness

What makes one person happy might bore or depress another. We are each so exquisitely unique in our likes and dislikes. One thing we do have in common, however, is the need for joy and happiness in our lives.

People often loose track of what makes them happy when they pass from one stage of life to another. This is a common experience for women who devoted their lives to raising a family. The children move out and that main source of purpose and fulfillment leaves with them. Add the hormonal shifts leading up to menopause, and emotional turmoil and depression often rear their ugly heads.

Find sources of happiness.

~

Another life passage that may require some redefining of our sources of happiness is the movement from a full and engaging career into retirement. This period can be especially trying for individuals who have loved their work and found their life purpose in it. They often have devoted such long hours to their career that they have not developed other interests or hobbies. If you are nearing retirement, it is crucial to begin creating a new and fulfilling lifestyle for yourself.

Find what gives you *joie de vivre.* Don't allow yourself to become mired in what have become, for you, life-draining rather than life-giving situations. Move on. As the words of inventor Alexander Graham Bell remind us, "When one door closes another door opens; but we so often look so long and so regretfully upon the closed door that we do not see the ones which open for us."

The happiest people are the ones who have the ability to be fully present and engaged in the moment. Do today what you always dreamed of doing tomorrow. It doesn't need to be something major. Even the smallest thing that gives us pleasure is important for sustaining our happiness. Don't limit yourself. Develop new interests. Moving forward and expanding are emotional keys to longevity. If you live alone and can't find a companion to share your interests, join a group that appeals to people with similar interest. A friend of mine was lost when her husband passed away. He had been the initiator of most of their avocational activities. A bereavement group not only provided support for her grief but also new companions with whom to share cultural events and travel excursions.

Humor

"A merry heart," wrote King Solomon, "doeth good like a medicine." Knowing this, the ancient Greeks built their healing centers next door to their theaters, so patients could be uplifted by the comedies performed there. The word humor comes from the Latin *umere,* which means to flow like water. While taste in humor is personal, humor itself is universal.

Today, we know about some of the physiological effects of humor-induced laughter. Laughter stimulates endorphin release, massages the internal organs and increases our ability to resist disease. Norman Cousins, in *Anatomy of An Illness,*[33] brought the healing power of humor and laughter to public attention when he wrote of how he used these tools. They became essential components in a program to successfully heal himself of an apparently "incurable" disease.

Weave humor and laughter into the tapestry of your life. Making light of an experience or situation changes things by moving your perspective from one place to the other. Fluidity keeps us young. Whenever things weigh very heavily on my shoulders, my colleague Janette Golden, an incredibly creative psychotherapist and true comedienne, pulls one of many jokes from her sleeve. I can't help but laugh, and soon the whole office is laughing with me. I can't agree more with Katherine Hepburn, who said, "…But whatever happens to you, you have to keep a slightly comic attitude. In the final analysis, you have got not to forget to laugh."

Take yourself lightly.

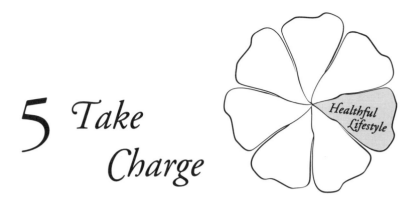

5 *Take Charge*

It's up to you.

Lifestyle Makes a Difference

*A*s I previously indicated, we can no longer blame only our genes for our illnesses. As you learned in Chapter 3, genetics is responsible for just 25% of our aging process after age 40. How we age and how fast we age is for the most part under our control. The three lifestyle factors that are the most accessible to change and have a tremendous influence on aging are stress, diet and exercise. By making health-promoting choices, we can remain vital and strong until we reach our naturally appointed time to leave this world.

Stress

When most people hear the word "stress," they think only of emotional triggers. The fact is that any stimulus can trigger the cascade of biochemical events, starting in the brain, that we call the stress response. Consuming toxin-laden or high-sugar foods and inhaling polluted air are also interpreted by our brain's stress detection centers as threats – and lead to secretion of stress hormones. Stress can also result from physical overexertion, as athletes so often experience.

Whatever the cause, the stress response starts with a signal to the hypothalamus – the perception center of the brain. From there, chemical messengers send alarm "fight or flight" messages all over the body through the involuntary nervous system. Our physiological and psychological equilibrium becomes disturbed, and, ultimately, cellular reserves become exhausted.

Stress is no longer related to food gathering, as it was with our cave-dwelling ancestors. Today, the grind of daily life exposes most of us to a myriad of toxic stimuli that can put us into a perpetual state of stress. Chronic stress impacts our health in many ways. It suppresses the immune system. It raises the levels of fatty acids and sugar in the blood, increasing the risk for many serious conditions, including stroke, heart disease and diabetes. By making our bodies acidic, stress also contributes to the depletion of calcium from our bones and increases our risk for osteoporosis.

Minimize and manage stress.
~

Manage Your Response

Stressors come in many different forms. Of course, we should avoid as many as we can, but as we all know, that is not always possible. *The one thing we can control, however, is our response to stress.* We are the masters of our response, and we have a choice. We can be reactive, like sailboats buffeted by every wind that comes along. Or we can be proactive and build structures that can support us when the winds unexpectedly change direction.

One of the most effective ways to minimize and manage emotional stress is to change the way we perceive external events. If we have a calm center and know that the events of our life are transient, we will be able to respond proactively rather than reactively to whatever life experiences may come our way. In Chapter 4 you were provided with a meditation technique, one out of the many available, which you can use to build a sense of stability at the core of your being. At our Centers, we often use biofeedback as a tool to teach our patients how to achieve the same result. Meditation and other relaxation techniques promote the balance of the energetic template, regardless of the source of the stress trigger.

Aromatherapy

Another useful and fun stress management tool is aromatherapy. Aromatic plants and the oils derived from them – essential oils – have been used since ancient times for healing. Advocated by the earliest Egyptians and Hippocrates, aromatherapy is still a common practice in India's traditional Ayurvedic medicine and it is also widespread in Europe.

Essential oils are the lifeblood of plants, and each oil has its own unique chemical properties. Some are antiviral or antibacterial. Some, like peppermint and rosemary, have a stimulating effect and increase adrenaline production. Others, such as lavender, prompt the secretion of the neurotransmitter, serotonin, and produce a calming effect.

The inhalation of these fragrant molecules transmits impulses to the limbic system – that part of the brain associated with learning, emotions and memories – and can produce profound beneficial effects. Our smelling apparatus, designed by nature to alert us to incoming danger, also has the capacity to transmit calming signals that can modulate or terminate the stress reaction.

The most common ways to use essential oils for stress management are inhalation, baths and massage. You can easily carry a small essential oil bottle in your purse, pocket or briefcase. Simply inhale deeply in the midst of your busy day and feel your energy immediately shift. For your home or office, you may want to purchase a diffuser (electric or candle-based), which disperses the aroma throughout a room. Adding an oil to your evening bath is another easy way to incorporate this powerful healer into your daily routine. Massage therapists often add several drops of essential oils to their base massage oil. You might want to do the same for home massages. Even a quick foot massage with an appropriate oil can make a big difference. The essential oil of sage is an overall balancer and is also helpful in relieving hot flashes. Lavender, bergamot, sandalwood, vetiver, fennel, neroli, rose and galbanum oils are all good stress relievers.

Sleep

Although most people don't think of sleep as a stress management tool, it is one of the best ways for restoring both our body and soul after a day "in the trenches." As we sleep, particularly in the earlier part of the night, our brains are very busy secreting serotonin, growth hormone, melatonin and even dehydroepiandrosterone (DHEA). DHEA, our most dominant cortical adrenal hormone, is also produced by our brain when not enough is available from our adrenals (see Chapter 12). The last three hormones together interact to reduce oxidative stress all over our body and modulate free radical production. At the same time, they facilitate enzymatic repair processes that rebuild what was torn down during our waking hours.

Sleep is not a static state. It progresses through four stages, with Stage 1 being the lightest and Stage 4 being the deepest. People who can move into the deeper Stages 3 and 4 quickly need less sleep than those who spend more time in the earlier phases. These deeper stages are also where the length of REM (rapid eye movement) sleep increases. REM sleep is a period of altered brainwave activity during which we dream (and are more receptive to soul messages), and process and store the memory of our daily events. Our muscles lose their tone in this stage. We are, in effect, in a state of muscle paralysis, which protects us from physically acting out our dreams. Adequate and efficient sleep is essential for maintaining the integrity of all three templates. It is necessary for modulating stress and slowing the aging process.

Diet

Today, we expend about 800 fewer calories daily than our parents did. We typically have sedentary occupations, and our busy lifestyles encourage us to take the elevator rather than climb the stairs. Our evening entertainment often keeps us glued to one spot, mesmerized by the computer, television or that great book we just can't put down. Combine this with the ready availability of tasty, calorie-rich food, and it is no wonder that more than half of us in the United States are overweight (and frequently undernourished on a cellular level).

Whether slim or overweight when young, most people tend to grow heavier as they grow older. This is due to a combination of wear and tear of our weight-controlling hormonal machinery, the tendency to be less physically active and, often, excessive calorie intake relative to our metabolic needs. As the amount of fat in our bodies increases and the amount of lean muscle mass decreases, our bodies become less efficient food metabolizers. Unless we take action, we will find ourselves gaining weight without increasing our food intake. Being overweight is one of the major risk factors for both accelerated aging and the serious degenerative diseases that plague our nation.

Obviously, we need to eat less, particularly as we get older. But we also need a nutrient-rich diet. Food is fuel for our biochemical machinery. Some foods are health-promoting; others are health-depleting. Clean proteins, for example, stimulate metabolism. Toxic, fatty and sugary foods, in contrast, make our metabolism sluggish. We need to be wise in choosing the type of fuel we feed to our organs and cells. If we think of ourselves as Chevy trucks and fuel our vehicles with high-calorie, low-nutrient-rich food, we will invite some damage to our organs that eventually will impact the quality and length of our lives. If we see ourselves as Maseratis, we will use the most refined and life-enhancing fuel to ensure that our finely-tuned machinery continues its peak performance for a very long time. As Hippocrates instructed his students a

Eat less,

but eat

the best.

~

few thousand years ago, "Let food be your medicine and medicine be your food."

Because of the broad scope of this book, I am unable to present detailed nutritional information. What I do want to share with you, however, are some general nutrition guidelines that I have clinically found promote wellness and longevity.

General Nutrition Guidelines

1. Eat food that is as close as possible to how nature made it.

We can try, but we will never be able to surpass nature's wisdom. She has provided us with a cornucopia of unadulterated nutrient-rich food in ideal combinations. Vitamin C always comes with bioflavonoids (the white material underneath citrus fruit skin that protects the vitamin from oxidation). Rice's husk contains vitamin B_1, necessary for digesting and metabolizing the grain's starch. This is why it is so important to eat whole foods, rather than refined products. Processing allows us to have quick meals, but it destroys so many vital nutrients. One example is whole oats, which contains soluble fiber that helps move LDL (oxidized, toxic cholesterol) out of the bloodstream. Instead of processed, quick oatmeal, we should eat steel cut oats, which provide all the nutrients and fiber of the whole grain. As for produce, it also should be consumed in a form that is as close to nature as possible – organic or at least pesticide-free. Eat vegetables lightly steamed or raw to optimize their nutritional value.

2. Eat a wide variety of foods.

Each food has its own unique combination of nutrients. A varied intake will ensure that you are obtaining an assortment of necessary nutrients. Eating the same foods day in and day out may lead to food allergies and sensitivities that weaken the immune system (see Chapter 8).

3. *Eat 40% complex carbohydrates, 30% proteins and 30% healthy oils.*[1]

It is best to include this ratio of nutrients in each meal, as it assists in maintaining healthy blood sugar levels and prevents post-meal fatigue.

∾ Complex carbohydrates should include a wide variety of vegetables and whole grains, which provide fiber, antioxidants, vitamin K and numerous minerals. Fruits should be limited (see Guideline 5: Limit Sugars) and preferably eaten separately from grains to avoid excessive fermentation.

∾ Flaxseed oil is the richest source of omega-3 essential fatty acids (EFAs), which have a wide range of health-promoting effects; while olive oil, of the omega-9 family, offers cardioprotective benefits (see Chapter 7 to learn more about these powerful healers). Olive and sesame oils are the best choices for cooking. Avoid saturated fats (solid at room temperature) and margarine (trans-fatty acid), which increase LDL (toxic cholesterol).

∾ Proteins derived from animal sources innately contain all the essential amino acids and are complete proteins. They also contain some very important minerals and vitamins, like zinc and vitamin B_{12}.

∾ Deep-water fish, and organic meat and chicken (especially free-range) are good sources of animal protein (see Chapter 6 for more details).

∾ Eggs are a highly-digestible, high-quality protein source, and are also rich in iron and vitamin A. Egg yolks contain the highest quality lecithin, which lowers total cholesterol. I only recommend eating eggs from free-range chickens.

∾ Grains and beans are lacking in certain amino acids, but they provide complete protein when they are combined. The most effective combinations are legumes and grains (e.g., tofu and millet, pinto beans and rice, chickpeas and barley, etc.).

∾ Although milk and some of its derived products are a good source of calcium and protein, dairy cows are given bovine growth hormone, which increases the occurrence of udder infections and, thereby, increases the need for administration of antibiotics (see Chapter 8 to learn about the dangers of antibiotics). Milk also contains xenoestrogens (foreign estrogens) associated with increased risk for breast cancer and male infertility. Some "clean" dairy products are beginning to appear on the market. Check your health food stores. Soy, almond and brown rice milks are healthy alternatives to cow milk.

4. Eat light at night.

In general, you should eat like a queen at breakfast, a princess at lunch and a pauper at night. Many of us, however, are not very hungry when we awaken because the body is in a detoxification stage. I always recommend starting the day with a detoxifying glass of warm water and lemon. This is best followed by a protein shake. The shake is quick and easy to prepare, and is packed with all the vital nutrients you need to start your Maserati on a good and happy race. Although I recommend different protein shakes, depending on the patient's condition and health goals, the recipe below is the one I most frequently recommend. It provides clean, digested proteins and is a balanced 40-30-30 zone meal.

Protein Shake
2 scoops high quality protein powder[2]*
2 tablespoons flaxseed powder or flaxseed oil
2 tablespoons mixed fiber powder (soluble and insoluble)
1/4 cup of organic berries (low in sugar, high in antioxidants)
8 to 12 ounces of purified water

1. Put all ingredients into a blender and, if you like it cold, add a few ice cubes.

2. Blend until smooth and drink it right away, as the fiber expands rapidly.

3. If you have problems with sugar metabolism (dysglycemia), add 2 tablespoons of predigested collagen protein (such as Twin Labs LPP). If this is unavailable, add ¼ cup of pumpkin or sunflower seeds.

4. Adding 1 or 2 teaspoons of a good probiotic (beneficial bacteria that facilitate intestinal health) makes this a formidable immune-enhancing meal. (See Chapter 7 to learn about probiotics).

If you have a protein shake for breakfast, have a small snack 2 to 3 hours later. Make lunch your heaviest meal. If you find yourself craving something sweet in the middle of the afternoon, eat a handful or two of pumpkin or sunflower seeds, or almonds, and an apple. This is a good blood sugar-stabilizing maneuver and provides many beneficial nutrients. Dinner should be a light meal and eaten, if possible, at least 4 hours before retiring to give the body enough time to burn off the calories. This last meal "sticks to your ribs" more than any other one. If you suffer from dysglycemia (sugar regulation problems), try to eat small, well-balanced meals every few hours to stabilize your energy levels. You can also consume half of a protein shake before retiring to avoid nocturnal hypoglycemia.

5. Limit sugars.

In the 1970s and 1980s, we became aware of the deleterious effect of saturated fats on our health. Many people are proud of having switched from the high-fat versions of cookies and cakes to the low-fat ones. The problem is that the low-fat ones, whether you buy them in the health food or the grocery store, are filled with sugars. Whether it's refined sugar or a "natural sugar," once they reach the intestine all these sugars become glucose.

Dysglycemia

In this decade, we are becoming aware that consuming too much sugar or foods that turn into sugar (white breads, white potatoes, etc.) can create a whole host of glucose metabolism problems, which fall under the general umbrella term "dysglycemia." Dysglycemia includes a wide variety of sugar processing problems, such as hypoglycemia (low blood sugar) and hyperglycemia (high blood sugar). The most common type of dysglycemia, which occurs primarily as we move towards maturity, is non-insulin-dependent-diabetes (Type 2 diabetes). Unmanaged, Type 2 diabetes can lead to serious consequences, including hypertension (high blood pressure), heart disease, stroke, neurological and visual problems, and severe infections. The causes of dysglycemia are multiple, but the most prevalent are obesity, and the overconsumption of sugars and foods that easily turn into glucose.

As we get older and heavier, we become more prone to developing insulin resistance, the hallmark of Type 2 diabetes. When we ingest foods that turn into sugar, our blood glucose level increases and our pancreas is forced to secrete more and more of the hormone, insulin. When our bodies operate normally, the insulin binds to specific receptors in our cell membranes to let the glucose come in and be burned as fuel for energy. When the insulin receptors become impaired, most often as a consequence of the body being overweight, they are unable to bind the insulin efficiently, and the action of the hormone is hindered. The pancreas continues to secrete more and more insulin in an attempt to overcome the cellular resistance. Its mass action eventually causes a sudden drop in the blood sugar level (reactive hypoglycemia). Incidentally, this is what happens during the early hours of the morning to most Type 2 diabetics. Physicians not well versed in the understanding of these "functional" cellular metabolic processes fail to suspect the disease, which can only be definitely diagnosed by a Glucose Tolerance Test (GTT) with the insulin curve.

Dysglycemia and Syndrome X

Excessive glucose in the blood is transformed into excessive fats (hyperlipidemia). When this happens, the small arteries can be narrowed by plaques, resulting in high blood pressure and cardiovascular disease. Syndrome X, marked by obesity (particularly abdominal fat accumulation), high triglycerides (blood fats) and hypertension is the natural consequence of untreated dysglycemia.

My clinical experience has proven time and again that people who develop Syndrome X have shown early signs and symptoms of dysglycemia that were missed. Subtle early manifestations of the condition include carbohydrate cravings, bouts of dizziness, irritability, progressive weight gain (especially around the abdomen) with little change in food intake, an increase in blood fats levels (triglycerides and cholesterol), a progressive (even if slight) increase in blood pressure, fatigue after an allergic meal, fainting episodes and frequent fungal infections.

Diagnosing Sugar Regulation Problems

Neither dysglycemia nor early stages of Type 2 diabetes can be diagnosed by the standard Fasting Blood Glucose Test because, as I have previously noted, there is often a burst of insulin before awakening, which will tend to lower the blood sugar level and give an inaccurate reading. The only way to diagnose these conditions is by a 4- to 5-hour Glucose Tolerance Test (GTT) that checks both glucose and insulin levels. If you have half or more of the symptoms noted above, ask your physician do a GTT with the insulin curve. Dysglycemia and Type 2 diabetes, one of its most serious manifestations, are among the most misunderstood and undiagnosed maladies of our day. The general nutrition guidelines I have presented are designed to prevent these sugar metabolism problems and reduce their impact if you suffer from them.

Sugars are Everywhere

Be aware that sugars are ubiquitous in canned and processed foods. Some foods release sugar (glucose) more rapidly into the bloodstream than others. The glycemic index (GI) is a ranking of more than 500 foods (on a 100-point scale) based on their blood glucose response.[3] The higher the number, the bigger the trouble. For example, a white potato ranks 85, while a yam ranks 51 and a sweet potato ranks 54. White rice ranks high at 88, while basmati rice is rated at 58, brown rice at 54 and pearled barley at 25. Grapefruit is rated at 25; apples, peaches and pears rank in the 30s, while watermelon is 72. The rating of pasta varies based on its protein content, shape, length of cooking and ingredients. Given the current state-of-the-art, I recommend eating whole grains with lower GI ratings and staying away altogether from white breads (rating = 100) and limiting white potatoes. In terms of fruits, I recommend the lower sugar ones, such as those noted above. I do recommend berries. Although they have not yet been included in the GI, they have a low carbohydrate content relative to other fruit and contain a number of health-supportive nutrients. Clinically, I have found berries to be well tolerated by people with sugar regulation problems. If you suspect you have dysglycemia, always eat tofu, nuts or seeds with your fruit.

I also recommend staying away from commercial fruit juices for a couple of reasons. A 12-ounce serving of juice contains the sugar of four to six pieces of fruit. Furthermore, the juice is produced from inferior grade fruits, which are often contaminated with molds and yeast. After the squeezing, the juice is cooked to kill these infective organisms. As a final step, a little synthetic Vitamin C is added, but the dead molds and yeast, with their powerful allergenic properties, are still there. In my opinion, children's high consumption of fruit juice is one of the major reasons for increased juvenile allergies. It is far better to eat the whole fruit, which contains beneficial fiber, antioxidant flavonoids and is free of infective microorganisms.

In terms of sweeteners, avoid the artificial variety. "Natural" sweeteners are not so great either. Honey has a GI rating of 73, which is even higher than white sugar (sucrose), ranked at 65. Fructose (fruit sugar), although scored at 23, increases triglycerides. Elevated triglycerides are a risk factor for both diabetes and heart disease. The ideal sweetener is the herb, stevia, which can be found in many health food stores in herbal and tincture forms.[4] If you don't have stevia, brown rice syrup is probably the least damaging alternative.

The Diet Theory Maze

It seems like there is a new diet theory almost every month. Like all theories, some are better than others, but most are based on what would happen in a perfectly balanced and healthy body. Since this eliminates 99% of us, we need to adapt any general theory to our genetic heritage, biochemical individuality and health status.

In designing dietary plans for my patients, I incorporate nutritionist Dr. Barry Sear's 40-30-30 Zone Diet Theory. I also take into account naturopathic physician Dr. Peter D'Adamo's Blood Type Theory.[5] It presents two generations of D'Adamo research documenting the link between blood types, the foods we eat and immune responses. According to the theory, people with different blood types do better with different types of food. For example, a person with Type O blood needs more animal protein than does a Type A person. My clinical experience has thus far validated this theory in its broad strokes. However, our nutritionists always adapt dietary recommendations to the patients' history, symptoms and clinical findings. A Type A, who is supposed to thrive on grains and milk products, will not do well if she has excessive *Candida albicans*, since this type of diet will accelerate the growth of yeast. And typically I would advise a Type O patient with cancer to limit or avoid meat.

Another popular plan, which has achieved remarkable results for individuals with heart disease, is the 10% fat, vegetarian diet, advocated by pioneering internist Dr. Dean Ornish.[6] The high quality protein found in tofu and sprouts may be sufficient for many, but a Type O person with controlled diabetes would not do well. Yet other considerations to take into account before adopting any dietary plan are your personal food allergies and sensitivities (see Chapter 8), and subclinical maladies.[7]*

After many decades as a practicing physician, I have arrived at the conclusion that when we are not too toxic and can get adequately calm and still, the inherent wisdom of our bodies will direct us to the right foods at the right times. Until you reach this ideal state, I advise you to follow my general nutrition recommendations and to start listening to your body carefully. As it gets cleaner, it will guide you wisely.

Nutritional Supplements

Even if we could eat a wide range of the highest quality organic foods every day, our diets would still not provide us with adequate nutrients for sustaining our health, let alone rejuvenating aging tissues. Because we are living in such a fast-paced and toxic environment, our bodies need additional nutritional support just to survive.

The Recommended Dietary Allowances (RDAs), established by the Food and Nutrition Board of the National Academy of Sciences, are defined as the amount of vitamins and minerals an individual needs to consume to avoid severe nutritional deficiency diseases, such as scurvy or pellagra. These diseases are very rarely, if ever, seen in the United States today. What we do see now are *nutritional insufficiencies* (also known as marginal or subclinical deficiencies), which manifest themselves in a variety of vague symptoms that are reflective of impaired organ function and accelerated aging.

Furthermore, the RDAs are calculated for the average person. But who is average? We know that each one of us is biochemically unique and that the need for specific nutrients varies enormously based on genetics, health status, and environmental and lifestyle stress factors. A 110-pound young woman in relatively good health certainly has very different requirements than a middle-aged man with multiple organ problems. Researchers are now discovering that some people have genetic enzymatic defects that make a higher intake of certain nutrients necessary. As a consequence of all of these insights, at our Centers we recommend nutrients based on an analysis of many interactive variables.

As I explained in the Prologue, this is not a prescriptive supplement book. I do, however, share some of the remedies that have been successful for a large number of my patients. With nearly 40 years combined experience as an orthomolecular psychiatrist and an integrative medicine practitioner, I have gained an in-depth knowledge of nutritional biochemistry. Like most other integrative healthcare practitioners, I purchase the best available products from many reputable companies. When I am unable to find a high quality, synergistic product to meet specific needs, I develop my own formulations. I refer to these products as Corsello Center (CC) Formulas. The Nutritional Supplement Appendix (Appendix A) lists their ingredients, therapeutic actions, and recommended dosages to assist you in finding similar nutrients on your own.

Choose Quality Products

Not all supplements are created equal. The source and quality of the ingredients are of the utmost importance. Manufacturing processes also impact the quality of the final product. Tablets require substances to bind the therapeutic ingredients together. The cost of these binders varies greatly, and some companies use those of a lesser quality to save money. The manufacture of capsules involves the use of fillers to facilitate the flow of various

Add high quality nutritional supplements to a well-balanced diet.

components. When poor quality fillers are used, the products suffer. All of these factors can have an impact on the absorbability and efficacy of the supplements, and, in some cases, on their safety. When buying herbal supplements, always buy from reputable companies and purchase "standardized" products. By labeling its product standardized, a manufacturer is committing itself to the concentrations of the ingredients the product is claimed to contain. By and large, standardized products have also passed a microbiological test to screen for infective agents and petrochemical residues.

Most importantly, manufacturers of nutritional supplements should have their products examined and certified by independent auditors, as well as have their own internal quality control procedures in place. Buy from reputable companies, which scrutinize raw materials, monitor manufacturing and assure quality. Generally, the best does cost more. Since your health is priceless, I am sure you will agree that buying quality products, in the final analysis, is a far better bargain than buying inferior and potentially harmful discount brands.

General Maintenance

In terms of general maintenance, I suggest you take a high-quality multi-vitamin and mineral supplement that exceeds the RDAs. Be aware that the research and development of nutritional supplements has outpaced the government's ability to establish RDAs. You will find many supplements with ingredients that have been shown to be effective but do not yet have RDAs assigned.

Antioxidants

In addition to a good multi-vitamin and mineral supplement, you need to make sure your body is well fortified with a wide range of antioxidants, also known as free radical scavengers. Our bodies are like burning candles. The rapidity with which we burn is dependent upon the amount of neutralizing antioxidants we possess. Our bodies use two groups of antioxidants to neutralize free radicals. Those produced internally are called *endogenous*, while those that must be ingested are called *exogenous*. Most people are far more familiar with the exogenous ones, such as vitamins C and E, but the endogenous ones are even more important in protecting us from the diseases of aging.

Superoxide dismutase (SOD), glutathione peroxidase and catalase are three of the most important endogenous antioxidants. Although they are internally produced, these antioxidant enzymes depend on our tissues' ability to constantly make them anew from ingested amino acids and trace minerals – copper, manganese and zinc for SOD, iron for catalase and selenium for glutathione peroxidase. When we have difficulty digesting and/or absorbing our food, or we eat food that does not have adequate nutrients, we cannot produce these important free radical buffers. Even if we ingest the appropriate building blocks, our individual requirements may exceed the supply. This may occur, for example, when diseases or medications increase our level of cellular stress and free radical production.

Any time we have an imbalance between internal antioxidant supply (endogenous or exogenous) and demand, we run the risk of oxidative stress. We can, however, still repair the body by supplying it with more external antioxidants and endogenous antioxidant precursors. Selenium is not only part of the important endogenous antioxidant glutathione peroxidase but is itself an antioxidant. Vitamins C (combined with bioflavonoids), vitamin A (and its carotenoid precursors), vitamin E, vitamin B_2, biotin, and lemonin (the oil of lemon peel) are all good exogenous antioxidants. The amino acid taurine and coenzyme Q-10 (ubiquinone) are powerful, more sophisticated antioxidants.

Interactive Effect

Individual antioxidants do not provide the protection we need. In donating electrons to free radicals, each antioxidant itself becomes oxidized and needs to be reconstituted. Vitamin C, for example, while fighting germs, loses electrons, and becomes ascorbyl radical. Vitamin E and glutathione are the best substances to correct this problem. Vitamin E not only regenerates vitamin C, but it is also part of the protective cell membrane shield. This interactive effect of antioxidants makes it difficult, if not impossible, to interpret the results of studies following the allopathic model, in which the effect of one antioxidant at a time is observed. This research model has led to many misconceptions, especially regarding vitamins C and A.

Liver-Supportive Antioxidants

The liver is the body's most important detoxification factory. It carries out this essential function in two phases. During Phase 1, it removes many chemicals by oxidation, but in the process often produces partially-biotransformed oxidant molecules that can be even more toxic than the original substances. The integrity of Phase 2 is essential to our well-being because this is where the toxic intermediaries produced in Phase 1 are transformed into nontoxic products and prepared for excretion. The ability of the liver to do this job is dependent on the endogenous antioxidant enzymes, which require both an adequate supply of raw materials and finely tuned cellular machinery to put these substances together. The powerful glutathione, along with SOD and taurine, facilitate this important work of the liver.

When the demand for antioxidants increases, the body utilizes what I call "third-line defenses," such as cholesterol and uric acid, to buffer free radicals. Protracted demands for third-line defenses can lead to life-threatening situations, since both uric acid and cholesterol are components of vital biological systems. Very low cholesterol levels are often found in people in the final stages of cancer and AIDS. Low uric acid is a sign of uncontrolled free radical pathology.[8]*

Comprehensive Antioxidant Protection

The defense of all living cells involves the interaction of many protective antioxidant substances.[9] City dwellers and people under chemical and psychological stress seldom can meet the body's demands for antioxidants from diet alone and require nutritional supplements to assure comprehensive daily protection. As the most basic protection, I recommend that you take 3,000 milligrams of vitamin C with bioflavonoids on the average (see Chapter 7 to learn about vitamin C and bowel tolerance) and at least 400 international units of vitamin E (mixed tocopherols) a day. To assure good Phase 1 and 2 liver detoxification and optimal overall protection, I suggest you add the more sophisticated antioxidants, such as those included in the **CC C.V. Antioxidant Formula** and **CC GlutaPath Formula** (see Appendix A), alternating between the two groups from day to day.

Exercise

Four of the most important biomarkers of youthfulness are lean body mass, strength, flexibility and endurance. As we grow older, these four physical characteristics are affected first and decrease the most rapidly unless we do something about them. Lack of exercise, hormonal imbalance and poor eating habits are the most common causes for their decline.

Regular exercise can play a very important role in enhancing these biomarkers. It can help us stay well, fit and strong as long as we live. Exercise facilitates bowel regularity and improves lean body mass by burning fat. It turns yellow (storage) fat into brown fat, the type of fat found most commonly in fit people. Brown fat is rich in mitochondria, the energy factories of the cells, and burns fat more readily. Not only is a more muscular body a stronger body, but it is also a body that continues to burn fat even on the days when it is not exercising. Exercise not only improves the biomarkers, but it can also enhance the hor-

Keep on moving.

mones that affect them. It increases the secretion of growth hormone (GH) and the binding of thyroid hormones to the tissues. Exercise also improves the fat-burning (antilipogenic) effect of DHEA and enhances insulin sensitivity.[10, 11]

A great stress-buster, exercise stimulates the release of endorphins – neurotransmitters that enhance relaxation and feelings of well-being. Exercise encourages deep, restful sleep. Its relaxing effects do not diminish as we age, researchers report.[12] Exercise also decreases the risk for osteoporosis and its associated fractures. Researchers, who conducted a recent study of more than 9,000 postmenopausal women, noted that moderately to vigorously active women had 42% and 33% less risk for hip and vertebral fractures, respectively, compared with inactive women.[13] When you put it all together, regular exercise (not once- or twice-a-week madness) is one of the most important tools for staying well and staying young.[14]

Flexibility

The American College of Sports Medicine (ACSM) has finally caught up with ancient Hindu wisdom. In its newly updated guidelines, it has, for the first time, recommended flexibility training for older adults.[15] Hatha yoga, in my opinion, is one of the most efficient and beneficial forms of exercise. It combines flexibility, isometric and weight-bearing training. At the same time, its slow, deep breathing reduces stress, balances the endocrine glands and facilitates the release of volatile toxins.

Although you can learn yoga on your own from a videotape or book, I recommend taking a class until you get the basics down. Having a teacher who can guide you assures optimal benefits from the postures. Ideally, it would be wonderful to do yoga an hour a day. For most of us busy folk, I recommend a 1-hour class once a week and a 15- to 30-minute home session every day. If you do yoga first thing in the morning, make sure to do a little muscle warming (e.g., running in place for 5 minutes), because a warm muscle stretches easier. Also, take care not to overdo it as you can knock your vertebrae out of alignment or create other injuries. Listen to your body – it will tell you when you are trying to do too much, too soon.

A Varied Program Is Best

In addition to yoga, I recommend that you incorporate some aerobic and weight-bearing exercise into your weekly schedule. To achieve the benefits of reducing your risk of numerous chronic diseases, the ACSM recommends engaging in aerobic activities that burn about 150 to 200 calories (about 30 minutes) on most days of the week. Heavy household chores, climbing stairs and gardening count. Walking at a moderate pace, biking or swimming will also get you to the desired weekly goal. If you want to increase your endurance and strength level, try to expend 250 to 300 calories, on most days of the week. Walking or jogging at a 15-minute-mile pace for 50 to 60 minutes (4 miles/hour) or bicycling eight miles in 30 minutes will do it. The ACSM recommends adding resistance exercises (e.g., lifting weights or using a strength-training machine) 2 to 3 times a week.

Personally, I combine fast walking and moderate weight training with yoga. Anything you want to do that pleases you is fine as long as you take into consideration the fact that aging causes some loss of flexibility in all of us. When the fibers of our muscles are less flexible, we are at a greater risk of injury. If you have skied all your life, you can continue enjoying the sport, but you should be a little less aggressive as you get older. If you have jogged all your life, you can continue well into your 70s and 80s, providing you take steps to protect your energy factories (the mitochondria) from burning out and your joints from wearing down.

One of greatest human skills is knowing your own body so well that day by day you are aware of how far you can push the machine to optimize its performance without punishing it. Even though habituated to a high level of exercise, you might wake up one day and find that your body tells you to go slow. Walk instead of run that day. Don't abandon exercise unless you are really sick or injured. Even if you are confined to bed, do some stretches. Daily movement is essential for maintaining wellness and staying young. Once the crisis is over, resume your routine at its least strenuous level and build up gradually.

Exercise and Nutrients

As our senior nutritionist, Colette Iannuzzi-Heimowitz, MS, tells our patients, "Exercising the body without the knowledge of its biochemical and nutritional requirements will only lead to harm in the long run." When we engage in aerobic exercise, we have a greater need for antioxidants. Aerobic exercise uses oxygen, and the more oxygen we burn the more damaging free radicals we produce. Antioxidants are essential for protecting our important cellular energy factories, the mitochondria.

Especially on the days when you engage in strenuous activity, I recommend that you take additional vitamin C with bioflavonoids (the amount depends on your personal baseline) and double your vitamin E. In addition, take the more sophisticated antioxidant ingredients found in the **CC C.V. Antioxidant Formula** and **CC GlutaPath Formula**. These formulations also include potassium and magnesium, to replenish these minerals which are lost in perspiration, and L-carnitine, necessary for burning fat and producing energy in the mitochondria. I also recommend taking essential fatty acids (EFAs) of the omega-3 family (flaxseed oil and fish oil), as they keep our joints and cells well lubricated and are powerful anti-inflammatories. Exercise inevitably produces some degree of inflammation. Adequate presence of these oils "cools" things down.

If our metabolic machinery were perfect, we would be able to rapidly release glucose from our carbohydrate stores to obtain the immediate energy we need when we exercise.

The reality is that as we grow older, the glucose-releasing machinery becomes impaired, and exercise without food may create hypoglycemic symptoms, such as dizziness, shakiness or headaches. This is why I recommend drinking a protein shake before strenuous exercise or other demanding events (on-stage performance, high-stress exam, etc.). This protective action is particularly important if you are very lean and have limited glycogen reserves.

6 *Protect Yourself*

Beware of toxins; they're everywhere.

The Downside of Modern Living

*M*any would say that we are living better now in this nation than ever before. Certainly, we are living faster; but we may not necessarily be living better. The same technology that allows us to do more in a shorter period of time and enjoy many modern conveniences also generates a variety of noxious stimuli that impair health and accelerate aging. These harmful environmental factors are cumulative and interactive with each other. We can, however, protect ourselves from many of their deleterious effects by taking some commonsensical, proactive measures.

Chemical Toxins

Chemical toxins are omnipresent. They are in our water and air, in the food and medications we consume, and in the cosmetic and personal hygiene products we use. These toxins are xenobiotics – substances that are foreign to our body and deleterious to our biological workings. Xenobiotics have been linked to a wide range of illnesses, including serious diseases such as cancer and degenerative neurological conditions. Scientists at the National Toxicology Program at the

National Institute of Environmental Health Sciences (NIEHS) recently announced the addition of 14 new substances to the current list of 184 known carcinogens – including some anti-cancer medications and immunosuppressive drugs used for organ transplants.

One of the saddest reminders of our collective environmental carelessness is the double-digit increase in childhood cancers during each of the last two decades. Every year, 8,000 children under the age of 15 are diagnosed with cancer. Biostatisticians warn us that one of every 600 newborns has a risk of contracting cancer by the age of ten. In 1998, Environmental Protection Agency (EPA) officials finally acknowledged a potential xenobiotic cause for this frightening trend and drafted a research plan to examine the toxicity of 75,000 synthetic chemicals.

Toxins in Our Water

The Federal Clean Water Act, passed in 1972, helped start the massive cleanup of rivers, lakes and streams. The Act, however, only applied to contamination coming from specific industries and industrial sites and had no impact on the rampant pollution emanating from agricultural ground water, rain drains, and leaking septic and gasoline storage tanks.

In 1974, the Safe Water Drinking Act mandated the EPA to ensure that public water systems met minimum standards of public health. The law was strengthened in 1986 and currently requires the states to establish "acceptable" contaminant levels in municipal drinking water supplies. The problem is that most municipalities test for less than 30% of the toxic chemicals on the EPA's list. That list, of course, does not include the 75,000 synthetic chemicals the agency is now planning to investigate for toxicity. Researchers in Los Angeles, California recently reported a higher rate of miscarriages among women who drank municipal water compared to those who drank purified water.[1] Long Island, New York's largest bedroom community, was populated for many years with potato farms in which high concentrations of pesticides were used to control blight. Today, Long Island women have one of the nation's highest rates of breast cancer. Finally, EPA officials have linked the high breast cancer incidence to the pesticides still residing in the underground water tables.[2]

Most water-borne toxins generally fall within four categories – microbial pathogens, organic chemicals, inorganic chemicals and radioactive elements. Pathogenic microorganisms include bacteria, viruses and parasites. Recently, some municipal water supplies have been contaminated with cyst-like organisms, particularly *giardia* and *cryptosporidium*, neither of which are destroyed by chlorine. Not only can they cause stomach cramps and diarrhea with the associated nutrient loss, but they also rob the body of vital vitamins and amino acids for their own metabolism. *Cryptosporidium* can be particularly deleterious to individuals with weakened immune systems and has been responsible for the death of many people suffering from AIDS.

As for toxic organic chemicals, only a few of those found in our drinking water supplies are regulated. This group of toxins includes pesticides (herbicides, insecticides and fungicides) and trihalomethanes (THMs) – well-known carcinogens, which are formed when chlorine combines with the microorganisms it kills. Volatile organic chemicals, such as solvents, degreasers and many other common household products are also known carcinogens. Petrochemicals, like gasoline and fuel additives, are yet another group of dangerous volatile chemicals. Inorganic chemicals include toxic metals like lead, aluminum, arsenic, mercury and silver. Nitrates, well-known inorganic contaminants, are commonly found in fertilizers, sewage, animal wastes and mineral deposits. Although not as common, radioactive contamination can occur in the form of radon, resulting from the decay of uranium in rocks and soils.

The impact of toxic chemicals can be devastating and far-reaching. Eisha, a young Nigerian attorney, who came to see me about infertility problems, informed me that her husband had a low sperm count with limited motility, a new and very widespread condition among Nigerian men. When I searched for the common denominator, I learned that Nigeria is rich in underground petroleum and that the government is very lax about protecting the water tables. As you will learn in Chapter 10, toxic chemicals disturb the delicate balance of sex hormones.[3]

It is clear that municipal water supplies are not a safe source of drinking water. Our local governments lack the funds to develop and install new and effective filtration systems. In fact, they do not even have the resources to monitor but just a few of the myriad of chemicals that poison our water supplies.

If you want to drink clean water, you must take the responsibility to make sure that it is purified. Installing your own home filtration system is the safest and, in the long run, the most cost-effective solution. Today, more than 500 companies sell water purification systems, and many of the products they offer combine two or more technologies. If you feel confused and overwhelmed, you are not alone.

Fortunately, an independent, nonprofit testing organization, the National Sanitation Foundation (NSF) International,[4] has set standards for drinking water systems. The NSF has two main standards for water filtration devices. One standard rates systems on chlorine removal and the other on removal of chemicals, pesticides, herbicides, cysts, lead, asbestos, turbidity and radon. NSF International ratings are now recognized as the industry standard nationwide. In California and some other states, manufacturers must include the filter's NSF International rating in their labeling. NSF International standards are far more comprehensive than those used by *Consumer Reports,* and the organization's ratings can assist you in your purchasing decision.

Purify your water.

∾

The most effective filters are the ones that combine technologies because each technology purifies a different contaminant. Granulated activated carbon, for example, removes organic chemicals, but leaves toxic metals and can breed bacteria. Ultraviolet light removes bacteria and some algae and protozoa, but leaves everything else. Reverse osmosis removes pathogenic organisms, organic and inorganic chemicals, and trace minerals, but some toxic molecules may slip through the filter.

If you buy bottled water, you should be aware that there are no laws requiring it to be any purer than tap water. Your best protection, again, is to buy water that is purified by a combination of technologies. However, I recommend that you do not purchase distilled water. Distillation removes trace minerals, including magnesium, which has been well documented as an element that protects the heart. Researchers, in a variety of countries, have found the death rates from cardiovascular disease are lower among people who live in areas where the drinking water contains magnesium compared with those people who drink water without magnesium.[5, 6] Because magnesium is instrumental in more than 300 enzymatic reactions, its deficiency has been implicated in a wide variety of conditions in addition to heart disease, including diabetes, fatigue, fibromyalgia, glaucoma, osteoporosis, and premenstrual syndrome (PMS).[7]

Toxins in Our Air

Our air is in as pathetic a shape as is our water. In 1998, the EPA updated its air quality standards, for the first time in 20 years for ozone, and for the first time in 10 years for soot (particulate matter). In describing its enhanced standards, the EPA acknowledged that air pollution is the cause annually of 15,000 premature deaths, 350,000 cases of aggravated asthma and 1 million cases of significantly decreased lung function in children.[8] Long-term effects include not only chronic respiratory disease and lung cancer, but also heart disease and damage to the liver, kidneys, brain and nervous system.[9] Outdoors, we are exposed to car exhaust fumes, industrial pollutants and pollens. Indoors, we face cigarette smoke, textile fibers, chemical residues, bacteria, viruses, fungi, human and pet dander, decaying organic matter, mold and dust mites. Many of us are ensconced during our workday in sealed buildings with contaminated air systems. Besides the obvious strain contaminated air puts on our lungs, it can make us more susceptible to infectious diseases, allergies and bronchial conditions, such as asthma.

The pollutants we breathe in go into systemic circulation, where they create free radical damage, leading over time to accelerated aging and degenerative diseases. Breathing in volatile petrochemicals is particularly dangerous for pregnant women because these toxins can cross the placental-blood barrier and damage the unborn fetus. The experience of Louise and her son is a tangible example of the impact of such toxins.

Louise was a very healthy 32-year-old, with two strong and healthy children, when she became pregnant for the third time. She was in the third month of her pregnancy when she and her husband found their dream house. In their excitement, they did not notice that it was adjacent to a petrochemical factory until after they had moved in.

Although Louise was disturbed by the irritating smell, she decided to ignore it and delivered a seemingly healthy baby 6 months later. Her infant son, however, soon developed many allergies and eczema, and was constantly irritable. He began suffering from serious asthma before he reached adolescence. In his late teens, when exposed to viral meningitis that did not harm those around him, he nearly died from it. Incidentally, the factory was subsequently condemned as a health risk to the community.

Obviously, the best strategy is to avoid as many air contaminants as possible. If you live in a city and work in a high-rise building, avoidance can be near to impossible, but there are a few steps you can take to protect yourself.

One is quite simple. Put plants in your home and office.

Not only do they remind you of your connection to nature, but they also absorb carbon dioxide and put oxygen into the environment. Whenever you can, escape to the country, mountains or ocean, where the air is fresher. Going to your local park, populated with trees, is an alternative when you can't get out of town. I adore the Sunday bustle of Central Park, an oasis of oxygen in polluted Manhattan.

Purify your air.

To protect yourself, you might also consider placing portable air filters in your office and home, or installing air cleaners in your home's heating and air conditioning system ductwork. Air filters work by trapping particles, such as dust, pollen, mold, etc. Some work mechanically, while others use electrostatic precipitation or particle ionization. High efficiency particulate arresting (HEPA) filters are very effective and reasonably-priced mechanical devices. They can trap up to 99% of particulates. However, they allow gas molecules, such as tobacco smoke, to pass through. As with water filters, the best solution is a combination of technologies – for example, a HEPA unit that also contains activated carbon or a charcoal filter to trap the gas molecules.

Another type of air filter, the negative ion generator, electrostatically precipitates particulates while releasing negatively-charged ions into the environment. An abundance of negative ions is what creates the clean, fresh- smelling air found in heavily forested areas, after lightening storms and in natural settings with moving water (oceans and waterfalls). In contrast, computer terminals, modern building materials, forced air ventilation systems and fluorescent lighting all generate an overabundance of positive ions, as do industrial pollutants and auto exhaust fumes.

Negative ion generators have been found to do far more than just cleanse the air. Scientific studies have shown that machine-generated negative ions can decrease irritability and tenseness,[10] improve memory and attention,[11, 12] and kill bacteria.[13] In a recent study, conducted at Columbia University, high-density negative ions were found to be effective in the treatment of seasonal affective disorder (SAD), commonly known as winter depression.[14]

Unlike water purification systems, no organization is currently setting certification standards for air purifiers. Parameters to consider when comparing air filters include clean air delivery ratings (CADRs) – how much air per unit of time does it cleanse – and maintenance requirements. I use ionizers manufactured by Wein Products,[15] a company that produces both room air purifiers and a portable unit, which I have found makes airplane travel much less toxic.

Toxins in Our Food

Because much of our ground water is polluted, and most farmers continue to use toxic herbicides and pesticides, our commercial produce is consequently contaminated. Animal foods also carry a variety of toxins. Fish live in contaminated waters. Most land animals are fed pesticide-laden grains with added antibiotics or graze on soil that is chemically fertilized. To top it off, the hormones with which they are injected to speed and enhance their growth are toxic to humans. One of the reasons we are seeing an increasing resistance to antibiotics among humans is the widespread use of these drugs in the animals that are raised for our consumption.

Go Organic

Organic Produce is Best

Organically-grown produce has fewer chemical toxins, and should be purchased whenever you can find it. You should be aware, however, that the organic food industry is currently unregulated by the federal government. The United States Department of Agriculture (USDA) recently proposed regulatory measures, but they have been sent back to the drawing board because they included provisions allowing irradiation, sewage sludge and genetically-engineered foods. These provisions were rightfully opposed by organic farmers, holistic medical practitioners and concerned consumers. Currently, 17 states have laws governing organic foods, and there are 33 private certi-

Consume the least toxic produce.

fication organizations. Lacking standardization, there is some variability in what organic means. Nevertheless, buy produce labeled "organically grown" whenever you can find it. Produce labeled "pesticide-free" is your next best choice.

Another reason to consume organic produce is its superior nutritional value. Commercial produce is typically grown in depleted soil, as the practice of crop rotation is no longer economically advantageous. Its nutritional value is further depleted by long lag times between harvesting and arrival at its final destination. In a recent study, conducted over a two-year period, the nutritional value of commercially- and organically-grown produce was compared. The foods were analyzed for 22 nutrients. On average, the organic foods had 90% more of the nutritional elements than did the commercial ones.[16] When you buy commercial produce, you are usually safer buying

Cleanse your produce.

items that are grown in the United States than those that are imported from other countries. Although current EPA standards and municipal regulation leave much to be desired, foreign countries that are major exporters of produce, such as Mexico, are

far less vigilant in protecting their food supplies. Because we still sell DDT to Mexico and other less-industrialized countries, we end up getting back in our imported produce supply what we have banned in this country!

Organic produce has many benefits, but because the soil in which it is grown is enriched by manure, it usually contains large amounts of parasites. When you intend to eat the produce raw, it should first be disinfected in a cleansing bath. This quick and easy practice also removes surface chemicals that might be present in some organic, and certainly are prevalent in nonorganic, produce. As the cleansing destroys molds and other decay-accelerating microorganisms, you will find that your produce will stay fresh longer.

Produce Cleansing Bath

1. Fill your sink with about 1 gallon of filtered water and add either 20 drops or 1 capsule of concentrated grapefruit seed extract[17] or 1 capful of Clorox bleach.
2. Put hardy produce (carrots, cucumbers, apples, potatoes, etc.) in the bath first.
3. Five minutes later, add medium hard produce (asparagus, zucchini, tomatoes, eggplant, peaches, etc.).
4. Five minutes later, add delicate produce (lettuce, parsley, basil, strawberries, blueberries, etc.).
5. Allow another 5 minutes (a total of about 15) and rinse with filtered water.
6. Your produce is now ready to eat raw or to be stored in a bleach-cleaned refrigerator vegetable bin. The fruit can be left on the counter to encourage its consumption in place of junk food.

Free-Range is Best

Organic meat and poultry are raised without pesticide-treated feed, antibiotics and hormones. Organic, free-range animals are raised uncaged, which means that products derived from these animals are clean and usually have the least amount of stress hormones. Buy free-range, whenever you can.

Deep-water fish, such as salmon, tuna and swordfish, are better choices than those that live in more contaminated coastal waters. Rich in health-promoting EFAs, fish also contain selenium, which facilitates Phase 2 liver detoxification. Shellfish

Consume the least toxic animal foods.

∽

are not a good choice, as they are bottom feeders exposed to high concentrations of waste. Particularly when eaten raw, they can transmit infectious diseases. There is also growing evidence that eating raw fish sushi presents a serious health risk, since raw fish is a common carrier of intestinal worms.[18]

Toxic Metals

Toxic metals are inorganic chemicals prevalent in our municipal water supply and the air we breathe. They also are found in other sources, including many commercially available products and foods. The most common of these harmful substances are aluminum, lead, mercury, cadmium and nickel.

Toxic metals have one of the most serious impacts on the human body as they poison all the intracellular enzymatic systems that are devoted to keeping the body machinery operating at an optimal level. They also age and destroy the architecture of cell membranes, limiting the efficacy of interventions that require membrane receptor binding, such as hormone replacement therapy.[19]

Metal toxicity is usually chronic, building up gradually in miniscule amounts, over the years. Since the body promptly moves the metals out of the blood and into fatty tissues and bones, symptoms may be vague or may not show up for many years. Initial symptoms of toxic metal poisoning may include fatigue, malaise, or increased susceptibility to infection. One inexpensive, initial way to assess metal toxicity is through hair analysis, which gives some indication of the amount the body is eliminating.[20]★ Urine and feces tests provide more precise information.

Accumulation of toxic metals can result in serious diseases. Researchers are now documenting the association between aluminum and a number of neurological diseases. My clinical experience has shown me that aluminum is just one of many toxic metals that accumulate in the lipids (fats) of the brain.

People with cancer usually have heavy metal toxicity, and I have yet to see a patient with multiple sclerosis (MS) who is not carrying high levels of toxic metals.

Lead

Although lead has been removed from our automobile gasoline supplies, leaded fuel is still used in some commercial vehicles, and lead is still used in a number of industries. Researchers at Baltimore's Center for Occupational and Environmental Neurology recently reported that smelter workers exposed to high levels of lead had greater levels of fatigue, confusion, tension, anxiety and depression than did co-workers with lower levels of exposure.[21] Lead is also found in paints and a number of other household products. According to Assistant Surgeon General Dr. Barry Johnson, lead poisoning affects more than 1 million American children and results in an 8-point decrement in standard intelligence tests. Lead and other toxic metals are capable of penetrating the blood-brain barrier. Once in the brain, they cannot be metabolized or excreted and can impair mental functioning.[22] Most of my young patients with learning disabilities have both excessive lead and cadmium in their systems.

Unborn children are also at risk from lead in the maternal skeletal system or from the mother's environmental or dietary exposure.[23]* Results of experimental studies have shown that their developing nervous system is particularly sensitive to the toxic effects of lead.[24]

Although the FDA has prohibited the use of lead solder in food cans, there are no controls over can manufacturing practices in other countries. Lead may also come from imported sources other than canned foods. The Centers for Disease Control (CDC) have found that some imported candy and powdered food coloring can contain extremely high lead levels.[25]

While domestically canned foods may not be a major source of lead, they have other problems. American researchers reported pitting corrosion and cannery residues that led to an interaction between a variety of food products and the cans in which they were packed.[26] Various amounts of aluminum were found in canned drinks by one group of researchers,[27] while others have reported the leaching of a potent xenoestrogen, bisphenol-A, into food from the lacquer-coating now frequently used on the inside of cans.[28]

Aluminum

Chronic exposure to aluminum is most prevalent, as this mineral is so ubiquitous. Many urban water treatment plants still use aluminum oxide for filtration purposes. This toxic metal can then contaminate our biological systems when we consume unfiltered water and food cooked with such waters. Aluminum is found in many common over-the-counter medications, such as buffered aspirins, douches, and anti-diarrhea and hemorrhoid medications. It is found in most deodorants and in many other cosmetic products.

Aluminum is hidden in many commonly consumed foods, including processed cheeses, baking powders, self-rising flours, pickled vegetables and table salt. Many restaurants still cook with aluminum pots, which practice should be outlawed since it readily releases the metal, especially into acidic foods. Beware also of baking or heating potatoes or other foods in aluminum foil. You will be poisoning yourself.

Like lead, aluminum can penetrate the blood-brain barrier. Aluminum toxicity, as I already noted, has been associated with a number of degenerative neurological diseases, most noticeably Alzheimer's disease, Parkinson's disease and Lou Gehrig's disease. I have also found it to be a factor in a wide range of other diseases, including anemia, suppressed immunity and conditions associated with impaired cellular energy production, such as chronic fatigue, diabetes and obesity.

Mercury

Mercury, like aluminum, poses a serious threat to brain integrity. If we have amalgam dental fillings, whenever we chew, mercury vapors are released into our biological fluids.[29] Given the proximity of the mouth to the brain, and since mercury vapors can cross the blood-brain barrier, they can readily damage the lipid-rich brain (the brain, in fact, has more lipids than any other body organ). The very toxic mercury vapors lead to cerebral oxidative stress and degenerative brain changes. Signs of damage can range from confusion and memory problems all the way to debilitating senile dementia. German researchers have also reported that infants whose mothers had amalgam fillings had higher levels of mercury in their tissues and that the early breast milk of these mothers also had higher mercury concentrations than that of mothers without such dental materials.[30] Based on such findings, German health authorities since 1992 have restricted the application of dental amalgam in women before and during childbearing age.

Insidious Sources

Toxic metals may enter the body in the most insidious of ways, as the saga of Jack and Tina illustrates. Jack and Tina are brother and sister, who are staunch vegetarians and strict adherents to a holistic lifestyle. Tina came to our Center with severe perimenopausal symptoms, while her brother's main complaint was cardiovascular problems. They couldn't understand why they ended up so sick, despite doing all the right things.

Urine tests[31] revealed in both of them the highest content of lead toxicity I had ever seen. The two siblings ate no canned foods and shared a house that didn't have lead pipes. It took a while to identify the contamination source, but we finally figured out that their organic garden, which was their main food source, was located less than a quarter of a mile from a railroad station. Consuming the vegetables toxified by the lead-laden fumes of the train fuel was poisoning them!

Be Proactive

As with all other toxins, avoid exposure to toxic metals as much as possible. Eating high-fiber foods that contain sulfa-amino acids, such as artichokes, broccoli, brussel sprouts, cauliflower and lentils, and foods rich in folic acid, such as beets and all dark green vegetables, assists in the removal of these toxic stores. Supplementing your diet with magnesium, zinc, selenium and vitamins B₆, E and C may also provide added protection against toxic metals.

Since the skin is the largest organ of elimination, it is a good vehicle for moving toxins out of the body. Chapter 6 provides you with some self-care techniques for doing this. Diet, supplementation, skin release and good kidney and bowel elimination are all useful measures for dealing with low level metal toxicity. However, with high levels of metal accumulation, as in the case of Jack and Tina, the most effective way to remove toxic metals is chelation therapy (see Chapter 14).

Avoid and protect yourself from toxic metals.

Radiation

In addition to the wide variety of chemical toxins that come at us from every direction, we are also continuously exposed to radiation – both ionizing and nonionizing. Medical X-rays are the greatest man-made source of ionizing radiation. We are also susceptible to a number of natural sources of ionizing radiation, including cosmic rays, emanating from the sun and remote parts of the universe. Radioactive minerals (e.g., uranium), and radon, found in soil, rocks and some building materials are part of the ionizing radiation load. The most widespread source of nonionizing radiation is ultraviolet light, a component of sunlight. Another continually growing source is the extremely low frequency (ELF) electromagnetic fields emitted from our electric wires, appliances and electronic gadgets. Both ionizing and nonionizing radiation create biological interference and are potentially harmful.

X-Rays

Cells that divide more frequently, such as those found in the skin, bone marrow and developing fetuses, are more susceptible to the damaging effects of ionizing radiation, such as X-rays. The DNA of these dividing cells becomes the target of such radiation, suffering genetic damage that can lead to abnormal cell replication. The risk from X-rays, as from chemical toxins, is cumulative and becomes yet another burden for the body to attempt to handle.

Limit X-ray exposure.

∽

If you do need X-rays for diagnostic purposes, take some precautions beforehand by increasing your intake of vitamin E and C with bioflavonoids. If you are not in the habit of taking these antioxidants, start with 400 international units of vitamin E and 500 milligrams of vitamin C per meal a few days before the scheduled procedure.

Additional precautions should be taken for radiation therapy. For years, I have advised my patients to massage large amounts of vitamin E the night before treatment into the area of the skin where radiation was to be applied to reach the target organ. This strategy has proven to be effective in diminishing surface radiation damage.

Thermography, which was popular for a while as a noninvasive way of checking for breast lesions, has not yet supplanted mammography. If you need a mammogram, make sure the equipment being used delivers the lowest possible dose of radiation and do the vitamin E treatment the night before.

Ultraviolet Radiation

Sunlight is a source of both ionizing cosmic rays and nonionizing ultraviolet rays. As the earth's ozone layer is continually being damaged by pollution, the sunrays reaching the earth are becoming more intense. Exposure to ultraviolet sunrays, both UV-A and UV-B, is associated with skin cancer.

Protect yourself from the sun.

However, if you take appropriate precautions, you will be able to enjoy and receive the heart-warming and healing gifts of the sun. Heliotherapy (sun therapy) is an old European remedy for many diseases. Moderate sun exposure is an immune-boosting measure. Sun exposure increases the synthesis of vitamin D. Most people know that vitamin D is good for the bones, but few are aware that this vitamin is also an immune stimulant.

German researchers recently reported that oral intake of vitamins C and E reduces sunburn reaction in humans, and concluded that the generalized effect of the antioxidant vitamins was superior to the application of topical sunscreens.[32] This study confirms the recommendations I have been making for years about using antioxidants, both orally and topically, for sun protection. Because I have such a strong affinity for sunny environments, I have developed some protective strategies to allow me to live with my predilection. I am pleased to share these measures with you.

Sunbathing Tips

1. Avoid the hottest time of the day, when the sun is directly overhead, and wear a broad-rimmed hat while sunning.
2. Prepare for your initial exposure of the season by taking nutritional supplements. Take, at a minimum, the oral antioxidants cited in the German study (2 grams of vitamin C and 1,000 international units of vitamin E [mixed tocopherols]) at least 8 days prior to exposure. Continue this dosage as long as you are spending long periods in the sun.
3. One of my oldest and best-kept secrets for safe and effective tanning is tyrosine. Tyrosine is an amino acid that

facilitates the formation of melanin, the pigment that protects the skin from sun damage and produces a beautiful tan. I recommend 1,000 milligrams first thing in the morning and another 1,000 milligrams between meals, starting the same time as the antioxidants (at least 8 days prior to exposure). ***If you have suspected melanoma, you should avoid both the sun and taking tyrosine.***

4. Mix approximately 1,200 to 1,600 international units of vitamin E (mixed tocopherols) with your favorite cream and apply generously to your entire body, paying particular attention to the most delicate areas of your skin (face, neck and chest).

5. If you are going to use a conventional sunscreen, use one that has a SPF of 15 or more[33]★ and that offers protection for both UV-A and UV-B radiation. Since most people's skin reacts to para-amino-benzoic acid (PABA), it is best to avoid products that contain this ingredient, despite the potential protective aspects of this vitamin. According to biochemist and skin specialist, Marie Badin,[34] the best and safest active ingredients in sunscreens are titanium dioxide and zinc dioxide. There is also a new micronized transparent form of zinc oxide (sold as Z-Cote) that offers extra protection for children and individuals who are sensitive to chemical sunblocks or who have skin lesions.

   Fair skinned people might need to take all of the above precautions. Be aware that the infrared heating rays can literally cook your skin, causing serious sun damage. This process, which is scientifically termed "cross-linking," refers to the permanent binding of proteins to each other that creates leathery skin.

6. Continuously drink filtered water with fresh lemon juice. Hydration is extremely important to diminish the cross-linking effect and the contact of damaging free radicals with vital cellular structures. The lemon, of course, is another protective antioxidant. Do not drink caffeinated drinks, as they are dehydrating. Avoid sodas, even if decaf-

feinated, since they contain phosphorous, which promotes tissue acidity. Among other things, this leaches calcium from the bones.

7. Eat lots of vegetables and small amounts of low-sugar fruits while sunning, as they contain antioxidants and are also high in fiber. Consuming sugary foods or foods that turn into glucose is especially dangerous in the sun because it accelerates the formation of glycosylated proteins, which promote tissue aging and hamper normal cell functioning. Avoid meat during the day. It requires more energy to digest than complex carbohydrates and produces more free radicals. Since the sun is already increasing your free radical load, you want to minimize other sources of these aging factors.

If you take my recommended precautions, you can safely enjoy yourself and the healing benefits of the sun!

ELF Electromagnetic Fields

Every time an electrical current moves through a wire, it generates a circular field of extremely low frequency (ELF) electromagnetic energy. These electromagnetic fields emanate in circles around the moving electrical current and decrease over distance, similar to ripples in water.

ELF fields emanate from the electrical distribution and transmission lines that bring electrical power to our homes and offices, and from all of our household appliances and office equipment running on the electrical current these lines supply. ELF electric fields are present whenever a piece of equipment is plugged in. ELF magnetic fields, which are induced by alternating current (AC), are created when the equipment is turned on. Your computer, for example, generates electrical fields all the time and magnetic fields when it is turned on.

Biological Impact

Our own biological workings also generate small electrical currents, and our bodies have their own weak electromagnetic field. Stronger external ELF fields can interfere with the weak electromagnetic field of our bodies, damaging our internal energy-producing machinery and biological systems.[35]

Scientists have been seriously studying the impact of ELF fields on health for more than two decades. Numerous studies have shown a relationship between ELFs and reproductive dysfunction, birth defects, neurological disorders, Alzheimer's disease, and cancers, particularly among children. A residential study conducted in Sweden, of more than half a million people, found a definitive link between childhood leukemia and exposure to electrical power lines.[36]

Recently, scientists have been linking ELF exposure to breast cancer in women.[37, 38] The EPA is currently funding a study at the State University of New York at Stony Brook to investigate whether the high incidence of breast cancer in Long Island women is caused not only by toxic pesticides in the ground water but by ELF exposure as well.[39] I am currently treating a young Long Island patient who has a very aggressive and unusual cancer. Her father died of cancer 2 years ago, and in half of the households in a cluster of 12 contiguous homes, someone is suffering from or has succumbed to cancer. The housing development is located a quarter mile from a powerful electrical generator.

More than 600 research papers were presented by leading scientists at the Second World Congress for Electricity and Magnetism in Biology and Medicine, held in Italy in 1997.[40] Even a quick review of the abstracts reveals a very interesting relationship between ELF fields, a variety of degenerative diseases and disturbances of the neuroendocrine system. Many of the studies documented that ELF fields adversely impact the pineal, thymus and thyroid glands. These three endocrine glands are essential for immune system integrity and the normal metabolic functioning of the body.

Mobile Phones: Another Threat

Two new European studies – one from Sweden and one from Germany – have documented less serious, but nonetheless, negative health effects from another form of radiation resulting from an increasing popular technological advance – the mobile telephone. Cellular telephones emit radio frequency electromagnetic fields (higher up the energy spectrum than ELFs). The Swedish study, conducted at Sweden's National Institute for Working Life, found that people who use mobile phones frequently experience more headaches and fatigue than do those individuals using them less frequently.[41] The German study found mobile phone use increased resting blood pressure.[42]

Government Regulation Inadequate

European countries have been the pioneers in implementing regulations to protect people from ELF fields. Sweden issued compulsory regulations regarding occupational exposure in 1989. Germany began developing its regulations in 1996. On the worldwide level, the International Commission on Non-Ionizing Radiation Protection (IRPA/INIRC) and the World Health Organization (WHO) have established exposure guidelines for electric and magnetic fields.

Although our government's National Energy Policy Act authorized the Department of Energy in 1992 to research the potential health effects of ELF fields, develop ELF mitigation technologies and provide public information, there are currently no federal standards in the United States. A few states, like Florida and New York, have established magnetic field limits for electrical transmission lines, and California is taking some measures to reduce ELF exposure from new or upgraded utility facilities. But such efforts are limited and far and few between. So, once again, as with chemical toxins, we cannot depend on our government to protect us.

Limit exposure to ELF electromagnetic fields.

~

The best strategy is to avoid as much exposure as possible to ELF electromagnetic fields. Remember, ELF fields are strongest near the source and dissipate with distance. Here are some commonsensical actions you can take to protect yourself.

ELF Protective Measures

1. Don't stand in front of the microwave while it is cooking.
2. Sit as far away from your computer as possible, and don't leave it turned on when you need to remain nearby but are not using it for a while.
3. Don't place electrical equipment at your bedside. Battery-operated clocks and radios are readily available.
4. If you really want to use an electric blanket, warm the bed and then unplug it.
5. Many companies claim that their products decrease or shield ELF fields. Be a prudent shopper and research these products thoroughly before making a purchase.
6. If you are relocating or buying a new residence, make sure to survey the surrounding area for power lines.
7. Finally – regarding radio frequency radiation – don't walk and drive around with a mobile phone glued to your ear!

7 *Tune-Up Your Detox Organs*

The body is the temple of the spirit; keep it clean.

Internal Toxins

*W*e have just taken a quick tour of the many sources of environmental toxins with which our bodies come into contact everyday. As if that were not enough, we also need to contend with our own internally-generated toxins. Every time we eat, we produce food debris. And most of us also harbor millions of microscopic guests that include bacteria, parasites and other microorganisms, which live in our intestines and generate waste products. As you will learn, the path to wellness goes through the intestine.

Toxin Impact

Excessive toxins, both environmental and internally-generated (endotoxins), result in oxidative stress, impaired metabolic functions, nutritional deficiencies, and hormonal imbalance. As you saw in Chapter 6, toxins can create a vast array of problems. They can build up in small increments, year after year, until the toxic burden disrupts normal functioning. I have yet to see a patient with a chronic inflammatory disease, such as allergies, arthritis, fibromyalgia or with a neurological disorder in which the toxic load (both internal and external) did not play a predominant role. Toxicity is also a major factor in chronic fatigue and all degenerative diseases, including aging.

Detox Organs

It is wise to take steps to avoid as many external and internal toxins as we possibly can. But, even with the best of efforts – cleansing our produce, eating organic food, purifying our air and water – our bodies still play the largest role in protecting us and removing toxins from our systems. Keeping our detoxification (detox) organs in top shape is a priority for maintaining our health now and in the future. The most important workers in the detox crew are the intestine (bowel) and the liver. The kidneys, skin and lungs are also more significant than most people imagine.

Bowel Health-Body Health

When I first came to this country in 1962 and began dealing with patients' multiple complaints, I was amazed at their surprise when I asked about their bowel habits. In Europe, where I was raised, bowel health was and still is recognized for the vital role it plays in overall health. We are so obsessed with bowel function, in fact, that it often becomes a preferred subject of discussion at social gatherings. I humorously recall the painfully resigned look on my mother's face as one of her friends proudly presented a prolonged and excessively graphic description of her bowel functions at a cocktail party!

The bowel, which refers to both the long, coiled small intestine and the shorter, large intestine (colon), is a remarkable multi-faceted organ. One of the bowel's best known and important functions is digestive – breaking down food, facilitating the absorption of food components into the bloodstream, and eliminating digestive waste products and other debris. When this function is disrupted, we end up with incompletely digested food particles, which are subsequently fermented in the lower colon. Putrescine and cadaverine are things you may think are found in the morgue, but actually they are metabolic byproducts of undigested food found in everyone's lower colon. The longer they remain in the bowel, the more they get reabsorbed through the intestinal walls into the bloodstream. As you learned in Chapter 6, commercially grown foods also bring man-made toxins (herbicides, pesticides, fertilizers, etc.) into our intestines. The combination of external and internal toxins can overwhelm the detox organs, primarily the liver, and make us very sick.

Although most people are aware of the bowel's digestive function, few know that nearly 60% of the body's total immune resources are housed in this organ in a vast network of blood and lymphatic vessels, and immune stations.[1] These immune stations, the gut-associated lymphatic tissue (GALT) and the mucosal-associated lymphoid tissue (MALT), are the first lines of defense against the microorganisms and toxins with which we come in contact daily.

Floral Imbalance

The human gut houses 100 to 400 different bacterial species, totaling 100 trillion viable bacteria. A healthy intestine maintains a balance among a variety of beneficial bacteria (probiotics), such as *Lactobacillus acidophilus, Lactobacillus bifidus*, and potentially harmful bacteria, such as *E. coli, streptococci*, and other microorganisms like the fungus, *Candida albicans*. This delicate flora balance is upset when the friendly bacteria are overpowered by the unfriendly organisms. Most often spoken about is the imbalance of too little *Lactobacillus acidophilus* and too much *Candida albicans* – responsible for the so-called yeast syndrome (for simplicity's sake, I often use *Candida albicans* and yeast interchangeably, but be aware that not all yeast strains are bad).

Other intestinal parasites (protozoa, spores, cysts, flukes, viruses, etc.) are also a major source of intestinal malfunctioning and imbalance. They are not just a Third World curse. Infestation is far more common than most people suspect and may come from a variety of sources, including food, infected municipal water supplies and inhalation.

The intestinal imbalance in which pathogens (the "bad guys") overpower probiotics (the "good guys") is known as dysbiosis. The unfriendly visitors exhaust our body's immunological resources and lead to still more free radical production and cellular damage (oxidative stress). They rob our bodies of nutrients for their own growth, especially the B vitamins, many of which – like B_2 – are antioxidants. Parasites and other microorganisms generate their own wasteful toxic byproducts. When they die, they create yet another toxic burden that aggravates preexisting conditions (Jarisch-Herxheimer reaction).

Leaky Gut Syndrome

Over time, excessive free radical and other toxins inflame and damage the intestinal wall, making it more porous. This state of affairs is known as the leaky gut syndrome. A leaky gut allows for the passage of pathogens (bacteria, parasites, etc.), toxins, and undigested food particles into the bloodstream. When pathogenic organisms (such as yeast) and endotoxins move into the circulatory system in large quantities, they can cause a wide range of serious health problems.

In one recent review article of 180 clinical studies, the authors noted the relationship between gut integrity and rheumatic disorders, such as arthritis and scleroderma.[2] Another group of researchers, in the same journal issue, reported the connection between bowel disease and eye problems.[3] Ultimately, uncontrolled intestinal leakage can result in multiple organ dysfunction syndrome (MODS) – a steady deterioration and shutdown of all the body's systems. Researchers, who recently followed critically-ill patients in an intensive care unit (ICU), concluded that, "Increased intestinal permeability on admission correlated with both the development and severity of MODS."[4]

Today, the research supports what I have intuitively suspected for a long time. Twenty years ago, a physician friend of mine, who had scorned the idea that yeast from the intestine could travel anywhere in the body and be responsible for organ failure, later on admitted to me that he had been wrong. His mother had been hospitalized with pneumonia and was given massive doses of intravenous antibiotics. Within 10 days she appeared well enough to be discharged, but suddenly died. An autopsy revealed that her meninges, the protective covering of the brain and spinal cord, was literally covered with a white gooky stuff – the unsightly *Candida albicans*. This illustrates how yeast waits for an opportune immunological climate (the protective "good" bacteria were destroyed by the antibiotics) to literally travel everywhere to steal the body's nutritional and energy reserves. In this case, the growth was so massive as to cause death. Large quantities of good bacteria (probiotics), taken orally, could have prevented her untimely death.

Bowel Imbalance Symptoms

A healthy bowel very much depends on the frequency and quality of bowel movements. When there is enough fiber[5] and oxygenation in the intestine, the stools are well formed but not compacted. When the bowels are in perfect health, they empty after each major meal. Evacuation is easy and there is very little or no unpleasant odor.

Constipation is the primary symptom of unhealthy bowels. If you do not move your bowels at least once or twice a day, you are constipated. When you move your bowels but have a sense of incomplete emptying, this also represents constipation. Constipation is caused by many factors, including inadequate fiber and water intake. Unhealthy bowel flora, food allergies, a sedentary lifestyle, and a sluggish thyroid are also typically associated with sluggish bowel movements.

Bloatedness and malodorous flatulence (gas) are also common symptoms of bowel imbalance. Frequent belching, bad breath and gastric heaviness after meals are signs of maldigestion, and are often associated with inadequate secretion of one or more digestive enzymes. Alternating between diarrhea and constipation is yet another message your body sends you that things are awry in your intestinal system. This condition, known as irritable bowel syndrome, can be symptomatic of many different forms of dysbiosis.

Fiber Important

A diet high in fiber content facilitates healthy bowel function by scrubbing and removing unwanted debris and toxic byproducts. Dietary fiber also promotes the growth of friendly intestinal bacteria, such as *Lactobacilli*, and reduces free radical production and inflammation of the intestinal lining. A combination of insoluble and soluble fibers has been proven to have the most beneficial effect.[6,7]

Insoluble fibers are plant materials that the body is unable to break down as they pass through the digestive tract, but that are capable of scrubbing out unwanted debris. Soluble fibers, on the other hand, do dissolve in the bowel's water reserves. They absorb toxic byproducts, bacterial debris and petrochemical residues, such as pesticides. Soluble fibers move dangerous oxidized cholesterol (LDL), responsible for hardening of the arteries (atherosclerosis), out of the body and reduce the reabsorption of cholesterol from the gut back into the liver.

The best sources of soluble and insoluble fiber are vegetables, fruits, beans, and grains. Complex carbohydrates, especially from vegetable sources, should comprise approximately 40% of your diet, barring limiting factors such as acute bowel disease (Crohn's disease, ulcerative colitis and other bleeding bowel disorders).

Eat a high fiber diet.

~

Corsello Centers Bowel Healing Program

Everyday, I see 70-year-old bowels in 30-year-old people. This is quite frightening because, as you now know, the intestine is an essential organ of detoxification and immune screening. When its immunological and digestive capabilities are impaired, the health of the entire body is jeopardized. Because intestinal

Tune-up your bowel.

health is so important, I have developed a self-care bowel healing program. This program has been very effective for thousands of patients with mild to moderate constipation or other signs of bowel imbalance. Absorption and toxicity problems have also been remedied by this intervention. Once the bowels are healed, all other natural interventions work far more effectively.

The Corsello Centers Bowel Healing Program has three components: **Step1: Bowel Scrubbing, Step 2: Bowel Soothing** and **Step 3: Bowel Repopulating.** The healing process is like the restoration of a castle. We must first remove the debris and then rebuild the walls before we take on any other task, like waging war against invading enemies. This self-care intervention does take a little discipline and time, but the rewards far outweigh the effort. ***If you have active Crohn's disease, ulcerative colitis, diverticulitis or any other acute digestive disturbance, you should consult an integrative physician before embarking on the program.***

Bowel Scrubbing: Overview

Our Bowel Healing Program begins with the very important process of removing stored toxins, which have resulted from years of improper eating as well as an overgrowth of yeast and other toxin-producing microorganisms. Yeast overgrowth is caused by a number of factors, but the first and foremost cause is a stressful lifestyle.[8] Other yeast promoters include diets high in sugar, alcohol and fermented foods (vinegar, aged cheese, etc.). Prolonged use of antibiotics, cortisone, birth control pills and many other drugs have a disruptive effect on the bowel flora.

The recommended fiber mixture (Scrubbing Procedure)

physically scrubs the intestinal lining, while it traps accumulated toxins and harmful debris. It also reduces artery-harden-
ing LDL. The powdered vitamin C-mineral combination
assists in gut motility and in enhancing the gut's immune
defenses. Since most people who need bowel cleansing have
inefficient absorption capabilities and would need an inordi-
nate number of tablets to stimulate bowel movement (peristalsis), we use a powdered form of the vitamin C-mineral
combination. The antioxidant minerals this powder contains
are a very important component of the process since they
scavenge the free radicals vitamin C produces as it does its
job of killing infective agents.

Step 1: Bowel Scrubbing Procedure

1. Preferably, start the day by drinking a glass of warm water
   with lemon, which facilitates the movement of mucus-
   trapped debris out of the bowels. (If you are just too
   rushed, start with 2.)
2. Place one teaspoon of a mixture of soluble and nonsoluble
   fiber mixture (such as **CC Fiber Max**) into a blender container and add 1 to 3 teaspoons of a Vitamin C powder
   with mineral antioxidants (such as **CC Minerals Powder**).
3. Add 10 to 12 ounces purified water. To make it more pleas-
   ant, you may add the juice of a freshly squeezed orange.
4. Blend all ingredients and drink immediately. (Stirring
   briskly also works.)
5. Follow this wonderful healing intervention with either
   another glass of warm water with lemon or your favorite
   herbal tea.
6. Wait at least 15 minutes before taking nutritional supplements or consuming breakfast food.
7. Continue doing the bowel scrubbing at least once a day,
   preferably first thing in the morning or between meals,
   until you achieve regular, healthy bowel movements.

8. Once you have obtained bowel regularity, continue with this health-promoting intervention at least one day a week. In case of dietary indiscretion, stress or any condition that brings back a less than healthy pattern (such as travel), resume until mission accomplished.

9. Change of seasons creates an increased immunological demand upon the body as it adapts to new environmental factors. Imbalance in the intestinal flora (dysbiosis) often occurs during these times. Since dysbiosis makes you more vulnerable to other health challenges, it is advisable to do a few days of bowel cleansing when one season changes into another, whether or not you feel you need it.

Bowel Scrubbing: Helpful Hints

After the body absorbs the amount of vitamin C it requires for its immune needs, the excess remains on the surface of the intestinal lining and acts as an irritant, which promotes elimination. The amount of Vitamin C you need to ingest to obtain its bowel motility benefits is very much dependent on your immunological need of the moment. For instance, if you have a cold, your body might need more than your customary daily intake before it can promote bowel movement. I have known of patients with cancer who have needed as much as 100 grams of vitamin C before they reached bowel tolerance level. The amount of vitamin C you require for improved peristalsis and ultimately maintaining optimal health varies from day to day, based on your general health status and whether you are constipated or have diarrhea. The amount of fiber that works for people also varies and should be adjusted to individual need.

If you are experiencing diarrhea rather than constipation, you will need to increase the amount of fiber and drastically reduce the vitamin C. For diarrhea, I generally recommend 2 to 3 teaspoons of the fiber mixture with a ¼ teaspoon of vitamin C or omitting it altogether. If the diarrhea persists, I recommend repeating the process twice a day. If the condition does not subside within 2 days or you have abdominal pain, consult a physician.

For best results during all three steps of the Bowel Healing Program and any time you want to upgrade your wellness, it is best to refrain from any yeast-producing, fermented or fermenting foods, such as vinegar, alcohol, sugar, starches and too much fruit. If you want to eat fruit, do so only in the morning after the bowel scrubbing, and eat no more than one or two low-sugar pieces. Since the pathogens feed on some of the B vitamins, it is best to avoid their oral intake until 3 or 4 weeks into the Program. It is important, however, to continue taking antioxidants, such as the ones recommended in Chapter 5.

Our Bowel Healing Program, although a very salutary intervention, might create some temporary discomfort, such as increased flatulence when the yeast, parasites and bacteria comfortably hiding in the intestinal crevices are killed. These dying organisms increase fermentation, often producing gas and some intestinal discomfort. If this should occur, the best way to deal with it is to increase rather than stop the intervention. Drinking calming teas, such as chamomile, peppermint, or linden is helpful in reducing spasms. If the flatulence becomes extremely uncomfortable, take activated charcoal tablets to absorb the gas and toxins. If you also have other symptoms of maldigestion (belching, gastrointestinal heaviness after eating or bad breath), I suggest you take a broad spectrum digestive enzyme, such as **CC Vege-Zyme** (see Appendix A), with your meals. Malodorous flatulence is always a sign of a toxic bowel and liver. Remedies for this condition will be presented later in this chapter.

Bowel Soothing: Overview

The bowel soothing step involves using flaxseed oil, rich in omega-3 (linolenic) essential fatty acids and also a source of omega-6 (linoleic) essential fatty acids,[9] in combination with olive oil, an omega-9 fatty acid. This combination both heals an irritated bowel and facilitates bowel movements. It has anti-inflammatory and a number of other healing properties.

Essential fatty acids (EFAs) are necessary for our survival and must be obtained from external sources. Flaxseed oil, which I call "the fish oil of earth," contains the same family of anti-inflammatory EFAs as do oily fish. In fact, flaxseed oil contains twice as much omega-3 fatty acids as fish, and is the richest source of these important fatty acids. Flaxseed oil also contains plant lignans, which can be converted by gut bacteria into mammalian lignans. The weak estrogenic and antiestrogenic activities of lignans have been found to be protective against estrogen-associated cancers.[10]

EFAs perform a number of important functions in the body, including the maintenance of cell membrane fluidity. They regulate the transfer of oxygen and promote the production of protein and red blood cell synthesis. They facilitate the recovery from muscle fatigue and weight loss. EFAs also play an important role in glandular activity, forestall menopausal symptoms, and keep the skin young and supple. They offer protection against cancer, and heart and autoimmune diseases, and are therapeutic in treating such diseases. Experts estimate that about 80% of us consume insufficient amounts of beneficial EFAs.[11]

Olive oil helps lower LDL cholesterol and prevents its oxidation,[12] and is also a powerful free radical scavenger.[13] People who eat Mediterranean diets, rich in olive oil, have a decreased incidence of heart disease despite other cardiovascular risk factors, such as smoking and obesity. Researchers have shown that regular consumption of olive oil also decreases the risk for some cancers.[14,15]

The Step 2 oil mixture combines stable, monosaturated omega-9 olive oil with easily-oxidized, polyunsaturated flaxseed oil. Together, they provide a plethora of healing benefits not only for the bowel but also for the entire body. I recommend using top quality, organic, cold-pressed flaxseed oil, bottled under low oxygen conditions and organic, extra virgin olive oil, extracted under similar conditions. Adding antioxidant vitamin E oil (mixed tocopherols) to the mixture provides another protection against oxidation of the oils. Garlic is included for more than the wonderful flavor it adds to the mixture. It has disinfectant properties, contains sulfa amino acids, which are necessary for Phase 2 liver detoxification, and has other beneficial effects.[16]

Step 2: Bowel Soothing Procedure

1. Start Step 2 as soon as you can assemble the ingredients.
2. In a wide-mouth jar, mix 8 ounces each of organic, cold-pressed flaxseed oil and extra-virgin cold pressed (green) olive oil.
3. Add 4 to 8 whole cloves (to taste) of fresh garlic (whole or crushed).
4. Squeeze the contents of 4 to 6 vitamin E (400 international units mixed tocopherols) capsules into the mixture.
5. Store in the lower portion of your refrigerator to avoid excessive thickening.
6. If you are not accustomed to these particular oils, begin with 1 tablespoon daily (otherwise start with 2 tablespoons) as a condiment for salads, steamed vegetables, cold soups or any food allowed on your diet. If you use it as a salad dressing, use lemon in place of vinegar. *This mixture should not be used for cooking, since the flaxseed oil is very unstable and prone to oxidation.*
7. After the first week, increase your daily intake to 3 or 4 tablespoons and continue at this level until you reach bowel regularity.
8. This oil mixture may be used indefinitely and is an ideal way to enjoy the many healing benefits the oils provide. Integrate at least 2 tablespoons into your daily diet.

Bowel Soothing: Helpful Hints

A tablespoon of this healing mixture contains approximately 120 healing calories. Since EFAs enhance fat metabolism and its breakdown, they ultimately assist in weight management. If you are concerned about calories, eliminate foods that have little nutritional value, such as starch, refined sugars and saturated fats. If you experience nausea when consuming this oil mixture, this may indicate poor gall bladder and pancreatic secretions, and the need to add pancreatic digestive enzymes to your diet (see CC Vege-Zyme in Appendix A).

Bowel Repopulating: Overview

Now that you have scrubbed out years of accumulated debris and toxins and soothed and lubricated the intestine, you need to bring back the healing bacteria. Repopulating the intestine with probiotics (good bacteria) contributes to the health of the intestinal tract and the entire body. One of the major activities of probiotics is the inhibition of the growth of all harmful intestinal organisms.[17] Since harmful bacteria and their toxic products can travel all over the body, damaging weak organs, it is important to restrain their growth in the intestine before they have an opportunity to spread.

Probiotics offer a number of other important health benefits. They facilitate nutrient breakdown and absorption,[18] lower cholesterol, inhibit tumor growth[19, 20] and generally improve immune function.[21] According to leading probiotics researcher and surgeon, Dr. Stig Bengmark, of Sweden's Lund University, consumed *lactobacilli* and *bifidobacteria* "are known to stimulate the immune system – macrophages, T-cells, B-cells, etc., most likely through production of nitric oxide and cytokine-like molecules."[22]

Step 3: Bowel Repopulating Procedure

1. Wait until you have been doing Steps 1 and 2 for 4 to 6 days before implementing Step 3.
2. Start with a ¼ teaspoon of probiotics mixed into water, and continue with this amount for 3 days. Read the label to learn if the culture needs to be taken with or between meals.
3. Increase your intake by a ¼ teaspoon every 3 days. It might take you 1 to 2 weeks to get to a full teaspoon, the amount needed, on the average, to repopulate a depleted intestine.
4. Thereafter, continue taking probiotics to maintain good flora balance in the amount of 1 teaspoon a day or, if you prefer, take 1 tablespoon on weekends.
5. Most good probiotics need to be refrigerated. They are live organisms, and high temperatures can hinder their effectiveness.
6. Probiotics may be taken indefinitely.

Bowel Repopulating: Helpful Hints

Probiotics, like most nutrients, need to be chosen very carefully. While there are many quality products on the market, there are also many that are less than reputable. Select probiotics that contain the highest quality and most researched strains of *Lactobacillus acidophilus*. A probiotic that also contains other beneficial bacteria, such as *Lactobacillus bulgaricus, Lactobacillus bifidus* and *Lactobacillus casei*, is more effective than a single bacterium product. A good culture contains approximately 10 billion live *Lactobacillus acidophilus* cells per gram.

Some probiotic products contain digestive enzymes, which are helpful in further facilitating the breakdown and absorption of nutrients. Colostrum is also now available in some probiotic products. Colostrum, a powerful immune enhancer[23] found in mothers' breast milk, enhances probiotic effectiveness. At our Centers, we use **CC ProBiotic Plus**, a product that contains colostrum, digestive enzymes and DDS-1, a *Lactobacillus acidophilus*, backed by voluminous clinical research and the reputation of one of the foremost probiotics experts, Dr. Kim Shahani of the University of Nebraska.

Probiotics accelerate the fight against toxic microorganisms and might cause transient bowel discomfort, such as bloating and gas. This is the reason we recommend starting with small amounts and gradually increasing the dosage until full bowel health is achieved. We prefer waging a "gentle war," and I am sure you will too. As noted earlier, drinking calming teas and taking activated charcoal will alleviate uncomfortable symptoms. If the probiotic product you are using does not contain digestive enzymes, you might want to add such a supplement to your diet.

Bowel Healing Program Summary

Step 1: Scrubbing

Use fiber and vitamin C-mineral mixture until you achieve bowel regularity. Then, do Step 1 once a week, indefinitely. Intensify program again with change of seasons, when you are under stress, and whenever you lose regularity.

Step 2: Soothing

Add the oil combination in the recommended dosage. Thereafter, incorporate at least a couple of tablespoons into your daily diet.

Step 3: Repopulating

After your body adjusts to Step 1 and 2 (4 to 6 days), add probiotics gradually, according to recommendations, and continue indefinitely.

Food Poisoning

Before I leave the subject of intestinal health, I would like to share with you a clinically-tested remedy for food poisoning.[24, 25] Food poisoning is generally due to an overload of toxins coming from a garden variety of bacteria – *Salmonella, E. coli, Streptococcus fecalis* and other pathogens that are present in contaminated foods. Common symptoms include severe malaise and nausea and, often, diarrhea. Since the perfect antidote for bacterial toxins are probiotics, I recommend that you take as much as 2 tablespoons initially. As long as the nausea and malaise persist, continue taking the probiotics, ingesting 1 to 2 tablespoons every 30 minutes until the symptoms subside.

If you should experience diarrhea as a result of food poisoning, I recommend the implementation of the bowel scrubbing strategy for diarrhea (2 to 3 teaspoons of the fiber mixture with or without a ¼ teaspoon of vitamin C). For best results, wait 15 minutes after the bowel scrubbing procedure before taking probiotics. To replenish the lost minerals, drink at least 1 to 2 cups of Veggie Broth.

Veggie Broth

1. Place 3 to 4 quarts of water in a large pot.
2. Add 3 to 4 large carrots, 3 to 4 parsnips, 1 bunch of parsley, the peel with some pulp of 3 large potatoes and 2 to 3 stalks of celery. Add dill to taste.
3. Bring ingredients to a boil and let simmer for 2 hours.
4. Add 1 cup of concentrated liquid amino acids.[26]
5. Strain and drink.
6. Refrigerate what remains to consume later.

The Liver

The liver, like the intestine, has multiple and important physiological functions. One of its major functions is to neutralize the toxins that have escaped the intestinal detoxification process. Every little bit we ingest and digest is transported from the intestine to the liver through a very large vascular communication network called the portal (circulation) system. The less well the intestine screens and inactivates pathogens, pesticide residues, drugs and food debris, the harder the liver needs to work.

Detoxification

As you may recall from Chapter 5, the liver does its important detoxification work in two phases. During Phase 1, the liver, through its P450 enzyme system, prepares toxic substances for elimination by increasing their solubility. In the course of doing so, however, the enzymes generate free radicals. A well-functioning liver can very well cope with neutralizing these free radicals during Phase 2, while it handles, at the same time, the fat-soluble toxins (pesticides, herbicides, drugs, etc.) that are not broken down in Phase 1. During the important Phase 2 (also known as conjugation) the liver binds and prepares these toxins for elimination through the kidneys via the urine and through the gallbladder via the bile.

The liver needs specific nutrients to properly do its clean-up work. Phase 1 requires an abundant supply of vitamins B and C. Dysbiosis can hinder the absorption of these important nutrients and affect the efficiency of both the Phase 1 and Phase 2 detoxification process. These life-saving processes also depend on the availability of substances that feed the liver's endogenous antioxidant enzymes. Glutathione peroxidase is the predominant endogenous clean-up enzyme, and it depends on adequate amounts of selenium and amino acids.

Detoxification becomes less efficient when our livers are

overloaded with chemicalized, high fat and processed foods. The beautiful-looking, nonperishable produce that populates our supermarket bins is loaded with pesticides and other damaging chemicals. Eating commercial produce can actually contribute more damaging toxins than helpful antioxidants to our overburdened livers! Taking drugs that further challenge our detoxification ability can lead to liver (hepatic) damage.

Immunity

When the detoxification pathways of the gut and liver are overburdened, the metabolism and storage of fat-soluble vitamins A, E and D are disturbed. These vitamins are of major importance in protecting us from aging and various disease states. Vitamin D, as you may recall, is not only required for healthy bones but it also supports our immune system. Vitamin A, among its many other protective properties, increases the activity of specialized white cells that gobble up infective agents.

The liver also has its own immune defense system – the Kufper macrophages. These specialized white cells are responsible for trapping infective agents (particularly viruses, such as the ones that cause hepatitis) that have escaped gut vigilance. This important protective system is hindered when the liver is underfed and overworked. A healthy intestine and adequate nutrient absorption are essential for the liver's immunological and detoxification work.

Other Roles

The liver plays several other important roles, including the processing of all nutrients, the storing of fat, iron and several vitamins, the synthesis of blood plasma proteins and the removal of cholesterol waste. Along with the muscles, it is a major site for the storage of glycogen, so necessary for proper levels of glucose in times of stress or strenuous exercise.

As if this were not enough, the liver also has a pivotal role in the metabolism and conversion of hormones through its sulfation pathway. Defects in this important pathway are often responsible for facial hair growth and other unpleasant symptoms in women on the threshold of menopause (perimenopause). This pathway requires an adequate supply of taurine, one of three sulfa-containing amino acids. Taurine is not an essential (internally unavailable) amino acid, since our bodies have the capacity to make it from cysteine. But because we need so much of it for the many biological functions in which it is involved, it often becomes "conditionally essential," and we need to depend on external supplementation to obtain adequate amounts.

Because the liver is involved in so many of the body's important metabolic processes, its impairment can lead to the rapid decay and aging of many biological systems. The so-called liver spots that appear most frequently on the backs of hands and the chest area herald damage elsewhere. Those ugly brown discolorations are the result of an overburdened liver and are signs of aging of our skin and, more importantly, of our brains.[27] They suggest the accumulation of lipofuscin – the free-radicalized lipid substances found in the fat-rich brain. Liver spots should serve as an early warning sign that your brain, the most important organ in your body, might be moving towards senility.[28*] Lightening creams are only cosmetic, not restorative. The only effective remedy is taking very good care of your intestine and liver.

Caring for Your Liver

Although we should limit toxin exposure as much as possible, it is even more important to ensure that our liver has an abundant supply of protective nutrients so that it can continue performing its many important

Nurture and protect your liver.

jobs. Eating artichokes, dandelion, beet tops and beets support the liver. In terms of liver protective supplements, functional medicine practitioners, like myself, use a wide variety of remedies. For prevention and mild malaise, I encourage you to follow the general maintenance recommendations in Chapter 5 – and to alternate between the ingredients in the **CC CV Antioxidant Formula** and the **CC GlutaPath Formula**.

Alpha-lipoic acid, although a bit costly, has emerged as one of the best liver protective nutrients currently available. It is a powerful antioxidant, and the body routinely converts some of it to dihydrolipoic acid. Dihydrolipoic acid neutralizes both oxygen and nitrogen free radicals, and unlike most other antioxidants, functions in both the watery and fatty regions of cells. According to Dr. Lester Packer, a molecular and cellular biologist at the University of California, Berkeley, alpha-lipoic acid helps the body renew and recycle vitamins C and E, glutathione and Co-Q10, extending the metabolic lifetimes of these other important antioxidants.[29]

When traveling in highly polluted areas, I suggest the addition of 2,000 milligrams per day of alpha-lipoic acid to your maintenance regime. For mild or early cases of liver spots, I recommend the ingredients in the **CC GlutaPath Formula** and 1,000 milligrams of alpha-lipoic acid daily. When our patients have combined this regimen with the entire Bowel Healing Program, the spots usually disappear within a month or two. I also like the detox and tonic tea recipe, developed by my associate, Dr. Ellen Kamhi, an expert in healing botanicals. It contains many liver supportive herbs that are also beneficial for all the other detox organs. I suggest you drink 2 to 3 cups of this tea for a few days or longer after overindulging or excessive exposure to environmental toxins, during the changing of seasons and whenever you feel a bit under the weather.

Detox-Tonic Tea

1. Place one tablespoon of each of the following herbs in a glass tea pot: red clover blossoms, burdock root, dandelion, chaparral, milk thistle, Oregon graperoot, licorice root, fennel and fenugreek. Add cascara sagrada if you tend to be constipated.
2. Add 8 cups of filtered water and bring to a boiling point.
3. Turn heat down and gently simmer (do not boil) for 10 minutes.
4. Strain into a cup. The remainder can be stored in the refrigerator and reheated (not microwaved) for later servings.

If you are not able to obtain fresh, bulk herbs, look for a packaged tea that contains as many of the above ingredients as you can find. Teas of this type are often packaged as "detox" remedies.

The Kidneys

The kidney's job is to filter blood and excrete waste products through the urine. What does not get cleaned out on the first passage through the urine goes back to the liver, thus the detoxification processes of the liver and the kidneys are intimately linked. When the kidneys are impaired or do not have sufficient fluid to eliminate toxins efficiently, the liver is forced to work so much harder. As a result, it becomes overburdened and is less able to perform some of its vital functions. Toxicity of the kidneys can also inhibit the secretion of hemopoietin (erythropoietin), which is necessary for triggering the production of red blood cells in the bone marrow.

Cleanse and support your kidneys.

Severe kidney impairment can lead to potentially life-threatening anemia.

The Importance of Water

Water is the primary component (more than 70%) of the body and the most frequently ignored nutrient. Not only is water essential for removing waste, it carries nutrients and oxygen to the cells, cushions joints, assists in the regulation of body temperature, and keeps our skin supple and young-looking. Despite its importance, a recent large, national survey revealed that we are taking in only about half of the water the body requires. Only 21% of us drink eight or more glasses of water a day.

Although people on the average drink nearly 13 8-ounce servings of fluids daily, almost half of the beverages contain alcohol or caffeine, which are dehydrating diuretics.[30] Soda pop is also a commonly consumed beverage, and even if decaffeinated, is detrimental to women's health. Carbonated sodas acidify the blood and ultimately leach calcium from the bones. Women who regularly consume sodas have been found to have twice the risk of fracturing bones after age 40 than do non-soda drinkers.[31]

Everyone should drink at least eight glasses of purified water daily. As we get older, we often need to drink "at command" rather than "at demand" because the hypothalamic center in our brain that regulates our sensation of thirst becomes less sensitive. I recommend adding the juice of (preferably fresh organic) lemons to your water. Lemon juice disinfects, rehydrates, quenches thirst, and facilitates the movement and release of toxins by the kidneys. It also contains the antioxidants, vitamin C and bioflavonoids. Since the oil of lemon (lemonin) found in the fruit's skin is also a powerful antioxidant, after squeezing the juice, I suggest dropping the whole fruit (if organic) in the water.

It is best to drink water between meals and first thing in the morning. The morning water, especially warm water with lemon, is an old remedy and one of the best to push out the intestinal mucus, loaded with toxic debris accumulated during the night. Drink only a small amount of water with your meals as too much hinders the efficiency of digestive enzymes. If you are attempting to lose weight, drinking two glasses of water 10 to 15 minutes before a meal will create a feeling of fullness that might limit the quantity of food you consume. If you do so, make sure you take digestive enzymes with your meals to prevent maldigestion.

Other Kidney Supporters

Flushing out the kidneys with adequate amounts of purified water and herbal teas that promote urination, such as Dr. Kamhi's Detox-Tonic Tea, is essential for maintaining kidney health. I also recommend nature's healing foods, such as organically grown asparagus, adzuki beans and watermelon. Juicing and drinking watermelon, seeds and all, first thing in the morning is a wonderful renal flushing remedy. Especially during the menopausal transition, when the tendency to urinary infections increases, I recommend the preventive use of kidney herbs, such as uva ursi. See Chapter 11 for more about this and other natural remedies for urinary infections.

The Skin

The skin is the largest organ in the body. It acts as a barrier, protecting our internal organs from environmental toxins and deflecting invading organisms. It is an essential organ of elimination, moving toxins out of the body through perspiration. Frequently forgotten, the skin is also an important organ of absorption. Medications, such as nitroglycerin, progesterone, estrogen and other hormones are best delivered through the skin.

When too many toxins overwhelm the liver, gut and kidneys, the skin – the last bastion of detoxification – gets into action. When toxins exit through the skin and combine with surface bacteria, the result can be acne. Acne is most frequently seen in adolescence, a time when the liver is flooded with hormones and its detoxification pathways are further overwhelmed by the consumption of junk food. I also see many women with acne during midlife transition. Like in adolescence, the liver can be overwhelmed by sudden bursts of estrogen. If the liver is not adequately supported by appropriate nutrients, the skin may wear the brand of toxicity.

Nourish the Skin

I often refer patients with acne and other skin problems to biochemist and skin specialist, Marie Badin,[32] who has developed a wide range of natural treatments and remedies for both problem and aging skin. To prevent skin aging, Badin recommends products that contain supportive and nourishing ingredients, such as natural oils (borage, black currant, sunflower and macadamia nut), hyaluronic acid, *Gingko biloba*, apricot kernel extract, honey, avocado, karite (shea) butter, sea kelp and RNA.

Release Toxins

Although it may not be "lady-like" to sweat, it is "healthwise" to do so. As the largest organ of the body, the skin offers infinite opportunities for releasing toxins. Exercise that is strenuous enough to make you sweat is a good way to move toxins out from the skin. Exercise is also a good tonic for bowel regularity.

Sauna and steam baths are wonderful ways to induce sweating. The use of sweat lodges by Native Americans was a wise indigenous practice that required no double-blind controlled study. A low-heat sauna is also a very salutary detoxification process. It is used in Ayurvedic medicine and in many European countries. The low heat allows the body to tolerate the intervention for hours. This process dislodges the volatile petrochemicals incorporated in the fatty tissue, brings them into circulation and allows them to escape

Sweat.

through the open pores of the skin. Anyone who has undergone this experience remembers the foul smell of escaping petrochemical residues. Best results are achieved when this practice is undertaken in conjunction with bowel and liver cleansing. Large amounts of water and minerals are necessary to support the body during this process.

Although not as deep a cleansing as a low heat sauna, an Epsom salt bath is an easy way to remove less deeply stored toxins that the warmth of the bath water moves to the skin's surface. As a routine preventive measure, I recommend you take a 20-minute warm Epsom salt bath, followed by a clean water rinse, 3 to 4 times a week.

The Lungs

The lungs are less often spoken of as a detoxification organ, but they do play a vital role in eliminating carbon dioxide (CO_2) and volatile toxic byproducts. Breathing is the vehicle for both oxygenating the body and releasing volatile toxins. The breathing process is directed by impulses from the respiratory neurons in the brain, which are affected by many factors, including emotions. Stressful living leads to chronic, shallow chest breathing, which is inefficient and does not move all of the stagnant residual air out of the lungs.

Healthy Breathing

Diaphragmatic or abdominal breathing is the most efficient way to breathe as it takes in about eight times as much air as chest breathing. It also balances the parasympathetic and sympathetic nervous systems, creating a sense of peacefulness. Longer-living animals, like tortoises, take only 3 deep breaths a minute, while more excitable and shorter-lived monkeys and hens take 30 shallow breaths a minute. Abdominal breathing is the method of choice of singers, and practitioners of yoga and the martial arts. In India, where yoga originated, breathing is associated with *prana* – the life-force of the body. The Chinese culture also values the prac-

Breathe deeply.

~

tice of proper breathing, associating the breath with *chi* or energy. Slow, deep breathing is the foundation of both yoga and *tai chi*.

Recently, I have been personally reminded about the wonders of abdominal breathing. In an effort to improve my diction, I have been studying with the renowned vocal coach, Elizabeth Dixon, whose student roster has included such luminaries as Katherine Hepburn, Margaret Thatcher and Rex Harrison, among many others. Dixon credits her superb health and vitality (she is 10 years my senior) to her Dixon "B" breathing techniques, which, as she says, "...not only improves the voice, but teaches not to take fresh air on top of stale air." I have also been privileged to study with Taoist master Stephen Cheng, author of *The Tao of Voice*.[33] Cheng incorporates tao toning and deep breathing exercises into his vocal instructions. After a training or practice session of either of these techniques, I am invariably simultaneously revitalized and calmed.

To learn if you are breathing from the chest or the abdomen, sit comfortably in a chair with your back straight and eyes closed. Rest your right hand on your abdomen and your left hand on your chest. Inhale deeply through your nose and pay attention to the movement of your hands. If your left hand rises more than your right, you are breathing from your chest. If your right hand rises more, you are breathing from your abdomen. If your breathing is shallow, practice until abdominal breathing becomes your normal pattern. Not only will you become more efficient at releasing toxins from your lungs and oxygenating your body, but you will also become calmer.

8 *Defend Yourself*

Keep the troops strong and responsive.

Multilayered Defense

Nature has endowed us with a complex, interactive and multilayered defense system to protect our bodies. The thymus gland and the intestine are two of the most important defenders. Others include the skin, and the mucus and fine hairs (cilia) of our respiratory and intestinal tract surfaces. Saliva, tears and other specialized white blood cells, called phagocytes, also play their roles. Our immune system is actually quite similar in structure to our nation's defense system. The army, the navy, the coast guard, the FBI, and the CIA all have the shared mission of protecting our country. Although interrelated, each also has its own unique function and arena of action.

Immunity and Aging

In early stages of evolution, the intestine was the primary site of immunological defenses. As simpler organisms evolved into more complex primates with increased defensive demands, nature took an embryonic organ of the intestine and promoted it to a five-star general – the thymus gland.

Although the thymus, a ductless (endocrine) gland located

just beneath the breastbone, has long been known to exist, it was believed by the medical community to be of no consequence until the last few decades. Its importance to the body's immune function has emerged most clearly since the AIDS epidemic. Now, some very exciting new discoveries are emerging regarding the relationship between the thymus gland and longevity.

The thymus releases several hormones that regulate many immune functions. It also primes the T-lymphocytes (white blood cells produced in the bone marrow), which have the job of directly attacking invading pathogens. Once the T-lymphocytes are primed, they stimulate the B-lymphocytes – another essential type of white blood cells, which produce antibodies. These cells not only limit the frequency and aggressiveness of infections, but also neutralize the damaging effects of free radicals. One of the main reasons our immune system inevitably becomes weaker as we age is because the thymus starts to shrink from puberty on. By the age of 40 to 45, the thymus is atrophied in most people. In my opinion, repeated infections, chronic stress and disease, trauma, and exposure to chemicals and radiation all accelerate the gland's decline. Older people who are healthy have stronger thymus glands and higher levels of T- and B-lymphocytes.[1]

The adrenal glands also play an important role in immunity. Higher levels of the adrenal hormone, DHEA are reflective of healthy adrenal glands and are also associated with stronger immune response.[2] As we age, DHEA declines. Its restoration is one of the most effective ways to support the immune system. The synergistic and compensatory actions of the thymus and the adrenals are yet another demonstration of my adage, "Nature is too smart to fly a one propeller plane."

Immune Dysfunction

The immune system is designed to recognize and attack any substance that is unlike the body's components. Its ability to do so can be altered by chronic exposure to stress and toxic substances, and by repeated infections. The immune system may become underactive, as in people with AIDS, or it may become overactive and indiscriminate, as happens in autoimmune diseases, such as lupus erythematosus and rheumatoid arthritis. CFIDS, AIDS, cancer and accelerated aging are all results of a weakened immune system. More than 65 million Americans suffer from one form or another of immune dysfunction, with allergies being the most common ailment.

Allergies

Allergies are an exaggerated or inappropriate reaction of the immune system to substances that are ordinarily harmless. They can be elicited by environmental stimuli, such as chemicals, dust or pollen, or by ingested foods. As with any external threat, the body responds to the allergen (antigen) by producing specific antibodies. Allergies, particularly those that trigger release of histamine cause suppression of the immune system. Allergies also release inflammatory chemicals (cytokines). Medical researchers are now implicating inflammation as a causal factor not only in immune disorders but also in most disease processes, including cardiovascular disease.

IgE Allergies

Allergies mediated by immunoglobulin E (IgE) antibodies are very common. They are easily recognized, as they produce an immediate reaction to the offending allergen, such as itching, sneezing, rashes, abdominal cramps, etc. When an allergen is introduced into the body for the first time, IgE antibodies coat the mast cells of the upper respiratory tract, the lining of the lungs and stomach, and the skin. When the allergen is reintroduced, the mast cells respond by releasing inflammatory chemicals that are responsible for the allergy symptoms.

Most IgE-mediated allergies are due to environmental factors like dust, molds, animal dander and pollens. They are also caused by foods, such as shellfish or strawberries, which can generate symptoms ranging from rashes to the frightening and potentially life-threatening bronchial or laryngeal spasms – the feared anaphylactic reaction. Asthma, eczema and hay fever are common IgE-mediated allergies. These diseases can also be the result of more insidious IgG allergies.

IgG Allergies

Although some adverse reactions to food are IgE-mediated allergies, most are delayed food sensitivities. They are not as easy to detect since the amount of time between the introduction of the allergen and the reaction is usually 24 to 48 hours. You may drink milk today, for example, but not feel achy, congested and bloated until a day or two later.

Delayed food sensitivities are mediated by the immunoglobulin IgG molecule, which operates a little differently than the IgE molecule. In the IgG response, one arm of the antibody binds to the allergenic food, while the other binds to phagocytic white blood cells. These phagocytes reach out and engulf the insulting substance attached to the other side of the antibody, expanding in size. This process leads to the formation of large molecules called immunocomplexes.

Immunocomplexes

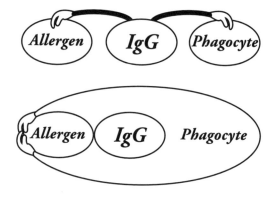

Figure 8-1

When these molecules are too large to be eliminated through the kidneys, they move back into general circulation. Once in the bloodstream, they can deposit on the surface of various organs, changing the organ's architecture. The cells of the immune system now perceive that organ as a foreign substance and attack. Autoimmune diseases, like rheumatoid arthritis, lupus erythematosus and insulin-dependent diabetes mellitus (Type 1 diabetes) are just a few examples of the immune system's inability to distinguish "self" from "nonself." Food allergens, bacterial and viral infections all cause the change in tissue architecture that confuses the immune system. Together, they are responsible for serious autoimmune diseases. When stress is added to the illness equation, it might be difficult to obtain healing unless all the causes are addressed.

The Food Allergy-Gut Connection

Some people have inborn intolerances to some foods. Those of Mediterranean origin, for example, are often reactive to gluten (found in wheat). And because there is a similarity in the structure of wheat and milk, people who are reactive to one are most often also reactive to the other. For most people, the most common cause of delayed food reactions, however, lies in a dysbiotic gut, a condition in which the intestine's friendly bacteria are overpowered by yeast, parasites and other pathogenic microorganisms. The immunological war that ensues leads to inflammation.

When the intestinal wall is inflamed, the pores of the intestinal lining become enlarged, allowing poorly screened pathogens, toxins and undigested food molecules to pass from the intestine into the bloodstream. If the dysbiosis is not promptly treated, the intestinal pores become even more enlarged, allowing more antigenic substances to move into the bloodstream. Stress makes this self-perpetuating cycle even worse, as it immediately stimulates the growth of yeast and weakens the immune response. Dysbiosis and a leaky gut may play a role in the pathogenesis of Crohn's disease and other serious inflammatory bowel conditions, and can initiate the autoimmune process described above.[3] The complex and interactive relationship among dysbiosis, a leaky gut, food allergies and stress is graphically illustrated by Sara's story.

Sara's Transformation

Sara, a very aware middle-aged patient, had for the previous year done the layer by layer cleansing work necessary to reduce her fatigue, anxiety and sense of impending doom. Like most of my patients, she had a dysbiotic gut and multiple food allergies. She had for the most part done very well by staying away from the most allergenic foods while we were working on diminishing her intestinal inflammation. The bloatedness and constipation were gone, and she was now able to eat, on a 4-day rotation cycle, most of the foods to which she was previously mildly or moderately allergic.

Sara was doing well when an extremely stressful situation occurred. A few days later, all the symptoms that she originally came with returned full-blown. Stress had diminished her intestinal immunovigilance, and the dysbiotic flora had a field day. Since the stressful circumstances could not be eliminated fast enough, we had her resume the entire Bowel Healing Program. At the same time, we had her abstain from most solid foods for a week and consume 4 drinks a day of an amino acid-fiber-probiotic-EFA combination formula, and eat one small meal of fish and vegetables. For a couple of weeks, we eliminated the oral B vitamins she was taking since the "bad microorganisms" feed on them and, instead, gave her weekly nutrient injections to support the immune system and promote liver detoxification. We added biologically active thymic protein[4], since the intestinal and thymic immune systems strengthen each other. Finally, she was instructed to make sure she utilized her relaxation technique on a daily basis.

By the end of the week, 90% of Sara's symptoms had disappeared. She recovered very quickly because her healing reserves were so much higher thanks to the work she had already done in the previous year. Her rapid recovery is a beautiful demonstration of the principle of accumulation of vital energy and restoration of organ reserves. Just like a business, our bodies accumulate deficits and surpluses. When the surplus is high, an unexpected deficit can be relieved quickly.

Impact of Allergies

Allergies, both IgE- and IgG-mediated, exert a tremendous strain on our body's resources. To neutralize the noninfective invaders, the body engages in chemical warfare, which uses a tremendous amount of cellular energy. Allergies damage important body systems components and divert resources from the ongoing work of neutralizing the free radicals. When the immune system is busy defending one front, it can forget to check its rear end. This is the same mistake Napoleon made in his Russian campaign – an error that brought about his demise.

Because they divert immunological resources, allergies also open the door to infections. When an allergic state causes an inflammation of the nose and throat, the mucus membranes that line these organs are less capable of containing the spread of infectious agents. Have you ever noticed how frequently allergic people succumb to the flu and develop serious respiratory system complications? Allergies also exert protracted demands on the adrenal glands, ultimately leading to varying degrees of adrenal insufficiency. Adrenal stress results in fatigue, a common symptom among people with allergies. When the burden of allergic stress is relieved and the individual is otherwise in good health, the energy level always increases, sometimes quite dramatically. Many people have both IgE- and IgG-mediated allergies. In such situations, symptoms can be very unpredictable, as Jean's experience demonstrates.

Jean's Transformation

Jean, a 55-year-old executive, originally came to our Center with a history of surgically- and chemotherapeutically-treated colon cancer, menopausal symptoms and a variety of other vague symptoms. She was highly allergic to molds, yeast and seasonal pollens, and also tested positively for a large number of food allergies. During the first year with us, she had dealt very well with her food allergies, and we had been successful in eliminating her menopausal symptoms and upgrading her overall immunity. She was doing so well, in fact, that she was about to be released from our care.

One afternoon, she arrived at the center in great distress during the height of the "spring bloom." She had a new and unusual symptom – an inability to keep her eyelids open. She reminded me of a patient I had treated many years ago for myasthenia gravis, a disorder of the involuntary nervous system. Since she had a history of multiple allergies, we felt it was appropriate to try allergy desensitization and performed, on the spot, the sophisticated Miller Skin Allergy Desensitization and Immunotherapy Process.[5]* A few minutes after the medical technician found the right neutralizing dose for the offending allergen, her eyelids lifted back to a normal position. Even to us, this was a dramatic example of the unpredictability of allergic responses.

The Gastrointestinal Defense

The gut is the largest immunological site of response to infective agents that enter our intestine through our food, water or contact with any contaminated surface. The gut is endowed with a very fine network of lymphatic stations that go under the global names of gut associated lymphoid tissue (GALT) and mucosal associated lymphoid tissues (MALT). You might be surprised to learn that the intestinal appendix, surgically removed so cavalierly in the not too distant past, belongs to the very fine and intricate GALT system. These lymphatic stations, in fact, produce nearly 60% of our antibodies!

The mucosal associated lymphoid tissue (MALT) is the site of a special class of immunoglobulins known as secretory IgA (SIgA), an extremely important first line of defense. SIgA binds to and forms immunocomplexes with pathogenic microorganisms, allergenic food proteins and toxins in an attempt to prevent them from entering the bloodstream through penetration of the intestinal tract surface. The immunocomplexes formed on the surface of the intestine are then easily moved out through the bowel. A good SIgA level is, therefore, very important to overall wellness. At our Centers, we frequently see patients with low SIgA levels. These patients, such as Michael, have serious dysbiosis. The inadequate SIgA is unable to protect them from infestation and multiplication of all sorts of pathogenic microorganisms, which cause both local and systemic symptoms.

Michael's Transformation

Michael, a young man of 30 years, who had the energy and looks of 60-year-old, came to us with a bloated belly, a very undernourished body, malodorous flatulence, a thrushy tongue and a look that initially made us wonder about AIDS. Since he had many gastrointestinal symptoms, we did a stool analysis and checked his SIgA. He had one of the most dysbiotic guts we had ever seen, loaded with bacteria, parasites, *Candida albicans* and more. His SIgA was below a detectable level, allowing all sorts of pathogens to take residence in his gut and poison his body. To top it all, the condition also created a severe malabsorption problem, rendering him unable to take in the nutrients necessary to improve his besieged immune system.

Since proteins and vitamins are necessary to make antibodies, and Michael had such severe malabsorption, we immediately started infusions of amino acids and vitamins, while he began the Bowel Healing Program. Within 3 months, Michael had gained 15 pounds. His SIgA level had moved up into a normal range, and he was well on his way to a complete healing.

Infections, Free Radicals and Aging

Infections are not just temporary inconveniences that take us out of commission for a few days here and there. They add to our internal toxic burden and, over time, weaken our organs. Whenever possible, we should avoid exposure to infective agents. If we do succumb, we should take some immediate steps to control them.

The one structure in our body that is most vulnerable to the damaging effects of the toxic load is DNA, the site of our genetic material. Just for fun – imagine the DNA as a damsel with long, golden braids ensconced in the tower of a medieval castle. She can only be reached if all the defenses of the castle are broken through – the moat, the drawbridge, the high walls, and finally the dedicated foot soldiers with their boiling oil and arrows. The damsel needs to be protected at any cost. The more numerous and aggressive the enemies, the more layers of defenses need to be put in place. In the end, this worthwhile defensive effort can save us from cancer and heart disease, as well as from accelerated aging. Like the medieval war image, our delicate genetic material is best protected by an immune system that has not been weakened by avoidable distractions (inadequately managed allergies, poor nutrition, smoking, negative attitudes, etc.). The shorter the immunological battles, the fewer the free radicals produced – the less chance is there for DNA damage.

Antibiotics

Overuse of antibiotics, both as prescribed medications and in animals raised for our consumption, has created a global health crisis. Today, more than 90% of *Staphylococcus aureus* strains are resistant to penicillin and other related antibiotics. In some parts of the nation, 40% of *pneumococcus* strains are partly or completely undeterred by multiple antibiotics, and a growing number of bacteria are developing resistance to Vancomycin, the antibiotic of last resort.[6]

Dr. Lida Mattman's *Cell Wall Deficient Forms: Stealth Pathogens*[7] opened my eyes to the insidious danger of antibiotics. Antibiotics initiate a viscious chain of events that result in the creation of cell wall-deficient bacteria. Most antibiotics work by destroying the bacteria's outer layer (the cell wall). Because our immune system recognizes invading bacteria by the structure of their cell walls, these wall-deficient bacteria go undetected and proceed to rapidly multiply. Concomitantly, these phantom microorganisms have the time to mutate into new species resistant to the original antibiotic. Cell-wall deficient bacteria are a most serious threat to the integrity of our immune system.

Commonly prescribed broad-spectrum antibiotics destroy not only the bacteria for which they were intended but also the friendly bacteria essential to the integrity of the intestinal immune system. With the protective bacteria destroyed, overgrowth of yeast and other pathogens is a common occurrence (dysbiosis). The combination of compromised intestinal defenses and an army of phantom cell wall-deficient bacteria place a great burden upon our immune system.

Good Immunity Starts in the Womb

When female patients let me know they want to become pregnant, I follow a three-fold strategy. First, I assist the mother-to-be in dealing with any underlying health problems. Once pregnant, I take steps to make sure she has sufficient nutrients to support both her health and that of her developing fetus. Lastly, I recommend breast-feeding, again ensuring that the mother maintains a nourishing diet, supplemented with whatever additional nutrients she biochemically requires. The result, time after time, is what I call "super-babies" – vibrant, alert and extremely healthy. I have helped many sick women (some with serious diseases like lupus, thyroiditis and cancer) regain their health, and conceive and deliver super-babies. Doing so is one of the greatest joys of my life.

Maintain a well-defended and vigilant immune system.

~

Breast-feeding is the best gift a mother can give her child. The power of emotional bonding between mother and infant has been well established. From an immunological standpoint, mother's milk contains antibodies to most of the infective agents to which the mother has been exposed. Since the infants' immune system is not mature and fully effective until 7 to 12 months of age, the passive immunity conferred by the breast milk is of the utmost importance.

Breast-feeding, in addition, gives babies very important nutritional advantages. Mother's milk contains a number of important nutrients, such as the amino acid, taurine, necessary for healthy brain, eye and liver functions; health-promoting omega-3 EFAs; and intestinal-protective probiotics. These three very important nutrients are seldom, if ever, contained in commercially-prepared infant formulas.

Furthermore, the ratio of amino acids to EFAs in cow's milk or soy formula is not conducive to proper development of the infants' intelligence and maturation of neurological functions. In a recent study published in *Lancet,* researchers reported that infants fed omega-3 EFAs showed significantly enhanced problem-solving ability compared to infants who did not receive the oils.[8]

If for some reason my patients are unable to breast-feed, I suggest that they give their babies goat milk, as it is the most similar to human milk. If that is not an option, I recommend that they "doctor" infant formula with flaxseed oil and probiotics, starting with a ¼ teaspoon of flaxseed oil and a ¼ teaspoon of a good probiotic per bottle. If the formula does not contain taurine (some of the newest ones now do), I recommend adding the content of ¼ of a 500 milligram capsule to the bottle. One of taurine's many beneficial properties is that of making infants less irritable. After the initial month, I recommend doubling all three additions and continuing supplementation at that level until termination of formula feeding. As you learned in Chapter 5, commercial fruit juices contain molds and other toxic substances. They should never be given to children, especially infants.

Supporting Your Immune System

The best way to maintain your immune system is to follow many of the strategies already presented in this book. A balanced lifestyle that includes a stress reduction practice, regular exercise, large amounts of antioxidants and an optimistic attitude supports effective immune function. A diet rich in nutrients that includes a wide variety of health-promoting foods is also essential.

Food Rotation

As most of us have some degree of dysbiosis, it is wise to rotate the foods we eat. Since it takes about 4 days for a food allergen to be totally erased, you should not eat any food more frequently than that interval of time. For example, if you eat salmon on Monday, don't eat it again until Friday. If you eat the same things, day in and day out, as many people do, you may unknowingly be exposing yourself to allergenic foods. The Standard American Diet (SAD) – a wonderfully descriptive acronym coined by pioneering biochemist and nutritional researcher, Dr. Jeffrey Bland – is based on a repetitive breakfast of wheat cereal and milk – two of the most common allergenic foods.

Keep Your Bowel and Liver Healthy

As you learned in Chapter 7, the Bowel Healing Program is essential for maintaining the health of your intestine and promoting generalized immune vigilance. Because our bodies are more vulnerable as one season transforms into another, remember to undertake the entire program (Steps 1 to 3) even if you are feeling well. This is also the time to drink the Detox-Tonic Tea and to make sure you are taking liver-supportive supplements. *An ounce of prevention is always worth a pound of cure.*

When you are under or anticipate being under unusual stress, I suggest some extra precautions. For example, when I travel by plane and know I am going to be exposed to poor quality air, infections, plastic food and damaging electromagnetic fields, I take a combination of natural disinfectants and immune supporters (see **CC Infection Nutrients Pack**, Appendix A) every 4 hours. I also add a packet of Biopro Thymic Protein A[9] every 4 hours (every 2 hours, if I'm not feeling well). To alleviate the common problem of water retention, I take 100 milligrams of Vitamin B_6 every 2 to 3 hours. I have never failed to arrive in top shape and ready to go work or play!

Extensive animal and laboratory studies, including testing at the National Institutes of Health (NIH), have shown Biopro Thymic Protein A to have the identical biological activity and function as the protein from our own thymus glands.[10] I am a firm believer in this intervention, and I have watched it shorten and reduce the impact of infections in so many of my patients.

Healing Allergies

You are usually aware of your IgE-mediated allergies, since they create immediate misery. We treat IgE-mediated allergies by a sophisticated desensitization process, which involves neutralizing the allergen with an appropriate dilution of the offending substance (Miller Desensitization). We use this method mostly for environmental allergies, and for *Candida albicans* and molds. Since environmental allergies aggravate food allergies, desensitization reduces one of the loads on the immune system.

Identify and desensitize allergies.

∼

Delayed food reactions (IgG-mediated) are identified by a blood test. The panel we use at our Centers tests for delayed allergic reaction to 83 foods. These most commonly eaten foods accurately represent other foods in the same family as the one tested. For example, if you have an allergic reaction to broccoli, you may also react to kale, kohlrabi and other members of that vegetable family. The IgG test identifies not only what foods an individual is allergic to but also the severity of the response.

When a patient has multiple food allergies, we recommend immediate elimination of the worst offenders. Since people need to eat to survive, we then advise patients to rotate the least offensive foods, eating them once a week or once every two weeks, depending on their allergenicity. This process of elimination-rotation may take many months for individuals who are allergic to numerous foods. Gradually, as the intestine is healed, allergenic foods are reintroduced on a 4-day rotation pattern.

Take quick action and fight infections naturally.

You will need to find a knowledgeable integrative health practitioner to help you with your IgE- and IgG-mediated allergies. In the meantime, using alkalinizing substances like Alka-Seltzer Gold, bicarbonate of soda or the ingredients of **CC Aller-1** (see Appendix A) will reduce the severity of the allergic response. Since allergies put a great strain on the adrenals and ultimately cause adrenal insufficiencies, supporting the glands with ingredients such as those found in **CC AdrenoMax** and **CC AdrenoSupport** (see Appendix A) are helpful in reducing fatigue and avoiding adrenal insufficiency.

Handling Infections

When you have even the vaguest suspicion you are succumbing to an infection, take quick action. Not only do you want to minimize your suffering, but you also want to limit free radical production and oxidative stress, responsible for the acceleration of the aging process.

At such times, it is prudent to implement the entire Bowel Healing Program, using 1 tablespoon of probiotics. You may also want to make prophylactic use of natural remedies, such as those found in **CC Infection Nutrients Pack** (see Appendix A). Eat lightly – primarily vegetables and soups. For protein, use protein drinks, tofu and fish. Drink plenty of purified water. I also recommend drinking ginger and ginseng teas, which are anti-inflammatory, supportive of the digestive system and energizing. If you find yourself with little or no appetite, consuming a healing broth (our grandmothers were right about chicken soup!), such as the one below, can provide good amounts of predigested protein to assist the immune system in rebounding to health. Drinking this broth is like having an infusion of amino acids, and my patients routinely tell me what a lift it gives them.

Healing Broth

1. Purchase 2 to 3 pounds of organic free-range beef.
2. Place the beef in a large uncovered jar and add enough purified water to just cover the meat.
3. Add a couple of cloves of garlic, some sliced fresh ginger and a teaspoon of sea salt. (These ingredients not only flavor the broth but also assist in the extraction process; garlic and ginger are also immune-supportive.)
4. Place the jar in a large soup pot with cold water. (You are creating a double boiler).
5. Cook the meat at the lowest possible heat for 5 to 6 hours.
6. Strain the liquid and drink a cup or two every few hours. (The meat has very little nutrient value at this point and should be discarded).

Additional Measures

If you have been unable to completely stop the infection in its tracks, add Biopro Thymic Protein A in large quantities – 2 packets, 3 to 4 times a day. Since the powder is absorbed under the tongue, you can take it even if you are nauseous. If your stomach is not in a sad state of affairs, use the natural antibiotic *Echinacea angustifolia* (echinacea). Take 1 capsule or 15 to 30 drops of extract every 3 hours.

If you are achy and feverish, don't take nonsteroidal anti-inflammatory drugs (NSAIDs), such as ibuprofen and aspirin. They irritate the gastrointestinal lining, opening the door to developing a leaky gut. Prolonged use has also been associated with the development of ulcers and other gastrointestinal maladies.[11] Instead, try white willow bark, a long-used herbal remedy for reducing both fever and pain. It contains the same active ingredient (salicin) that has been synthesized for aspirin, but is a gentler anti-inflammatory and is also rich in minerals and vitamin B_{12}.

If you find yourself in the dire predicament of suffering from an infection that is very severe or life threatening, a combination of natural interventions and pharmaceutical antibiotics is usually the most effective approach. Make sure to take probiotics along with your antibiotics to protect your "good" intestinal bacteria and prevent dysbiosis.[12]

9 *The Hormonal Symphony*

A magnificent biochemical orchestration.

The Neuroendocrine System

*T*he intricate relationship of the involuntary nervous system, the glands and their secretory messengers – hormones – is, to me, the ultimate example of *divine orchestration*. The neuroendocrine system has an impact on more body processes, and has more interactive checks and balances than any other physiological system. Growth, metabolism, temperature modulation, immunity, response to stress, sexual activity and, of course, the aging process are all regulated by its actions.[1, 2, 3]

The hormonal symphony begins in a small but most significant part of the brain called the hypothalamus. The hypothalamus is the major hub where information from the nervous system and all endocrine glands converge. It is here that all involuntary commands for life function, such as ovulation, are initiated. Through biochemical messengers (hormones), the commands travel to the various endocrine glands. Once stimulated, the glands produce more specific biochemical messengers, which reach various target organs through the bloodstream. The hormones each gland secretes into the bloodstream interact with each other through a feedback mechanism. This allows for the appropriate amount of specific hormones to be released in response to the body's continually changing needs (dynamic homeostasis). I affectionately liken the endocrine glands to shimmering butterflies winking at each other with fragile, sensitive antennas. The glands and their messengers are powerful in their action, and yet very vulnerable to interference. Disruption in messaging can lead to many diseases and can accelerate the aging process.

Our glands become less efficient as we age. Most of the hormones they secrete diminish in quantity and quality, and all parts of the body begin to deteriorate. In fact, hormone levels that are most closely related to overall stress response and daily life functions – DHEA, melatonin and the sex hormones – are becoming more accepted as biochemical markers of aging. Maintaining the health of each gland and the proper interactive feedback among all of them is key to retaining organ function and vitality as we mature, for a disturbance in one affects all the others. *Neuroendocrinological research has now provided us with the knowledge of how to maintain the glands and restore them to the peak efficiency of a 30-year-old – essentially, turn back the hormonal clock.*

Each of the ductless glands that comprise the endocrine system plays a vital role in our well-being. It is, however, the individual and combined health of the thyroid, adrenals and gonads (ovaries and testes) that, in my opinion, provide the biochemical infrastructure for maintaining youthfulness and productivity. At our Centers, we call this infrastructure "the triad." In this chapter, the focus is on the first two members of the triad – the thyroid and adrenals. Chapters 10 and 11 are devoted to the ovaries, and Chapter 12 to the exciting anti-aging hormones – DHEA, melatonin, and growth hormone.

The Thyroid

The thyroid gland, which sits just below the voice box, is to the body what the starter is to the car. It secretes iodine-containing hormones, mostly T_4 (tetraiodothyronine) and some T_3 (triodothyronine) – the biologically active thyroid hormone. Thyroid hormones stimulate and synchronize all metabolic cellular functions.

The thyroid has a very important function in glucose metabolism, breaking it down into fuel for brain and muscle activities through a process called glycolysis. Thyroid hormones stimulate all tissues of the body. Thus, for example, inadequate thyroid stimulation of bone marrow can lead to anemia. Thyroid hormones also stimulate the neurotransmitters, the chemical messengers of our moods. A sluggish thyroid can cause depression. Poor utilization of blood fats and an increase in cholesterol can result from an inadequately functioning thyroid. The thyroid also secretes calcitonin, a hormone that regulates calcium metabolism and has a very important role in the prevention and control of osteoporosis.

During childhood, the thyroid promotes normal physical growth and mental development. Many cases of avoidable childhood mental retardation are due to a failure to identify a poorly functioning thyroid gland.[4]

Thyroid secretion, like all endocrine gland secretions, is regulated by an initiatory hormone from the hypothalamus – thyrotropic-releasing hormone (TRH). TRH travels to the pituitary gland, activating the secretion of thyroid-stimulating hormone (TSH). When the thyroid gland is activated by TSH, it responds by secreting T_4 and some T_3. Under normal circumstances, T_4 and T_3 secretions are regulated by a feedback mechanism. When blood levels of T_4 are too low, the hypothalamus starts the chain of events that leads to increased thyroid hormone production. When the levels are too high, the hypothalamus diminishes its initiatory command for thyroid secretion.

Thyroid Hormone Pathway

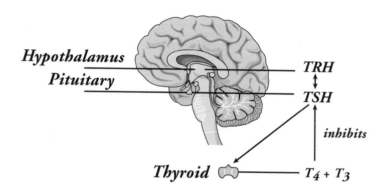

Figure 9-1

Thyroid Malfunction

Never, as in recent times, has so much thyroid malfunction been reported in the medical literature. The most frequent disorders are hypothyroidism (low function), but we are also witnessing an alarming increase in Graves disease (severe hyperthyroidism) and in thyroiditis, an autoimmune disease of the thyroid that usually leads to low circulating hormones.[5]

In my opinion, chronic stress plays a major role in thyroid dysfunction. Under normal circumstances, the thyroid gets primed in the wee hours of the morning to increase the secretions that will activate all cellular metabolic processes we need to get up and go. During stressful events, the thyroid gets a super jolt, which stimulates the entire body and increases glucose breakdown (glycolysis). This process provides more available energy, needed for the "fight or flight" response. Given the pace, at which most of us live, our thyroid glands are continually in a state of over-reactivity and become vulnerable to depletion and subsequent malfunction. An overworked thyroid is also more susceptible to viral attacks. A combination of viruses and toxins is responsible for the increase in inflammatory thyroid disease (Hashimoto disease).[6]

Another cause of thyroid problems is a lack of adequate nutrients. To produce adequate amounts of thyroid hormones the gland has to be supplied with sufficient amounts of the amino acid, tyrosine and with iodine. Tyrosine, combined with iodine, produces tetraiodothyronine (T_4). If the diet does not include enough of these two substances, the gland will lack the building blocks for hormonal production. Vitamins E, A, C, B_2, B_3 and B_6 are also necessary for the manufacturing of the thyroid hormone.

Hypoconversion Hypothyroidism

Even if the thyroid produces adequate amounts of T_4, the tissues still need to convert T_4 to T_3, the biologically-active thyroid hormone. This conversion process requires the enzyme deodinase to remove one iodine from T_4 to make T_3. The deodinase contains selenium and zinc as components of its structure. Inadequate amounts of these trace minerals hinder the availability of the enzyme.[7, 8] Many people, unknowingly, have subclinical deficiencies of these two important trace minerals. Inadequate conversion of T_4 into the biologically-active T_3 is the result (hypoconversion hypothyroidism).

The transformation of T_4 into T_3 takes place not in the transporting blood serum, but in various tissues of the body. Thyroid, like most other hormones, exerts its action only if it can properly bind to the cells of the target organ. Toxic substances interfere in this process. Toxic metals, in particular, disrupt the cellular architecture and limit hormonal binding.[9] The organic hydrocarbons and chlorinated compounds found in our water can displace thyroid hormones from cellular receptors.[10, 11] Pentachlorophenol (a wood preservative) is even more harmful, since it binds to thyroid hormones and crosses the blood-brain barrier.[12] As the brain is the regulator of all endocrine functions, this chemical can have a major detrimental impact, not only on the brain structure itself but also on thyroid cerebral activity.[13, 14]

Common in Women

Thyroid disorders are more common in women than in men.[15] In women, adequate T_3 binding is also dependent upon sufficient progesterone.[16, 17] A low level of progesterone, so common in young women today, interferes with thyroid efficiency and is one of the most frequent causes of infertility. All cellular functions, including egg maturation, are dependent on the overall health of the thyroid and the capacity of our tissues to utilize the hormone. Because progesterone levels rapidly decline during the time around and after menopause, this form of hypothyroidism is also common during this life transition (see Chapter 11).

Identifying Thyroid Malfunction

When physicians understand that the thyroid is not only the starter but also the gearbox of the body, interacting with the adrenals, gonads and all other glands, they can easily write a laundry list of subtle clinical symptoms. Most physicians today, however, are either not trained in functional medicine or don't have the time to ask the right questions. Burdened by managed care pressures, they are typically forced to perform only limited diagnostic blood tests, such as the TSH Test, to determine thyroid malfunction. Unfortunately, this test fails to identify all possible problems, including often subtle, but significant, clinical hypothyroidism.[18] As a result, many patients remain undiagnosed until their conditions become serious.

A malfunctioning thyroid can either be sluggish (hypothyroidism) or too active (hyperthyroidism). Common symptoms of these two types of disorders are summarized in Figures 9-2 and 9-3.

Signs and Symptoms of Hypothyroidism

Early morning fatigue	Recurrent infections
Weight gain	Low body temperature
Dry, brittle nails	Cold extremities
Dry skin	Scanty periods
Skin changes (edema and thickening)	Menstrual disorders
	Infertility
Hair loss	Hoarseness
Loss of the outer third of the eyebrow	Poor vision and hearing
	Anemia
Mental sluggishness	Elevated cholesterol
Memory and concentration difficulties	Muscle aches and weakness
	Labored and difficult breathing
Depression	

Figure 9-2

If you have four or more of the above signs or symptoms, you should see a physician who understands the subtleties of clinical hypothyroidism.

Although hypothyroidism is far more common than hyperthyroidism (the overproduction of hormones), it too can be missed by standard laboratory tests. If you have three or more of the signs or symptoms listed in Figure 9-3, you should see a knowledgeable physician.

Signs and Symptoms of Hyperthyroidism

Anxiety	Heart palpitations
Sweating	Bulging eyes
Weight loss	Insomnia
Heat intolerance	

Figure 9-3

When thyroid malfunction is compounded with other hormonal imbalances and toxic metal burden, conventional lab tests rarely identify the problem. Diane's story is an example of this all too often encountered situation.

Diane's Transformation

Diane, a 35-year-old woman, who had the demeanor of a woman double her age, came to our Center with the clinical symptoms of hair loss, brittle nails, constipation, menstrual irregularities, some weight gain, and a sense of impending doom and gloom. Her TSH lab test was within normal limits, and her physician had refused to acknowledge she had a thyroid dysfunction, despite her large array of clinical hypothyroidism signs and symptoms.

We embarked upon our usual medical detective journey to discover which of many possible factors could have caused Diane's problems, and we found a couple of very significant ones. She had a very low progesterone level and high levels of toxic metals (aluminum and cadmium), both of which were interfering with the tissue binding of the thyroid hormone. Our lab work revealed a couple of other indicators of clinical hypothyroidism – mild anemia and slightly elevated cholesterol, despite a good diet. Her adrenal function test indicated marginal adrenal reserves.

Given our overall understanding of the clinical hypothyroidism picture, we felt thyroid hormonal supplementation should not be the first course of action. With Diane's level of toxicity, the hormone might not have been able to adequately bind to the tissues anyhow and might have caused heart palpitations. At best, we would have achieved poor results.

We began by dealing with the intestinal toxicity and the toxic metal load through the Bowel Healing Program, diet and special nutrient infusions. At the same time, we started her on a progesterone cream and supported the thyroid with homeopathic remedies. We made certain that she had enough zinc and selenium in her supplement regime. Her diet was adapted to correspond with her blood type, and foods to which she was allergic were removed and rotated. We recommended **CC AdrenoMax** (see Appendix A) and DHEA to support her adrenal glands. Within a few months, we watched her blossom into a chic and confident woman, who now looked and felt younger than her chronological years. At this point, we added a small amount (30 milligrams per day) of the whole thyroid gland (Armour Thyroid). One month later, her cholesterol returned to within normal limits and her anemia disappeared.

Supporting Your Thyroid

As with all the body's organs and glands, a proper choice of foods is important for maintaining optimal thyroid function. Seaweed, rich in iodine, supports the gland. Beans, sprouts and cruciferous vegetables (brussel sprouts, cauliflower, broccoli, etc.) reduce the toxic load and provide good antioxidant protection. Unless you eat a couple of pounds of cruciferous vegetables a day, you don't need to worry about their ability to block thyroid hormones. It is also wise to include foods rich in selenium (e.g., fresh tuna, sunflower seeds and whole grains) and in zinc (e.g., pumpkin and sunflower seeds, soybeans and fish). Exercise is also an important thyroid health strategy. Sustained aerobic exercise raises your body temperature, which allows proper binding of the hormone to the tissues.[19] If you feel tired and depressed, I recommend tyrosine supplements. For the best results, take 1,000 milligrams before breakfast and a repeated dosage before lunch.

Maintain thyroid health.

The Adrenals

The adrenals, a pair of triangular-shaped glands that sit on top of each kidney, are to the body what the fuel tank is to the car. Proper functioning of the adrenals is necessary for sufficient energy production, efficient metabolism and normal response to stress and infections.

Adrenal stimulation begins in the hypothalamus, which responds to input from our five senses and secretes an initiatory hormone called cortico-releasing hormone (CRH). Through the nervous system, CRH stimulates the inside of the adrenals (adrenal medulla) and the brain to release adrenaline. At the same time, it travels to the pituitary gland to stimulate the secretion of adrenocorticotropic hormone (ACTH). ACTH is a very busy chemical messenger. When it reaches its target, the outer layer of the adrenal glands (cortex), it activates three types of hormones – mineralocorticoids, glucocorticoids and steroids – collectively known as adrenocorticoids.[20]

Adrenal Hormone Pathway

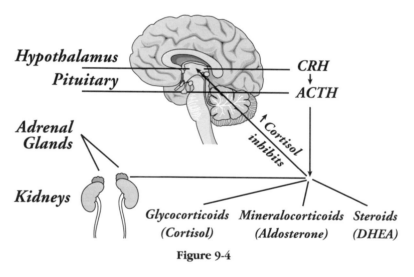

Figure 9-4

The main function of mineralocorticoids (primarily aldosterone) is the maintenance of water balance in the body through the regulation of sodium, magnesium and potassium. Glucocorticoids (cortisol is the most abundant) are powerful anti-inflammatories. They are essential for the utilization of carbohydrate, protein and fat by the body, and for a normal response to stress. Excessive cortisol, however, is one of the major threats to our survival because it inhibits immune cellular response, increases blood glucose and mobilizes calcium from the bones. Because of these deleterious effects, it has been called the "death hormone." The third type of adrenal hormones stimulated by ACTH is the sex-related steroids (androgens), of which DHEA is the most abundant and important. DHEA has many vital functions, first among them being the ability to counterbalance the detrimental effects of excessive cortisol. It also has the capacity to become estrogen in women and testosterone in men. DHEA is one of the primary players in anti-aging medicine (see Chapter 12).

Although excessive amounts of adrenal hormones are released in response to stress (the fight or flight response), they are routinely secreted in the body for adaptive survival purposes. The rise in the level of mineralocorticoids in the early hours of the morning increases our blood pressure and allows us to stand up and get going.[21] The time of its peak secretion, 3:00 a.m. to 6:00 a.m., is known as the "hour of the wolf" because many people with cardiovascular problems die at this time of heart attacks. (Interestingly, this happens most frequently at the beginning of the workweek, on Monday mornings.) The increased adrenal cortical secretion of DHEA is responsible for early morning sexual arousal, most common among young people (and those who keep themselves young!).

Of all the interconnecting hormonal highways, the highway between the hypothalamus and the adrenal glands is one of the most important and also the one that bears most of the brunt of our hectic lives. For this reason, nature has put buffering mechanisms in place to protect it. Under normal circumstances, when the level of cortisol gets too high, the hypothalamus and pituitary respond to this chemical signal by respectively decreasing the production of CRH and ACTH.

Constant exposure to a diverse variety of stressors, however, can have an adverse impact on this feedback loop, creating a vicious cycle that, over time, can have devastating effects. The hypothalamus is constantly stimulated not only by the perception of stressful events but also by excessive activation of the five senses. Loud noises, bright lights, offensive tastes and odors, or being shoved in a crowded street – all common experiences of urban living – trigger a cascade of hormonal events that result in the overproduction of CRH, ACTH and cortisol. This overproduction of cortisol ultimately damages the hypothalamus, rendering it less and less able to modulate the activity of the adrenal cortex.[22]* The result is adrenal overwork and consequent malfunction, which manifests in a wide variety of symptoms.

Adrenal Malfunction

The wear and tear of our glands ultimately leads to their damage and the reduction of their capacity to produce the substances for which they are responsible. The adrenals and the thyroid are the most used and abused glands in the body, and they are the first ones to show signs of wear and tear. It is unfortunate that mainstream medicine only recognizes complete adrenal failure (Addison's disease). In all my years of practicing medicine, I have only encountered a couple of cases of total adrenal failure, while I have seen thousands of people suffering from varying degrees of adrenal insufficiency.[23] Allergies, as you may recall from Chapter 8, greatly strain the adrenals, and are often responsible for the subclinical adrenal insufficiencies physicians such as myself commonly see. As you may be aware, people with severe allergies, including asthma, often need emergency injections of adrenaline or cortisone. Chronic stress combined with allergies is a sure formula for adrenal insufficiency.

Identifying Adrenal Insufficiency

Respected longevity researcher, Dr. Ward Dean, calls adrenal insufficiency "adrenal maladaptation syndrome," since we are unable to adapt to the stresses of life once our glands reach this state of exhaustion.[24] As with hypothyroidism, signs and symptoms are numerous and varied, as you can see in Figure 9-5.[25] Those of us who practice functional medicine have been aware of them for a long time.

Adrenal Insufficiency Signs and Symptoms

Fatigue	Weakness
Nervousness	Poor memory
Severe PMS	Palpitation
Salt craving	Abdominal discomfort
Depression	Alternate diarrhea and constipation
Inability to concentrate	Obesity
Carbohydrate cravings	Poor wound healing
Allergies (hay fever, asthma)	Glucose intolerance
Anxiety	Moon face
Headache	Purple striae
Alcohol intolerance	Loss of bone density
Muscular pain and tenderness	Joint pain and tenderness (arthritis)
Skin discoloration on cheeks	

Figure 9-5

People with adrenal insufficiency not only are prey to all the symptoms of maladaptation listed above, but they also have great difficulty in bouncing back from infectious diseases and stress. Fatigue is the most common of all the symptoms and is most often experienced in the early afternoon, when adrenal response is physiologically tempered. Early morning fatigue is more reflective of thyroid insufficiency, a condition that is often accompanied by sluggish adrenals.

The actions of the thyroid and adrenals are intimately connected. The *Physician's Desk Reference* states, "… Synthroid is counterindicated in patients with uncorrected adrenal insufficiency, since thyroid hormones increase tissue demands for adrenal cortical hormones and thereby may precipitate acute adrenal crisis when adrenal insufficiency has not been corrected."[26] It is, indeed, unfortunate that most physicians, even endocrinologists, have probably never read this important passage and seldom, if ever, check the status of the adrenals prior to thyroid supplementation.

The simplest way to identify adrenal insufficiency is to measure DHEA levels, both total and sulfate. DHEA is always low when the adrenal glands have been exposed to persistent and excessive demands. Since low DHEA levels have been associated with breast cancer and menopausal symptoms in women, and with accelerated aging in both sexes, we focus a great deal of attention on this hormone at our Centers.

In a clinical setting, we can also test the reserves of the adrenals by checking the cortisol levels first thing in the morning, then challenging its release with an injection of ACTH (Cortosyn Test). We subsequently measure the cortisol levels 30 and 60 minutes later. Very often, people with chronic fatigue have low levels of cortisol before stimulation and sluggish or delayed response. Some have paradoxical responses, showing higher levels at the 30-minutes rather than at the 60-minutes mark. It is as if they can make the initial jump, but they just can't keep going. Like the Glucose Tolerance Test that checks the ability of the body to respond and adapt to a load of carbohydrates, the Cortrosyn Test checks the ability of the adrenal glands to respond and adapt to ACTH stimulation. It mimics what occurs when we wake up, drink a cup of coffee, and start our day.

Supporting Your Adrenals

Maintaining the health of the adrenal glands is essential to the maintenance of our overall wellness, particularly as we grow older.

Reduce and Manage Stress

Because the effect of stress is cumulative and devastating, reducing and managing it is the most important step we can take to reduce the wear and tear of our adrenals. I have presented you with a number of stress-reducing strategies in earlier chapters. I suspect I'm sounding like a broken...CD by now, but stress continues to rear its ugly head again and again as one of the most serious underlying causes of disease and accelerated aging. Adequate restorative sleep and a nourishing diet are also essential for maintaining the health of the adrenals.

Helpful Supplements

If you are exposed to infections or are under a great deal of unavoidable stress or anticipate that you will be – business travel, school exams, extended work hours, emotional conflict – I advise that you supplement your diet with some specific nutrients. The adrenals under normal circumstances contain large quantities of vitamin C and B$_5$ (pantothenic acid) – important ingredients for the hormonal factory. Any supplements taken to support the adrenals must contain these two vitamins. Make sure to also take a good multi-vitamin and mineral supplement. In addition, take vitamin C with bioflavonoids to bowel tolerance, vitamin E (at least 400 milligrams) and 100 to 500 milligrams of vitamin B$_5$ two times a day. It is also important to replenish vitamin B$_6$ (100 to 200 milligrams), potassium (70 milligrams) and zinc (25 to 50 milligrams), since their urinary excretion is accelerated during periods of stress. Adding an adrenal extract supplement, such as **CC AdrenoMax** or **CC AdrenoSupport**, provides additional support for the glands. DHEA can also help, but as it is a powerful hormone, it is prudent to use it wisely and preferably under medical supervision (see Chapter 12).

Maintain adrenal health.

Digestive Support

Since stress breaks down protein to make sugar for the "fight or flight" response, make sure you consume adequate amounts of easily digestible proteins. I recommend the protein shake, described in Chapter 5, which immediately puts predigested protein into your system. Since stress reduces the secretion of digestive enzymes, enzyme supplementation can assist the digestive process. As you well know by now, stress promotes dysbiosis (yeast overgrowth and bowel problems), so engage in the Bowel Healing Program and take 2 to 3 teaspoons of probiotics until you have completely regained your energy. Of course, if you are one of those rare Martians who never experiences stress, all this hard work is none of your concern!

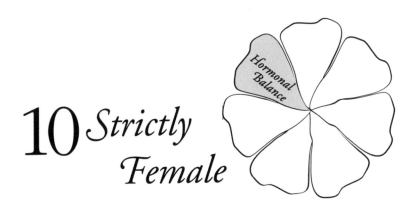

10 *Strictly Female*

What complex and magnificent beings we are!

Doing It All

*W*e women are quite remarkable creatures. Our bodies have been designed to give new life. Innately, we have a strong intuitive sense – as nurturers and caregivers, we need it to "know" when our loved ones are in trouble. This quality that served us so well while we were cave-women, today makes us more vulnerable in the fiercely competitive, male-dominated business world. Surviving in such an environment often requires control and tempering of our sensitive antennas, even though they register the subtlest imbalances. Such adaptation doesn't come without a price. As we step into the 21st century, many of us are mothering (children and often parents, as well) and engaging in fast-paced careers, all at the same time. Yes, we may have the ambition to do it all, but living such expanded and complicated lives takes its toll on our intricate hormonal systems and accelerates our biological aging clocks.

Today, there is an increasing rate of infertility – partially because working women are waiting longer to start a family and partially because modern living is taking a toll on our complex hormonal pathways. More women are having premenstrual symptoms and bumpy mid-life transitions. It doesn't need to be this way. *We just need to know about and be committed to implementing the natural remedies and lifestyle enhancements that will support our chosen lifestyles.*

Let's first familiarize ourselves with the workings of our hormonal system. We'll then identify some of the symptoms of imbalance and the strategies we can adopt to bring our system back to a healthy balance, and ultimately to maximum wellness and sustainable vitality.

The Female Cycle

Once we reach puberty and our female hormones kick into gear, we begin to menstruate and, hopefully, soon get into a regular 28-day fertility cycle. The hormonal orchestration underlying this cycle, just like the regulation of the adrenal and thyroid glands, begins with the secretion of an initiatory hormone – hypothalamic gonadotropin releasing hormone (GnRH). GnRH signals the pituitary gland to secrete follicle-stimulating hormone (FSH), which makes its way to the ovaries. Once prompted by FSH, the follicles (the encased eggs) begin to secrete estrogen. When estrogen reaches a certain level, the hypothalamus gets the message and signals the pituitary to secrete luteinizing hormone (LH).[1] As LH rises, it alerts the pituitary to reduce the production of FSH. When LH peaks (around day 14 of the cycle), the egg, that had been targeted and has moved towards the periphery of the ovary, is released from its follicular casing (ovulation).

A new type of hormonal orchestration then begins. The empty follicle is filled with cholesterol and is now called the corpus luteum (yellow body). Progesterone is made from this cholesterol through the intermediate step of conversion to the hormone pregnenolone. During the first 14 days of the cycle (follicular phase), the high levels of secreted estrogen build up the lining (endometrium) of the uterus. After ovulation (luteal phase), the newly-secreted progesterone enriches the uterine lining with mucus and lots of nutrients (secretory endometrium). If fertilization doesn't occur, the lining is sloughed off around day 28 in response to the drop of both hormones (menstrual period).

The Female Cycle

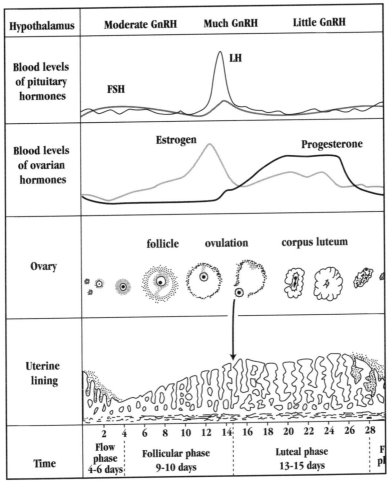

Figure 10-1

If the egg is fertilized, the corpus luteum keeps on growing and is now called the corpus luteum gravidarum. It secretes much more progesterone to build an abundant and enriched uterine lining to receive and feed the newly fertilized egg, and to support the development of the placenta and fetus. During the second and third trimester, the placenta produces most of the progesterone needed to sustain the pregnancy, up to 300 times the level produced by the ovaries during an unfertilized cycle. This high level of progesterone plays the important "pro-gestational" role of abortion prevention by relaxing the uterine wall. Progesterone also promotes maternal fat metabolism and stabilization of blood sugar, which allows for the increased energy production required for the development of the fetal brain.[2]

Power of Progesterone

Progesterone is quite an amazing hormone. As we have seen above, it plays an essential role in the female cycle and in pregnancy. But it does so much more! Progesterone is involved in a wide range of important physiological activities. It is necessary for the proper binding of thyroid hormone to the tissues, and it modulates glucose metabolism. It reduces blood clotting and water retention, promotes cell division, and stabilizes our moods. Its cardinal role in the bone building process and the prevention of osteoporosis is still widely unrecognized by mainstream physicians, although this function has been well documented in the medical literature (see Chapter 11).

This versatile hormone is also capable of transforming itself into estrogen and, during stress, into adrenal hormones. It is truly a masterpiece of nature and the female hormone, unfortunately, most neglected by mainstream physicians. Dr. Jonathan Wright and John Morgenthaler describe the socioeconomic reasons for this phenomenon in *Natural Hormone Replacement for Women Over 45*.[3]

Estrogen and progesterone are both necessary in the female cycle. Progesterone has an anti-estrogenic effect, especially at the breast and uterine sites, where its presence blocks the over-proliferative effect of estrogen that may lead to cancer. Many female cancers and endocrine system problems, including premenstrual syndrome (PMS), breast and uterine fibroids, endometriosis, infertility and some of the uncomfortable symptoms that occur around and after the cessation of periods (perimenopause and menopause), are the result of too little progesterone and too much estrogen.[4] In functional medicine, this state of hormonal imbalance is known as "estrogen dominance."

Even when both hormones are within the so-called normal reference range, estrogen dominance may occur when estrogen is on the high end of the reference range and progesterone is on the low end. Because of the potential risks associated with this hormonal imbalance, I have for years measured both estrogen and progesterone, and consequently incurred the wrath of insurance companies, content with the minimalistic and improper mainstream approach of assessing only estrogen. Without measuring both hormones, the problem of estrogen dominance cannot be identified.

Renowned British gynecologist Dr. Katherina Dalton noted many years ago that PMS results from inadequate progesterone in the second half of the cycle (luteal phase).[5] In this country, Dr. John Lee, a respected family practitioner, awakened us to the wide ranging effects of inadequate progesterone in his first book *Natural Progesterone: The Multiple Roles of A Remarkable Hormone.*[6, 7] Figure 10-2 summarizes the potential deleterious effects of excessive estrogen and the counterbalancing power of progesterone.

Hormonal Impact

Excessive Estrogen	Progesterone
Increases salt and fluid retention.	Acts as a natural diuretic.
Interferes with thyroid hormone binding to cells.	Facilitates normal thyroid hormone cell binding.
Can cause excessive blood clotting.	Normalizes blood clotting.
Increases insulin resistance, which can lead to blood sugar regulation problems, weight gain and Type 2 diabetes.	Normalizes insulin resistance.
Increases body fat.	Uses fat for energy.
May cause depression.	Acts as an antidepressant.
Stimulates breast and uterine tissue growth, which may result in fibrocystic breasts or uterine fibroids.	Protects against formation of fibrocystic tissue.
Increases breast cancer risk by stimulating excessive breast cell growth.	Helps prevent breast cancer by opposing estrogenic proliferative action.
Increases uterine lining proliferation, which can lead to endometriosis.	Maintains uterine lining suppleness and normal cell growth.
Increases risk of uterine cancer by stimulating building of mucosa.	Prevents uterine cancer by promoting shedding of mucosa.

Figure 10-2

Hormonal Imbalance

Estrogen dominance, whatever the source, is largely responsible for most of the dysfunctions of menstruating women, from premenstrual syndrome (PMS), fibrocystic breast disease (FCBD), uterine fibroids and endometriosis to infertility, ovarian cysts and cancer. The growing phenomenon of estrogen dominance is caused by a number of factors, with protracted stress leading the pack.

Stress

Stress affects all female hormones, but first and foremost, progesterone. I call progesterone the "masochistic mother hormone," because it readily transforms itself into adrenal cortex hormones when stress puts demands on the adrenals beyond their capacity to cope. Nature puts procreation on the back burner during stressful periods and uses progesterone to support our overworked survival glands: the adrenals. Excessive stress also affects the estrogen side of the hormonal equation. It stimulates the overproduction of hypothalamic GnRH, which promotes FSH production and subsequent estrogen secretion. Furthermore, as you may recall from earlier chapters, whenever we are under stress, the intestine grows more yeast. Yeast produces estrogen-like substances that introduce further imbalances into the estrogen-progesterone equation.

Inadequate Progesterone

To add insult to injury, while estrogen is produced during the entire menstrual cycle, progesterone is only produced from ovulation to menstruation, and many women have frequent anovulatory cycles. So, we start out with far less progesterone than estrogen, and chronic stress further depletes it. As a consequence of all of the above, women in industrialized countries have far less progesterone than they need to balance the overabundance of estrogen, both endogenous (internal) and exogenous (external).

Liver and Intestinal Malfunction

The liver and the intestine also play vital roles in estrogen dominance. Estrogen, like all hormones, passes through the liver. The liver has, among its many functions, that of binding (conjugating) excessive estrogen so that it can be eliminated through the bile into the intestine and be subsequently released through good bowel function. When the conjugation pathway is overloaded by other processes, such as elimination of toxic substances, this binding does not occur, and the level of estrogen rises. When there is an excessive amount of dysbiotic flora in the small intestine, the conjugated estrogen that has reached this site is released through the breaking of the bond by an enzyme (B-glucoronidase). This released estrogen then gets reabsorbed in the liver, creating a hazardous and viscious cycle. These combined processes are major contributors to estrogen dominance.

Exogenous Estrogens

There are even other more insidious and dangerous threats to the tenuous estrogen-progesterone balance. One such threat is the estrogens routinely fed to our livestock. Our livestock are plied with synthetic growth hormones to increase lactation and with estrogen to make them heavier at a quicker rate. When we consume the meat, the milk and its byproducts – cheese, ice cream and even yogurt – we also ingest large quantities of exogenous estrogens. The Europeans are way ahead of us in being aware of the danger of these hormones. Several years ago, the European Common Market refused to buy our meats unless they were raised in a free-range fashion and without hormones.

Xenoestrogens

The worst of all exogenous estrogens are xenoestrogens (toxic exogenous estrogens) – xenobiotics that exhibit estrogen-like activity. The worst xenoestrogens are those that come from petrochemical sources. These insidious toxic estrogens come from environmental pollutants, pesticides, toxic fumes and plastic-coated cans. The lacquer-coating, used on the inside of many canned foods, contains bisphenol-A. This plastic is a potent xenoestrogen, which can leach into the contents of the can.[8] Researchers recently reported that fetal exposure to bisphenol-A in the range currently being consumed by people can alter the adult reproductive system in male mice.[9] Whatever their source, xenoestrogens are metabolized by the body into carcinogenic forms of estrogen, which compete with our own estrogen to bind to our cell receptor sites.[10] When we add up all the various sources of xenoestrogens, exogenous estrogens, as well as our own excessive estrogen generated under stress and by impaired intestinal and liver functions, we end up with the dangerous imbalance – estrogen dominance.

Early Menarche

At this point, I want to comment on another ominous sign of our toxic times – the precocious onset of menstruation (menarche) in many of our girls. Not too many years ago, girls in the United States usually had their first menstruation around ages 13 to 16. As Dr. John Lee has noted, the onset of menarche as early as age 10 is now commonplace.[11] During the last few decades, our children have been bombarded with television ads promoting fast food, laden with exogenous estrogens and other toxic estrogenic byproducts. The consumption of large quantities of these toxic estrogens stimulates the production of LH and early ovulation, robbing our girls of their childhood.

Our girls, from the very earliest ages, are also exposed to explicitly sexual media messages. Everyone knows that viewing sex is sexually stimulating. I firmly believe that the taking in of these sexual messages triggers early hypothalamic secretion of GnRH and is another major factor contributing to the premature onset of menses. Young girls who become sexually mature before a sense of discernment and restraint has been firmly established are at risk of having babies while they are still babies themselves.

If this was not enough reason for serious concern, early menarche also increases the risk of breast and uterine cancer.

The longer a female is exposed to large quantities of estrogen, especially in the presence of inadequate progesterone (estrogen dominance), the more chance she has of developing these types of cancer.[12, 13, 14] Given the current state of affairs, I feel parents need to be proactive in monitoring their daughter's food and media intake.

Hormonal Mapping

As you can see in Figure 10-3, hormones undergo individual and unpredictable transformations. When patients come to me with hormonal imbalance problems, I order lab tests that provide me with a complete picture of what is happening with all their interconnected hormones. I call this process "hormonal mapping."

Although the number of hormones that I check varies somewhat depending on the condition I am treating (infertility, perimenopause, etc.), I always include adrenal and thyroid testing because these glands are intimately connected with the sex hormones. Since all sex hormones, female and male, are manufactured from cholesterol, I typically also include a lipid profile. In terms of female hormones, I often start with the precursor of all the sex hormones – pregnenolone – and then look at its derivatives, which include estrogen, progesterone, testosterone, DHEA and cortisol. I also assess IGF-1, an indirect measure of growth hormone (GH), when clinically indicated (see Chapter 12).

Hormone Pathways

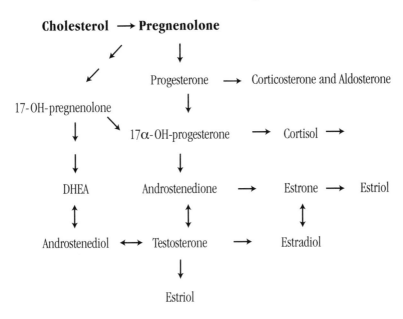

Note: ↓ = one way action,   ↕ = two way action

Figure 10-3

Natural Hormone Replacement

Let me share with you why I believe natural hormones are better for us than those adulterated by chemical manipulations. Over the millennia, human beings have evolved in synchrony with their environment. At some point, the environment consisted mostly of shrubs and forests. This habitat provided food and medicine for all, and cave-dwellers learned to rely on these natural substances for the maintenance of their physiological functions.

One example of what I call "symbiotic phytoadaptation" is the ability of phytosterols (plant estrogen-like substances), such as black cohosh (*Cimicifuga racemosa*) or dong quai (*Angelica sinensis*), to exert beneficial estrogenic effects without the negative consequences of synthesized "look-alikes." Another is the progesterone-like properties inherent in wild yam (*Dioscorea*), soy and herbs, such as *Agnus castus* (also known as vitex or chaste berry). These natural hormonal substances have been successfully used for millennia in traditional cultures.

Progestins Are Not Progesterone

Some pharmaceutical companies have recently begun to go "natural," or so they claim. In the United States, anything that exists in nature cannot be patented. Industry scientists, therefore, take natural substances, such as soy or wild yam, and add some chemical bonds. The now altered substances are patentable products, which become sources of substantial revenue for the companies that own the patents. The most dramatic example of this practice is the progestins, chemicalized progesterone-like substances. Progestins, such as Provera, are not progesterone and, in fact, have many of the side effects of estrogen. The warnings for Provera in the *Physician's Desk Reference (PDR)* read like the worst estrogen dominance nightmare you could imagine. While progestins may be good for the coffers of the pharmaceutical companies, they are far from good for our bodies because our cell receptors often are unable to recognize and utilize these altered substances.[15]*

Same Structure As Our Own

A number of years ago, some like-minded physicians and I began using, with astounding results, the natural progesterone from which pharmaceutical companies create progestins. Innovative compounding pharmacists, to whom I am extremely grateful, produce hormones, such as progesterone, pregnenolone and estrogen, through biochemical manipulations that respect the integrity of the natural products from which they are derived.

Use natural remedies to treat hormonal imbalance conditions.

∽

Unlike progestins, natural progesterone has the same chemical structure as the progesterone our bodies produce. With access to natural pharmaceutical grade hormones, carefully prepared by compounding pharmacists,[16] physicians like myself can prescribe formulations that provide hormones that operate in the same manner as the ones our bodies naturally produce. They are wonderful rejuvenation tools for both women and men when our own production capabilities run out.

Treating Hormonal Imbalance

In most women, if the conditions are mild, they can be remedied by a combined program of intestinal and liver detoxification, dietary modifications, nutrient supplementation and herbal remedies. More complicated conditions require the intervention of an experienced integrative physician.

Premenstrual Syndrome (PMS)

Premenstrual syndrome (PMS) is one of the most common disorders of women of reproductive age.[17] Although its existence first appeared in the medical literature more than 60 years ago, it didn't receive much attention in the United States until the 1980s. In 1987, the American Psychiatric Association (APA) defined PMS as a solely psychiatric disorder by calling it "late luteal phase dysphoria" (a mood disorder occurring during the second part of the menstrual cycle). This definition, unfortunately, ignores the biochemical, nutritional and hormonal factors underlying the syndrome. Although I have treated mild to severe emotional distress associated with PMS, I don't consider it a psychiatric disorder. As you can see in Figure 10-4, emotional disturbances are just one of the many symptoms of PMS.

Common PMS Symptoms

Tension and mood swings	Fatigue
Depression	Headaches (premenstrual migraines)
Bloating and water retention	Sleep disturbances
Carbohydrate and chocolate cravings	Skin eruptions
Breast tenderness	Bowel changes
Irregular periods	

Figure 10-4

PMS symptoms are mostly a manifestation of estrogen dominance and its consequences (see Figure 10-1). The overload of estrogens creates a negative feedback with the hypothalamus, which, in turn, impairs ovulation and the subsequent production of progesterone. Many girls and young women who have severe PMS menstruate without ovulating (anovulatory cycles). With very little or inadequate progesterone, they are even more vulnerable to stress. Stress, in turn, increases the excretion of important nutrients, such as zinc, magnesium, potassium and vitamin B_6 – necessary for hormonal balance and the metabolism of essential fatty acids (EFAs).

PMS is probably triggered and made worse by a fast food diet loaded with exogenous estrogens. In addition, these foods are low in vital nutrients and high in saturated fats – the precursor of the pro-inflammatory arachidonic acid series 2 hormone-like prostaglandins (PG2s). Researchers have documented that a predominance of PG2s can stimulate PMS, particularly the symptom of painful menstruation (dysmenorrhea).[18, 19, 20]

PMS Remedies

Mild Symptoms

The first step in restoring hormonal balance is the reduction of exogenous estrogens through the consumption of a clean diet. The diet should exclude nonorganic meats, milk products and canned foods – all sources of exogenous estrogens. This is necessary at least until the syndrome is resolved, and ideally should be continued thereafter, as much as possible. Eating whole grains and lots of dark, green leafy greens, rich in B vitamins and fiber, is an important healing strategy. Soy foods and flaxseed contain good estrogen-like substances that impede toxic xenoestrogens from binding to our tissues. Anti-inflammatory EFAs from flaxseed oil or fish both reduce painful uterine spasms and have a general calming effect on the body. Bowel cleansing will scrub out the excessive estrogen that has been excreted with the bile into the intestine, and keeping the liver clean will assist the organ in its estrogen-binding process. For mild forms of PMS, these actions will generally take care of the problem.

Moderate Symptoms

If symptoms are more severe, I recommend including nutrients and herbs, such as those found in the **CC Female Pack**. I also recommend using an over-the-counter natural hormonal cream, such as **CC Hormonal Balance Natural Body Cream**. The cream should be massaged into any area of the body (except the breasts)[21]* from day 14 to 28 of the menstrual cycle to compensate for inadequate progesterone. Many of my patients have also found that massaging the cream above the pubic area relieves their menstrual cramps.

Severe Symptoms

Women with the most severe form of PMS are generally those who ovulate infrequently, if at all (anovulatory cycles). With an undetectable level of progesterone, pharmaceutical grade progesterone needs to be added to the healing program. Depending on the results of the hormonal map, I might prescribe transdermal creams, micronized oral capsules or rectal suppositories, to be used from day 14 to 28 of the cycle.

Sleep disturbance often accompanies moderate to severe

forms of PMS. Poor sleeping patterns aggravate the syndrome, adding more stress to an already biologically-distressed system. When sleeping is a problem, I recommend melatonin, a multi-faceted pituitary hormone, which induces sleep, and also reduces estrogen dominance (see Chapter 12). I recommend 1 to 3 milligrams (sublingual, for better absorption) 15 to 30 minutes before bedtime. I usually recommend that it be used just before or around ovulation until menstruation. For those who suffer from more severe sleep disturbances and aggressive behavior, I also add gamma-aminobutiric acid (GABA). GABA is a modulating neurotransmitter that has finally entered the consciousness of mainstream medicine.[22]*

Allergies

Women with PMS often also suffer from allergies. Taking 500 to 1,000 milligrams of calcium at bedtime is a good way to reduce the tension-producing histamine. Reduction of histamine also promotes restful sleep.

Rapid Resolution Possible

When comprehensive and individualized recommendations are followed, the turn-around from PMS can be very rapid, as Lisa recently experienced.

Lisa's Transformation

Lisa was a typical 17-year-old high school senior, who skipped mom's homemade meals and went out almost every night to join her friends at the local dispensary of plastic foods. In the company of her peers, she gorged on fried and fatty foods and cokes, and stayed up late. By the time her mother brought her to our Center, Lisa had gained 30 pounds, had terrible menstrual cramps, severe premenstrual headaches, irregular periods, acne, and constipation, and was inappropriately aggressive. She was a perfect example of the combined effect of the Standard American Diet (SAD) and adolescent rebellion to parental guidance.

After appropriate testing, we started Lisa on the Bowel Healing Program, along with melatonin at night and GABA in the afternoon. We also negotiated a dietary agreement with Lisa – she would eat out only one day a week and the remainder of the time she would consume the elimination-rotation diet our nutritionist had designed for her, based on the results of her food allergy panel. In a far better frame of mind two weeks later, Lisa started the **CC Female Pack**. She also began taking additional magnesium (500 milligrams in the morning) and 1,000 milligrams of calcium in the evening to assure proper balance between these two minerals. Since Lisa had anovulatory cycles, she also needed exogenous progesterone. In her case, because of her poor gut status, we used progesterone cream.

I had promised Lisa that she would be free of PMS within 3 months if she followed all of our recommendations. Lisa was symptom-free after 2 months – far exceeding our expectations. We were a little concerned that she might backslide when she went off to a residential college. But, again, she surprised us! The fast results she had obtained and my "tough love" approach had converted her. Having maintained relatively healthy eating habits and her supplement regime, Lisa laughingly reported, during her first break from college, that she was in far better shape, both in body and mind, than most of her peers.

Fibrocystic Breast Disease (FCBD)

According to the American Academy of Pathology, 50% to 80% of North American women suffer from some form of fibrocystic breast disease (FCBD), which includes fibrocystic mastitis (lumpy breasts) and mastodynia (painful breasts). FCBD often accompanies PMS, and it can also exist as an independent condition. Although FCBD is considered a benign condition, it may be a predisposing factor for breast cancer. It also makes it difficult for both women and their physicians to distinguish a benign cystic lump from a cancerous one by manual breast exam.

Estrogen Binding

Many years of clinical experience have proven to me that, here too, estrogen dominance is a major culprit. Estrogen binds to the breast tissues, causing excessive cell proliferation. In the presence of inadequate amounts of opposing progesterone, cell multiplication of milk-producing breast tissues becomes rampant. These overgrown tissues turn then into cysts. Month after month, the reoccurrence of this condition, often accompanied by mastodynia, leads to FCBD.

For resolution of symptoms, I start with the basic PMS strategies – cleansing the bowel and liver, following the PMS dietary guidelines, taking supportive nutrients and herbs, and using a natural hormonal balance cream. I recommend applying it in varying locations but not directly to the breasts, as it may increase breast pain. The hormones know where to go, regardless of application site.

Iodine

The role of iodine in FCBD has been made clear by a dear colleague, Canadian women's health specialist Dr. Carolyn DeMarco in her book *Take Charge of Your Body.*[23] According to DeMarco, at least 25% of North American women are iodine deficient at some point in their lives. Adequate amounts of elemental iodine prevent FCBD. Iodine's beneficial effect is due to its capacity to diminish estrogen binding to the breast tissues.

Iodine dietary intake depends on the types of foods consumed as well as the iodine content of the soil and water in which foods are grown. Some foods, such as seaweeds and seafoods, are rich in iodine, but vegetables and fruits are often deficient in iodine because they are grown in depleted soil. The Great Lakes area, with little or no iodine in the soil or water, is known as the "goiter belt," and the incidence of both FCBD and breast cancer is higher there than in other areas of North America.[24]

Researchers have verified the beneficial effect of elemental iodine in healing FCBD.[25, 26] Integrative clinicians, including Dr.

DeMarco, Dr. Jonathon Wright and myself, have achieved successful results with the addition of this remedy. At our Centers, I usually recommend 6 to 8 drops of tri-iodine (I-3) in the morning.[27] ***Do not take iodine if you have thyroiditis.***

Uterine Fibroids

Uterine fibroids, in my opinion, are often the consequence of inflammation of the uterus. Estrogen dominance, however, is a major underlying cause as well. Many times, fibroids remain small and present no problems. As estrogen levels decrease when we approach menopause, they often shrink. If they grow large, however, they can cause a number of problems, including pressure on the bladder and bowel, infertility, miscarriages and, of course, heavy or prolonged bleeding episodes that often lead to severe anemia.

Fibroids, especially in the early stages, can be successfully treated with natural strategies. As a foundation strategy, I suggest you follow the recommendations for severe PMS. One important addition is Wobenzym N, a German product that contains a combination of powerful proteolytic enzymes.[28] These proteolytic enzymes, which break down protein, are also natural anti-inflammatory substances. When taken between meals, they effectively digest the newly-formed soft part of the fibroid that surrounds the often-calcified core. I have had great success in shrinking uterine fibroids with this approach. The calcified core that remains is usually small and causes no problems. In any event, it can be easily removed by an uncomplicated laser procedure if necessary.

Joan's Transformation

Joan, a 37-year-old executive, had been experiencing very heavy menstrual cycles for a couple of years. During the past year, the bleeding was so severe that she required transfusions. Her physician diagnosed multiple, large fibroids and, alarmed by her chronic life-threatening anemia, advised her to undergo a hysterectomy. Instead, Joan came to our Center to explore alternatives to such a drastic remedy.

Our work-up revealed extremely high levels of estrogen and almost no progesterone, a dysbiotic gut with parasites and an overgrowth of yeast, a toxic liver, food allergies and a high level of aluminum. As a successful executive with a demanding position, Joan frequently ate in restaurants, which exposed her to both excessive aluminum and perhaps to parasites, as well. (I find it frightening that kitchen workers need to be reminded to wash their hands. And what if they don't?)

We began Joan's treatment with the Bowel Healing Program, while our nutritionist designed an elimination-rotation diet, and an individualized protein shake to help her deal with her food allergies and malabsorption problems. As the fibroids had doubled in size during the previous 3 months, it indicated the existence of newly-formed soft tissues around the hard cores. This fact led to the prescription of Wobenzym N. We started with a dosage of 5 pills, 3 times a day and increased it the following week to 10 pills, 3 times a day.

To counterbalance the extreme estrogen dominance, I prescribed pharmaceutical grade natural progesterone suppositories, to be used from day 14 to 28 of the cycle, and recommended the use of a mildly antiestrogenic over-the-counter hormonal balance cream (see **CC Hormonal Balance Natural Body Cream**) to be used throughout the cycle. In the ensuing weeks, we gave her injections of liver extracts to help the anemia, along with B vitamins and antioxidant infusions. Eventually, we used toxic metal chelation (see Chapter 14) to remove stored aluminum.

Her severe menstrual bleeding began to diminish within 2 months, and her anemia was subsequently resolved. Her hormonal map, repeated 3 months later, showed a dramatic reversal of the estrogen dominance condition. A sonogram, performed 4 months after that, revealed that her fibroids had shrunk to half their previous size. Within 12 months, the only remnants of Joan's fibroids were some insignificant calcium cores.

Endometriosis

Endometriosis is probably the most complex and, often, the most severe of all gynecological problems. It has multiple causes, including the possibility of an autoimmune factor. It is a condition in which the uterine lining (endometrium), under estrogenic stimulation, keeps growing – often expanding outside of the uterine boundaries. Islands of endometrial tissues are found surrounding the ovaries and fallopian tubes, and often around the rectum. These tissues can travel anywhere through the general circulation and can cause very unexpected symptoms. I recall one patient, who would cough up blood during her menstrual periods. She, of course, was tested for tuberculosis, but the result was negative. Further investigation revealed she had endometriosis of the lungs – a rare, but nonetheless possible condition.

The most common symptoms of endometriosis are abnormal or heavy menstrual bleeding, accompanied by severe abdominal or lower back pain. If endometrial tissue has migrated to the intestine or rectum area, it can cause digestive tract symptoms, such as diarrhea, constipation or rectal pain during bowel movements. Endometriosis is one of the primary causes of dysmenorrhea and infertility. Unfortunately, diagnosis often occurs when the disease is so advanced as to require surgery to remove the imbedded tissues.

If you have any of the above symptoms, I recommend that you schedule an appointment with a specialist in endometriosis before the condition progresses. Early detection requires intra-abdominal examination with a laparoscopic instrument and the eye of an experienced examiner. In the early stages, endometriosis can be remedied by the same general strategies as those recommended for severe PMS, under the guidance of an experienced integrative physician.[29]* In advanced cases, surgery and complex hormonal and other biochemical manipulations are necessary. Many of my patients with endometriosis have been victims of physical or emotional abuse connected with their female being. If this aspect of their condition is not healed, very little else will work.

Infertility

Infertility affects one of every six women in the United States today. The causes of infertility, like endometriosis, are multiple and complex. Insufficient progesterone, very often from anovulatory cycles, and estrogen dominance are two of the major causes, but many other factors may be involved. Various forms of thyroid problems leading to clinical hypothyroidism, malabsorption and chronic stress are all important contributing factors. One of my early successes in treating infertility was a young drug sales representative, who had undiagnosed thyroiditis. Proper treatment of the condition led to an easy pregnancy and a beautiful healthy child.

As I have developed a reputation for successfully reversing infertility through natural interventions, I see many women who come to me after consulting a myriad of fertility experts. Laura's case is perhaps the easiest way to give you an idea of what a natural approach to infertility treatment looks like in a patient who had closed the door on motherhood.

Laura's Transformation

Laura initially came to our Center solely to alleviate her migraine headaches and her chronic respiratory infections. At the age of 40, she had never had a regular cycle since she first menstruated at age 12. Not only were her periods irregular, she would often have to stay in bed for a week when she did get a period because the blood loss was so substantial. The birth control pills she was prescribed at age 13, and continued for 10 years, failed to relieve many of her devastating symptoms.

During the course of the next 10 years, she saw more than 20 gynecologists and fertility specialists, endured two laparotomies, surgical removal of a fibroid tumor, a dilation and curretage (D & C), and more than 3 years of fertility drugs, to which she had adverse reactions. She remained infertile, and she and her husband had given up on ever becoming parents. Laura thrived on junk food, and was addicted to chocolate and sweets. She suffered from frequent migraines, had a negative outlook on life, and constantly took to her bed, debilitated by cold and flu-like symptoms.

We were obviously in the presence of a multisystem imbalance and disruption of the hormonal orchestration. I believe this disaster was promoted by her horrendous eating habits and liver toxicity. This led to estrogen dominance which, in turn, contributed to her severe PMS, endometriosis, fibroids and infertility.

We needed to rebuild this woman from the inside out. We started with shifting her negative attitude, drastically changing her eating habits and, of course, painstakingly peeling the layers of toxicity and hormonal imbalance. Our nurse-nutritionist at the time, Barbara Schiltz, took Laura under her wing as her own personal project. She helped her rework her eating and thinking patterns, administered injections and cuddled her.

Laura's liver toxicity was very high, not only because of her dysbiotic gut, but also because she had, for many years, taken so many medications and repressed so much anger. The Bowel Healing Program, a very comprehensive liver detoxification program that included both intramuscular (IM) injections and sophisticated oral supplements were part of her healing journey. Since Laura was a highly-stressed individual, biofeedback and training in meditation were essential components of our comprehensive approach.

And then the unexpected happened 8 months later: Laura became pregnant. As her healing was not yet complete, we gave her weekly antioxidant and mineral infusions to compensate for her still slim cellular reserves. Nine months later, we witnessed the entry into this world of a beautiful, calm, smiling, well-developed baby! He was a super-baby – endowed with the biological and, most likely, spiritual capacity to make a smooth transition into the new millenium.

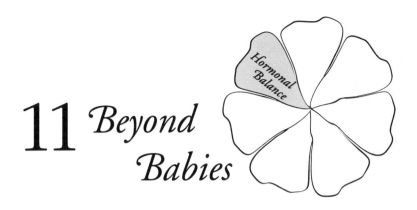

11 *Beyond Babies*

Older can be better!

Mid-Life Transition

*W*omen, by nature, have a tremendous amount of creative energy. For many, a good portion of that energy is channeled into birthing and raising children during the reproductive years. When reproductive capability ceases, women have the opportunity to redirect their creative energy. Many women, including myself, have found this stage of life to be most fulfilling. We have the opportunity to blossom anew with the assurance of earned wisdom unavailable in younger years.

Perimenopause

Before reaching this potentially liberating stage of life, women go through perimenopause – the transition time between regular menstrual cycles and their complete cessation (menopause). On the average, women move into menopause around ages 50 to 52. If all were well, perimenopause should not exceed a year. Over the course of my lengthy clinical practice, however, I have witnessed a dramatic increase in both the length and intensity of this transitional phase. I now see women in their 30s beginning to show early menopausal signs. For women who are chronically stressed – such as high-powered city dwellers – this transition can be debilitating and go on for many years, unless remedial actions are taken.

Mainstream medicine defines menopause as the mid-life cessation of menstrual periods for at least 6 consecutive months. At this point, the common recommendation for a resolution of symptoms, and the prevention of heart and bone disease is pharmaceutical hormone replacement therapy (HRT). We have a very different perspective at the Corsello Centers. We view the earliest and most subtle of perimenopausal symptoms as the beginning of the menopausal continuum, and mark this as the time to begin using natural remedies to facilitate smooth sailing to the new shore.

Perimenopausal Symptoms

Perimenopause is an all-encompassing physiological phenomenon that simultaneously affects all three templates – energetic, chemical and physical. Whether perimenopause is uncomfortable for you and what symptoms you experience is dependent on a number of factors. Lifestyle, diet and stress play significant roles. Women in traditional societies, who have clean, healthy diets, live close to nature and have low stress levels, move uneventfully into menopause. Traditional Japanese women, who have consumed a diet low in saturated fats and high in soy all their lives, also make a smooth transition. The more depleted, the more stressed, the more burdened the body is with toxins and allergies, and the more sensitive the brain is to hormonal fluctuations – the more tumultuous and lengthy is the menopausal transition.

Earliest Symptoms

One of the earliest symptoms of perimenopause is a change in the character of the menses. Commonly, periods start getting somewhat irregular. Some women, who bled a lot, begin having shorter periods and less blood loss. Others may start having clots and interrupted flow. Subtle emotional shifts may begin to occur. Family, work and other stressors that were previously manageable now trigger irritable responses. Some women begin to have insidious recall or short-term memory difficulties that threaten their livelihood. Sleeping patterns may be disrupted and sex drive may dwindle. Intercourse may become painful as a result of reduced vaginal lubrication and thinning of the vaginal mucosa. Unexpected weight gain while maintaining the same eating habits may add to the distress of this often unrecognized early transitional stage.

Hormonal Confusion

Perimenopause is marked by a disruption of the hormonal feedback loop, which inevitably increases as we age. The ovaries begin to receive confusing messages and go through bouts of estrogen overproduction. Concomitantly, progesterone rapidly declines as the frequency of anovulatory (without ovulation) periods increases. Irregular FSH spikes begin to occur, as if a whirling dervish is trying to awaken the last few eggs to their final hurrah. And for a brief moment here and there, while the ovaries forget that they are about to conclude their reproductive dance of life, they get into a frenetic state that sends estrogen up to the sky – not very functional, but what a dance!

Estrogen Impact

These bursts of estrogen can cause unpleasant PMS symptoms – mood swings, anxiety, irritability, depression, acne and carbohydrate craving. An overproduction of estrogen leads to excessive insulin production, which in turn is responsible for inexplicable weight gain. If uncontrolled, this hyperinsulinism can lead to Type 2 diabetes. With falling progesterone levels unable to balance the estrogen bursts, the result is further estrogen dominance. If the liver has lost its capacity to bind and clear estrogen out of the system, the levels may get high enough to eventually bring about cancer of the breasts, ovaries or uterus.

When the frenetic hormonal seesaw tips the other way, inadequate estrogen is the result, leading to a variety of symptoms. Unlike progesterone, estrogen naturally occurs in three forms – estrone (E1), estradiol (E2) and estriol (E3). While some symptoms, such as hot flashes and other vasomotor instability reactions, are related to total estrogen decline, others are more specifically related to a particular form of the hormone. Confusion, memory difficulties, impaired creativity and insomnia are all the result of reduced estradiol, which affects the proper working of the neurotransmitters. Vaginal dryness and urinary problems, in contrast, are predominantly due to reduced estriol. Estriol, in fact, governs the harmonious workings and the suppleness of the lower third of the urethra, located in the vagina.

Inadequate Progesterone

When we stop ovulating, we no longer form a corpus luteum – the predominant site of progesterone production.[1]* As ovulation becomes less and less regular, progesterone levels decline rapidly. As you may recall from Chapter 10, progesterone sacrifices itself to produce adrenal hormones under stress – so most urban women unknowingly have deficient progesterone levels even before ovulation becomes sporadic.

Since progesterone plays a role in many important body functions, including glucose metabolism, mineral balance, cell division, good thyroid function, mood stability and bone metabolism, inadequate levels can have a myriad of consequences in mid-life. Symptoms can be very surprising – like mid-life asthma. Since progesterone is an involuntary muscle relaxant, its decline can result in constricted breathing in women who have allergies or an inherent lung weakness.

Decreased Testosterone

Testosterone, produced marginally in the ovaries, but mostly as a product of the metabolism of adrenal DHEA, also begins to decline. Low testosterone plays a major role in osteoporosis, decreased libido, and loss of initiative and drive. Fifty percent of postmenopausal women have substantially decreased testosterone levels.[2]

Thyroid Interaction

The thyroid gland, which has been subject to much wear and tear, becomes less efficient as we mature, especially because its hormonal assistant, progesterone, is low. One of the causes of clinical hypothyroidism, you may recall from Chapter 9, is low progesterone. Disturbances in the thyroid-adrenal axis are aggravated by the concomitant disruption in the hormonal feedback loop between the hypothalamus and the ovaries.

A sluggish thyroid worsens both the weight gain and fatigue of the menopausal transition. Fat distribution takes on more of a male pattern, with accumulation of fat at and above the waistline (apple shape). Besides the loss of the appealing feminine waistline, an apple shape is associated with a greater risk for heart disease.[3]

Dr. John Lee was the first to report that natural progesterone supplementation relieved symptoms of hypothyroidism in estrogen-dominant women.[4] I have verified his clinical experience, as have many of my integrative medicine colleagues. Women who are estrogen dominant have poor thyroid efficiency. At this point in time, we know that estrogen increases thyroxine-binding globlulin – the transport system for both T_3 and T_4. Globulin-bound thyroid is biologically inactive. The more thyroid hormones are globulin-bound, the less of the active form available.[5] Adequate amounts of natural progesterone reduce estrogen dominance and, consequently, increase the biologically active form of thyroid hormones.

If a patient's thyroid blood levels are not below the normal reference range, but she has mild symptoms of clinical hypothyroidism, I don't rush to give thyroid supplements. Instead, I focus first on balancing the estrogen dominance with adequate natural progesterone. I clean the tissues to diminish resistance to whatever circulating thyroid hormone is present. Usually, this takes care of mild clinical hypothyroidism. I also recommend tyrosine and iodine drops to upgrade the functioning of the gland. If these interventions do not resolve all of the symptoms, I add thyroid extracts and/or homeopathic thyroid drops.

Proactivity is the Key

I hope you haven't become too disheartened by learning about all the symptoms that may occur during perimenopause. *Remember, knowledge is power. If you are aware of the very earliest indicators, you can proactively take measures to mitigate symptoms and decrease the length of the perimenopausal storm.* Appropriate lifestyle changes, such as smoking cessation, restriction of alcohol, nutritional modifications and natural hormonal interventions make a big difference. Usually, once you have been period-free for 6 to 12 months, the wild estrogen fluctuations subside. As your body becomes adjusted to the new you, fewer interventions are needed to keep you vital in your "wise woman" years.

The Corsello Centers Approach to Mid-Life Transition

At the Corsello Centers, we approach mid-life transition in two phases. Phase 1 is usually sufficient for women who are generally in good health and have mild to moderate symptoms. It includes bowel and liver detoxification, lifestyle modifications, some hormone-mimicking herbs and foods, bone nutrients, and an hormonal cream. Additional nutrients are recommended for specific concerns, such as "brain fog," insomnia and urinary problems. For women who are experiencing a more challenging transition, we add what we call a Phase 2 intervention – which includes individualized natural hormone prescriptions, based on clinical symptoms and the results of hormonal mapping.

Manage perimenopause naturally.

~

Phase 1 Interventions

Bowel and Liver Health

As you learned in earlier chapters, a healthy bowel and liver is essential for overall body health. It is particularly important during perimenopause. Nourishing and keeping the liver clean enables the organ to efficiently process and release excessive estrogens from the body.[6] The three steps of the Bowel Healing Program remove xenoestrogens and the estrogen byproducts produced by pathogenic microorganisms, while assuring a balanced intestinal flora. This is the first important step in Phase 1.

Diet and Phytonutrients

Although it is always wise to eat a highly nutritious and balanced diet, it is particularly important during this major hormonal transition. This is a time to go even further – adding some foods that are protective and limiting or avoiding potentially damaging ones, such as refined carbohydrates.

The risk for osteoporosis and heart disease increases substantially after menopause, when ovarian hormone secretion has totally ceased. However, since hormonal decline and associated disease risk occur gradually over a time period that may be very extended, appropriate preventive precautions are effective and should be taken as soon as you notice any symptoms of perimenopause.

Soy and Flaxseed

If you are not already doing so, you should include soy products in your diet. Soy products (soybeans, soymilk, tofu, tempeh, soy protein powder, etc.) are rich in phytoestrogens – plant estrogens. Soy is high in a type of phytoestrogen called isoflavones (primarily genestein and diadzein). Intestinal bacteria convert isoflavones into hormone-like substances, which have weak estrogenic activity. These phytoestrogens have been shown to bump toxic forms of estrogens out of receptor sites and, thus, counteract their harmful effects.[7] Researchers have found that soy offers a wide range of benefits for mature women – decreasing perimenopausal symptoms, lowering the risk of a wide range of cancers, and preventing osteoporosis and heart disease.[8, 9, 10, 11, 12]

Another food I have recommended for years, and that should have a preeminent place in the diets of mature women, is flaxseed. In addition to its many healing properties described in earlier chapters, flaxseed contains a type of phytoestrogen known as lignans. Lignans, like soy isoflavones, are acted upon by colonic bacteria to produce weak estrogenic-like substances. Lignans have been shown to offer protection against both cancers and heart disease.[13, 14] Incorporating flaxseed into your daily diet is an easy way to obtain these disease prevention benefits.

Researchers have confirmed that eating one serving of soy (45 milligrams) a day decreases cancer risk and helps mitigate hot flashes. It appears, however, that larger quantities are necessary to reduce the risk of heart disease and osteoporosis.[15, 16, 17, 18] A cup of soymilk has about 20 to 30 milligrams of isoflavones, while a half of cup of tempeh or tofu have about 35 milligrams. A tablespoon of flaxseed is roughly equivalent to one serving of soy.

Limit or Avoid Harmful Foods

Refined carbohydrates and sugars should be limited or avoided, as they can increase hot flashes.[19]* And as you already know, they have a tendency to be turned into fat when they can't be utilized for energy production. Refined carbohydrates also make the blood acidic, promoting calcium removal from bones (osteoporosis) and the formation of blood clots. Many women suffer unexpected strokes after menopause because they don't know they need to adapt their diets to compensate for the loss of cardioprotective ovarian hormones. In fact, any food or beverage that increases blood acidity should be limited or avoided. This includes an overabundance of animal proteins, alcohol, coffee and caffeinated tea. Red meats and sodas, besides being acidic, are also high in phosphorous – an element which also depletes skeletal calcium.

Natural Hormone Supplements

Since consistently consuming large amounts of phytoestrogen-containing foods is difficult for many of us, I recommend combining dietary phytoestrogens (20 to 45 milligrams) with the phytoestrogens and hormone precursors found in herbal members of the plant kingdom. Herbs, such as black cohosh, licorice, chaste berry, wild yam, dong quai and ginseng have been found to relieve menopausal symptoms and promote overall health and vitality. I recommend you supplement your diet with these powerful healers (see **CC Meno-Pack**, to learn about these and other synergistically supportive ingredients, such as vitamin E).

I also recommend the use of an over-the-counter natural hormone cream, (see Appendix A: **CC Hormonal Balance Natural Body Cream**) which contains progesterone, a small amount of pregnenolone, and a small amount of DHEA (included to modulate the shunting of progesterone into testosterone). My perimenopausal patients, using 1 teaspoon a day, have found it helpful in relieving a variety of symptoms. To prevent osteoporosis, I recommend supplementing the diet with calcium and other nutrients essential to bone health. Read more about this important topic later in this chapter.

Other Phase 1 Interventions

Stress Management

Managing stress during perimenopause is crucial. Your progesterone is already waning, and stress accelerates its decline. Women who have been able to manage stress and preserve their adrenals have adequate DHEA levels. As a consequence, they have an easier menopausal transition since their DHEA can both continue to produce necessary testosterone and also become estrogen. Unfortunately, by mid-life, most of us have depleted our DHEA reserves by repeatedly responding to the complicated demands of modern living.

Do you remember the studies in Chapter 4 that reported that meditators had higher DHEA levels than nonmeditators? Reducing and managing stress spares the adrenals. Find some way to incorporate a stress-management technique into your daily life – meditation, yoga, deep breathing, biofeedback, music, etc. You have lots of choices. Move it to the top of your priority list.

In Chapter 5, you learned how essential oils (aromatherapy) can be used as a stress reducer. Sage *(Salvia officinalis)* is an overall energy balancer and has been used in that capacity for centuries in Native American healing rituals. It has also been found to be effective in relieving hot flashes and other perimenopausal heat reactions. To obtain its healing benefits, add 10 drops of sage oil to a warm bath or keep a bottle with you and inhale whenever you feel a heat wave coming on.

Exercise

Exercise, as you learned in Chapter 5, is an essential longevity strategy. It is especially important during the female hormonal wind-down as a stress-releaser, energizer and heart-protector. Its role in the prevention of osteoporosis is well documented.[20, 21]

Yoga is one of the best exercises for the prevention of osteoporosis. The slow, deep stretching of the muscles facilitates bone rebuilding by improving reabsorption of calcium. Yoga tones the endocrine glands and provides overall body relaxation, which decreases blood acidity (one of the causes of osteoporosis).

Some yoga postures are also weight-bearing. Weight-bearing exercises reduce the rate of bone loss by stimulating bone cells (osteoblasts) to increase calcium utilization. Walking, moderate jogging, cycling and weight lifting are all good weight-bearing exercises. And, of course, all types of aerobic exercise are also cardioprotective.

Mental Symptoms

If you suffer from mental symptoms, such as forgetfulness, fogginess, depression or impaired creativity, I recommend that you add phosphatidylserine (100 milligrams, 2 times a day). Phosphatidylserine is the main lipid (fat) in the brain. It is essential for maintaining the integrity and fluidity of brain cell membranes and facilitates the smooth working of the neurotransmitters. It has also been shown to reduce the secretion of cortisol in response to stress and to improve the release of acetylcholine, an important neurotransmitter involved in memory and other brain functions.[22] *Gingko biloba* extract is also useful for improving brain clarity (40 milligrams, 3 times a day). *Gingko biloba* is extracted from the leaves of the gingko tree and has been used in China for thousands of years. Gingko increases the brain's blood circulation and the utilization of glucose for mental activity. French experiments have shown that it restores the communication ability of brain neurotransmitters.[23] Researchers have found both phosphatidylserine and gingko to be effective in treating Alzheimer's disease.[24, 25]

Sleep Disturbance

Insomnia can have many causes. As I mentioned previously, it can be due to a decreased estradiol level, which affects the workings of the neurotransmitters. An overall drop in estrogen that causes hot flashes or other heat symptoms in the middle of the night is also frequently responsible for awakenings. Decreased melatonin, characteristic of this transitional phase, also plays a role in insomnia. One of the many functions of this pineal hormone is the promotion of deep, restorative sleep (see Chapter 12). Taking 3 to 6 milligrams of sublingual melatonin at bedtime, 4 to 5 times a week, is extremely efficacious in managing menopausal insomnia.

Since calcium is a natural tranquilizer, taking your calcium supplement at bedtime will also help relax you (see the section titled Osteoporosis later in this chapter). For women who are very anxious or tend to ruminate once they get into bed, I often recommend Stabilium 200 (*Garum armoricum*).[26] *Garum armoricum* is a natural product, derived from fish viscera, which the Romans gave to their battle-fatigued veterans in their famous spas to speed their recovery. It has been researched internationally[27] and is currently widely used in France and Japan. Recently, its effectiveness in relieving anxiety was validated in an American study.[28] Stabilium 200 decreases the production of the stress hormone, epinephrine. It works the same way as Valium, but without the side effects.

Urinary Problems

The menopausal transition is sometimes accompanied by the embarrassing loss of urinary control and frequent urinary infections. Decreased vaginal mucus, which traps and expels bacteria, and thinner vaginal walls and lining make us more vulnerable to infections.

Early signs of a low-grade urinary tract infection (UTI) are increased urgency and frequency of urination. When the UTI is more advanced, it can cause a burning sensation, and chills and malaise, when the bacteria move into the bloodstream.

At our Centers, at the first sign of a possible infection, we recommend 2 capsules of the urinary protective herb, uva ursi (1 capsule, 2 times a day on an empty stomach) and 4 cranberry capsules (2 capsules, 2 times a day with meals). Uva ursi, taken on an empty stomach, develops ippuric acid, a powerful urinary disinfectant. Cranberry not only acidifies the urine, making it difficult for some bacteria to multiply, but it also keeps bacteria from sticking to the bladder's wall.

Urinary leakage is a sign of stress incontinence – the loss of bladder control when you cough, sneeze, laugh, etc. This problem is related to weakened muscles, usually the result of childbearing, which is aggravated by the drop in estrogen.

Kegel exercises, which contract the muscle that stops urine flow, are very useful in the early stages of stress incontinence. You can make the muscles stronger by contracting them repetitively 20 times, 3 times a day until they are toned. Then exercise them once a day to maintain the tone. You can do your repetitions wherever you are – while waiting for a red light to change, watching a movie, standing in line, etc.

Phase 2 Interventions

When the combined Phase 1 interventions don't relieve perimenopausal symptoms, we move into Phase 2. In Phase 2, we do a complete hormonal map that includes total estrogen, estrone (E1), estradiol (E2), progesterone, testosterone, pregnenolone, and DHEA (total and sulfate). If I am unsure as to whether the ovaries have stopped producing hormones, I add FSH and LH levels to the map (high levels indicate menopause). In Phase 2, I use the information of the hormonal map, in conjunction with the patient's symptoms and general history, to design a prescription-grade natural hormone replacement therapy.

Natural Hormone Replacement Therapy

About 90% of our patients who need a Phase 2 intervention choose natural hormone replacement therapy rather than pharmaceutical hormones. The source of these natural hormones is from either wild yam *(diascorea)* or soy, usually in the form of transdermal creams or gels. This is a very individualized strategy, and the ingredients and their proportions vary from patient to patient.

I prescribe natural progesterone for all women, as this preserves the bones and prevents the symptoms of estrogen dominance. Pregnenolone, the first step in the hormonal metabolic pathway, is usually part of the formula. It has its own brain-activating and energy-enhancing properties.[29] If a woman is perfectly healthy and has an optimally-functioning liver, progesterone can also transform itself into the estrogen the body needs. In this phase of life, progesterone alone is rarely able to supply the estrogen needed, so I combine progesterone with triestrogen (80% estriol, 10% estradiol and 10% estrone) in the same formula. This distribution of the three estrogens replicates their natural occurrence in the body, and a small amount of estradiol is necessary for brain integrity, vascular stability, and bone and heart health. Depending on the need, I may also add DHEA and testosterone to the same formula to improve energy, libido and will power.

Because hormones affect the entire body and they can shunt (move) from one form into another, we routinely perform follow-up hormonal mapping every 3 months, until the symptoms are controlled and we have learned enough about our patients' hormonal shunting propensity. Most women have their symptoms resolved within a few months. Then, we recommend follow-up mapping every 6 months, and then yearly once all is well. At that point, as long as they have incorporated Phase 1 interventions into their lifestyle, most of our patients can replace the prescription cream with an over-the-counter hormonal-balancing cream.

Natural hormone replacement therapy works very well, except when patients have uncontrolled stress, high levels of toxic metals or severe dysbiosis. In such cases, nothing works unless we remove these impediments. Very thin women also may run into difficulties since they lack adequate fat reserves to store the hormones. For the remaining 10% of our patients who prefer pharmaceutical hormone therapy, I recommend that they add natural progesterone to counterbalance the potentially carcinogenic effects of high-dose pharmaceutical estrogen (Premarin).[30]*

Natural hormone replacement requires a sophisticated appreciation of the subtleties of hormonal orchestration. I have been involved in this arena for more than 15 years and enjoy immensely the complicated blending of science and art it requires. If you need this type of assistance with your mid-life transition, I advise you to find an integrative physician well versed in this specialized field.

Sheila's experience provides a good example of the complexity of what we call the "perimenopausal storm" and our multi-faceted Phase 2 approach.

Sheila's Transformation

Sheila's main symptoms were severe memory and concentration problems. A bright, 42-year-old woman, who had juggled family and work for many years, she now was terrified of losing her job and feared she was slipping into Alzeihmer's. For nearly 9 months, she had also suffered from painful menses, low libido, constipation, sleep disturbances and anxiety. She had never had an easy time as a female – suffering from PMS, painful menses and a fibroid uterus. She also had all the symptoms associated with dysbiosis. The hormonal map showed low estrogen, very low progesterone, low DHEA and testosterone, and normal FSH and LH. She was in the midst of the perimenopausal storm.

Our first intervention was the Bowel Healing Program to reduce the toxicity that further confused all her hormones. Because Sheila's dysbiosis was very severe, we set about to starve the unwanted yeast, bacteria and parasites inhabiting her gut. We avoided the oral B vitamins and, instead, used intramuscular (IM) injections of B vitamins and powerful liver detoxifying substances (glutathione and taurine). By detoxifying the liver, we improved its ability to bind and eliminate xenoestrogens.

She was placed on a nutrient-rich, high fiber diet, and on a baseline of oral antioxidants and minerals. We also started her on phosphatidylserine, the **CC Meno-Pack** and added a natural hormone cream (progesterone, pregnenolone and DHEA). Sheila was also given melatonin and Stabilium 200 to regulate her sleeping patterns and reduce her anxiety. Given the extent of her emotional distress, biofeedback and counseling were also instituted.

Two months later, Sheila had painless, regular periods and

regular bowel movements. Sleep and most of her other peri-menopausal symptoms were 90% improved. Since her memory at that point was only 50% improved, we doubled the phosphatidylserine and added gingko. When she came for a follow-up visit two months later, her transformation was astonishing. The changes were evident not only in the physical and chemical templates, but also in the energetic one. She had achieved a level of psychological and spiritual balance, the likes of which she had never experienced. Sheila is now well on her way to being an *Ageless Woman*.

Hypothalamic Castration

Not too long ago, we had a rather simplistic view of hormones and their behavior. A new world of understanding has opened up with the study of psychoneuroimmunology (PNI).

Hormones are quite versatile and exert different actions, depending upon the cells they activate. Binding to the white blood cells, estrogen promotes heightened immune responses, whereas in the brain, it improves memory, sleep and concentration. Thyroid hormones binding to the same cells might direct them to break down glucose to produce energy to increase the white blood cells fighting ability and enhance the brain's thinking processes. Conceptually, it is similar to a violin that can be used to play a magnificent Mozart concert or to produce the disturbing and sensuous notes of a gypsy lament.

Since all hormonal commands originate in the hypothalamus, subtle damage of this enormously important brain structure can affect all body functions and the complex orchestration of the body's interacting glands. After years of cortisol floods caused by chronic stress, the hypothalamus becomes insensitive to the feedback that regulates and modulates hormonal secretions.[31] This insensitivity leads to confusion and the shut down of many hormonal systems at once. Most importantly, the hypothalamus loses the capacity to down-regulate the flood of cortisol – the most aging of all hormones. I call this all encompassing, unhealthy condition "hypothalamic castration."

Hypothalamic castration is the ultimate result of wear and tear on the regulatory hub of our hormones. Unfortunately, I am seeing it with increasing frequency in young women in their late 20s and early 30s, who seek my counsel regarding fatigue, infertility and other women's issues. Typically, the young woman has been living a high stress life for years. When I map the hormones, I find the female vitality triad – adrenals, thyroid and ovaries – completely depleted.

Women who are able to manage until the mid-life transition often push a stressed hypothalamus over the edge at this time. Many of the women who require more than Phase 1 interventions suffer from hypothalamic castration. Because menopausal symptoms are mixed with others, diagnosis is difficult if one is not aware of the interactive hormonal highways. Rachelle's story is illustrative of just such an experience.

Rachelle's Transformation

Rachelle, a 46-year-old beauty expert and make-up artist, always knew how to create an attractive appearance. Although she looked fabulous, it was a well-designed façade that covered up her extreme fatigue, mental fogginess, muscle weakness, insomnia, volatile moods and sexual disinterest. She had become a shell of the energetic Rachelle everyone knew and sought out for advice.

An intelligent and aware woman, Rachelle tried to heal herself with a healthy lifestyle of a balanced diet, nutritional supplements and regular exercise. Discouraged by her inability to improve her health, she consulted many physicians, who after extensive testing, found nothing to justify her overall malaise. They told her that she was probably reaching menopause and might have chronic fatigue – a condition for which they had no remedies.

Like many other executive women who engage in a high-stress lifestyle and live in a toxic environment, Rachelle had become hypothalamically castrated. Her hormonal protection had disintegrated as she approached menopause – all of her female vitality triad hormones (thyroid, adrenal and ovarian) were extremely low. Viruses were having a "field day" with her, as her immune system had become marginally effective in fighting infections. Her sense of centeredness and well-being had disappeared, leading to a subtle depression.

Rachelle, an intelligent and studious pupil, understood the importance of our initial interventions – cleansing the intestinal reservoir of toxicity, and battling against bacteria and parasites – and how this improved the detoxification capacity of her liver. We then began to work on her vitality triad hormones. Her thyroid needed to be supplemented, her adrenals were shot, and she needed DHEA, melatonin and, eventually, GH. Since Rachelle, like most city-dwellers, also had a high level of toxic metals, we implemented a course of toxic metal chelation therapy (see Chapter 13) to obtain complete target tissue hormonal binding.

Rachelle followed our recommendations step by step. She not only understood everything but she also became a valuable source of feedback regarding the efficacy of each intervention. Rachelle has rebuilt herself during the past year and has emerged as an extremely functional, vibrant and youthful woman. She is now considering cell therapy (see Chapter 13) as the ultimate rejuvenation stimulus for her organs. Rachelle has many ambitious and worthwhile dreams, and I have no doubt that she will make them all come true.

Postmenopause

The good news about moving into the postmenopausal stage is that the body has now adjusted to different levels of hormones. Some peri-menopausal symptoms, such as urinary incontinence and vaginal dryness,

Maintain yourself naturally during postmenopause.

may, however, appear for the first time postmenopausally. In general, however, in postmenopause you need to do less to maintain your health and vitality if you have properly handled the hormonal storm. During postmenopause, preventing heart disease and osteoporosis are the most important concerns.

Heart Health

Risk factors for heart disease include high levels of triglycerides and total cholesterol, high LDL and low HDL levels, obesity (particularly apple-shape), smoking, diabetes, chronic stress and lack of exercise. Healthy eating habits, regular exercise and managing stress are the most effective strategies for decreasing the risk of heart disease at any age – and are a "must" at this stage.

The relationship between our body's own estrogen and heart disease is unclear. The fact that the incidence of heart disease increases in postmenopausal women may simply be related to age – not the assumed protection of ovarian estrogen. However, researchers have found that women who take estrogen after menopause have lower rates of heart disease than those who don't.[32]

The amount of exogenous estrogen should be, however, as little as necessary, as researchers have also shown that women taking pharmaceutical estrogens and progestins for 5 or more years have an increased risk of breast and endometrial cancer.[33, 34] For this reason, my patients and I prefer natural hormones. It is safer to use natural forms that don't have the potential side effects of the powerful pharmaceutical hormones. To prevent estrogen dominance and its detrimental consequences, any supplemental estrogen needs to be appropriately balanced with adequate natural progesterone.

Since foods and nutritional supplements high in phytoestrogens have been demonstrated to be cardioprotective, they should be part of any postmenopausal woman's diet. Vitamin E, the premier lipid antioxidant, is a well-documented heart protector, as is coenzyme Q-10 (ubiquinone), another powerful antioxidant. As a preventive measure for postmenopausal women, I recommend 400 international units of vitamin E (mixed tocopherols) 2 times a day and 50 milligrams of coenzyme Q-10 (co-Q10) daily. (The lipoidal form is much more powerful.) Both these supplements should be taken with food.

Osteoporosis

Our bones are constantly remodeling themselves. Two crews of cells are at work all the time – the osteoclasts that break the bones down and the osteoblasts that rebuild them. Under normal circumstances, our bones have reached their peak mass by the time we are in our mid-30s. From that point on, they begin to get thinner in both men and women.[35] * After menopause, unless we take appropriate action, the breaking down (osteoclastic) activity of our bones exceeds their rebuilding (osteoblastic) activity.

Bone health is dependent on the interaction of many factors: hormones, diet, exercise and lifestyle. Calcitonin from the thyroid and the opposing parathyroid hormone, and progesterone, estrogen and testosterone all have a powerful affect on our bones. When we go through menopause and our ovaries stop producing hormones, our bones have a tendency to get thinner faster. If remedial action is not taken, we may lose 30% to 40% of our bone mass by the age of 70. This condition of accelerated bone loss and increased brittleness is known as osteoporosis. Osteoporosis is responsible for over a million bone fractures each year. More women die annually from complications of such fractures than from breast and cervical cancer combined.

Caucasian and Asian women, women who have a history of eating disorders and amenorrhea (lack of periods) during adolescence, and athletes have an increased risk for osteoporosis. Other risk factors are listed in Figure 11-1.

Osteoporosis Risk Factors

Refined carbohydrates	Alcohol
Smoking	Coffee
Stress	Caffeinated tea
Lack of exercise	Soda pop
High animal protein intake	Low ovarian hormones
Low calcium intake	Dysglycemia
Diabetes	

Figure 11-1

Osteoporosis Prevention Tools

Diet

To prevent osteoporosis, avoid calcium-depleting foods, such as excessive animal protein. Excess consumption of animal protein causes the production of strong acids. The process of neutralizing and eliminating these acids requires large amounts of sodium. Once the sodium alkaline reserve is depleted, the body turns to calcium in the bones to continue its alkalinizing work.

While animal protein has an acidifying effect on the body, vegetables and fruits are alkalinizing. Italian researchers, who evaluated the effects of diet on bone health, recently recommended that the daily intake of animal protein should not exceed 20 grams a day.[36] I believe that this is particularly important for menopausal women. Coffee, black tea, alcohol, sugar and sodas are also calcium depleting and should be limited or avoided. Adding calcium-rich foods to your diet, such as dark green, leafy vegetables, soy foods, salmon and sardines, is a wise move.

Stress Management

Stress increases the breakdown of protein, the secretion of cortisol, and the production of glucose and free radicals. All of these processes, like the food and beverages noted above, make the body more acidic and the bones more prone to calcium depletion. Stress management, therefore, is an essential tool for the prevention of osteoporosis.

Exercise

As discussed earlier in this chapter, regular exercise is an excellent way to stimulate the bone-building osteoblastic cells to increase calcium utilization. A combination of yoga and weight-bearing exercise is a powerful deterrent to osteoporosis.

Calcium Supplementation

Proper supplementation of calcium can significantly reduce bone loss.[37] Since it is usually impossible to obtain the amount of calcium necessary for prevention (1,000 to 1,500 milligrams a day) solely from dietary intake, I recommend that you add a calcium supplement.[38]*

Not all calcium supplements are equally beneficial. Some are difficult to absorb and incorporate into the bony structure. Supplements made from animal bones may contain toxic metals, such as lead, arsenic and cadmium.

The supplement that has emerged as the most advantageous is microcrystalline hydroxapatite (MHCH), which has a similar structure to our bones. In addition to calcium, MHCH contains protein, mucopolysaccharides, phosphorus, fluoride, magnesium, and iron. It also contains a number of trace minerals, such as zinc, copper and manganese, all of which facilitate bone building by assisting in enzymatic activity. Combined with vitamin D, MHCH has been proven to actually increase bone mass.[39]

Other nutrients that insure optimal bone health include the mineral, boron, which increases calcium uptake and has mild estrogenic properties, vitamin D, also needed for calcium uptake, and vitamin K, which improves calcium binding. Researchers recently found that women of any age were at increased risk of fractures with a low dietary intake of vitamin K, even if they had high levels of vitamin D.[40] Lysine, an amino acid that inhibits viral multiplication, has also been demonstrated to be part of one of the enzymes that assists in bone formation.[41]

To assure adequate nutritional support for your bones, I recommend that you add a supplement, with ingredients such as those found in **CC Bone Plus** (see Appendix A), to your diet. Since calcium is also a relaxant, taking it before bedtime promotes a good night's sleep.

Ipriflavone

Fosamax and other bisphosphonates are pharmaceuticals that bind and neutralize the osteoclasts – the cells responsible for rapid bone remodeling. In recent years, Fosamax has been heavily promoted as an alternative to estrogen for preventing bone loss in women with established osteoporosis. It, however, causes serious ulcers of the esophagus unless it is taken precisely according to the manufacturer's directions, and it has a number of other unpleasant side effects. I have found that most of my patients cannot tolerate the drug.

A more promising alternative is Ipriflavone, synthesized from isoflavones, the bioflavonoids primarily found in soy.[42]* Ipriflavone is a registered medication for the treatment of osteoporosis in Japan, Argentina and Italy. It both inhibits osteoclasts and stimulates bone-building osteoblasts. Researchers have found Ipriflavone to be both a safe and effective treatment for established osteoporosis in postmenopausal women.[43, 44] In the United States, integrative practitioners have access to it as a "natural product" to replace poorly tolerated Fosamax. Most researchers recommend 200 milligrams, 3 times a day. In combination with other bone-building substances (see **CC Bone Plus**), 50 to 100 milligrams, 3 times a day is equally effective. I primarily recommend its use for women with early (osteopenia) and advanced osteoporosis.

Ovarian Hormones

The fact that estrogen supplementation after menopause slows down bone loss has been overemphasized. Estrogen, however, only works by binding to the cells that break down the bones (osteoclasts) and not to those that build the bones (osteoblasts). This later attribute belongs to the neglected progesterone.[45] Furthermore, researchers are now documenting that we need very little estrogen to obtain its bone protective benefits. A recent *New England Journal of Medicine* editorial concluded that 0.25 milligram of micronized estradiol daily was as effective as the current standard of 1.0 milligram in reducing osteoporosis risk in postmenopausal women.[46]

For women who have stabilized their hormonally-related symptoms, a diet rich in phytoestrogens supplemented with other substances that have progestenic properties is usually sufficient to decrease bone loss. I generally recommend that my patients take the CC Meno-Pack weekdays and jilen ginseng on weekends.

Integrative healthcare practitioners, such as myself, are bringing forth the notion that progesterone supplementation is even more important than estrogen in preventing osteoporosis.[47] Natural progesterone has also been shown to have a positive effect on total and HDL cholesterol.[48] As the leading authority in natural progesterone, Dr. John Lee notes that the lipid profiles of postmenopausal women on combined estrogen and natural progesterone have been shown to be better than those on estrogen combined with progestins. His clinical experience has shown that lipid profiles improve when women include natural progesterone. Dr. Lee also notes the importance of natural progesterone for maintaining brain function.[49] Because progesterone plays such important and diverse roles, I recommend continual use of an over-the-counter hormone cream that contains natural progesterone.[50]*

Other Nutritional Supplements for Postmenopausal Health

Life continues these days well past the menopausal transition. This is a relatively new phenomenon that brings forth a re-evaluation of what is normal for a 70-year-old lady. I'll be there in 4 years, and I don't expect to be less productive and vibrant at that magical point. Following my postmenopausal recommendations has kept me functioning at this high level, and it will for you, too.

Whatever else you do should depend on your specific symptoms. If you want to continue living in the "fast lane," symptoms may flare up from time to time. You may need to go back to what worked for you during perimenopause until your symptoms stabilize or you decide to slow down. If you are still going strong mentally, take phosphatidylserine or gingko to support your brain. If you have warmth sensations, take dong quai and extra vitamin E for a week or so until your symptoms subside. If you are fatigued and have normal blood pressure, drink licorice tea. I also suggest you routinely take 1 uva ursi and 2 cranberry capsules at least 5 days a week to prevent urinary infections. No matter what you do, don't forget to smile.

12 *The Magical Anti-Aging Hormones*

Sophisticated and interactive rejuvenation tools

Three Rejuvenators

*W*hen people hear the term "anti-aging hormones," they most often think of DHEA, melatonin and growth hormone (GH). These three hormones – one from the adrenals, two from the brain – are multi-faceted, interactive, powerful tools for turning back the biological clock and are the subject of this chapter. In reality, calling some hormones and not others "anti-aging" is arbitrary. It is, in fact, the maintenance of the producing glands and all the hormones they secrete that keeps us young. As you have seen in the last few chapters, when the hormonal secretions of the female vitality triad – the thyroid, adrenals and ovaries – decline, interventions often involve the repair and support of all three by natural hormone supplementation. You may have already noticed that, when needed, DHEA, melatonin and GH are included as components of my comprehensive rejuvenation approach.

When we combine the bountiful gifts of nature with the sophisticated and escalating research in endocrinology, we can facilitate miracles. For the reversal of biological age to take place, it is necessary to restore our hormones to the levels of a healthy 30-year-old – an age when ideally they are at a maximum level of efficiency. When all is finally in place, the result is the *Ageless Woman* – endowed with boundless energy, vibrant, vital and highly productive.

DHEA

DHEA (dehydroepiandrosterone) is the most dominant steroid in the body. Produced by the adrenal cortex, DHEA reaches its zenith around age 25 to 30 and then declines progressively. By age 60, DHEA is down to about 5% to 15% of its peak level, probably because it has to work so hard to buffer the life-long cortisol production.

As you may recall from earlier chapters, researchers have reported that individuals who regularly engage in stress-reducing meditation have higher DHEA levels than nonmeditators. In a new study, in which participants were taught emotional self-management tools to eliminate negative thought loops and promote positive emotional states, researchers reported that the experimental group showed a 23% decrease in cortisol and a 100% increase in DHEA compared to a control group which did not engage in the program.[1]

Because of its progressive decline, DHEA is used as a biomarker of aging. Poor lifestyle, illnesses, exertion and all forms of stress reduce DHEA. Researchers have concluded in a number of studies that DHEA levels are lower in unhealthy aging individuals compared to their healthier peers.[2,3,4] When we look at DHEA's multi-faceted roles, we begin to understand why this is so.

Increases Energy and Sense of Well-Being

People with low DHEA levels typically feel the fatigue associated with adrenal exhaustion. Two of the clinical responses to DHEA supplementation are, in fact, higher energy and feelings of well-being.[5,6] In one double-blind, controlled study of men and women, aged 40 to 70, researchers reported that 82% of the women and 67% of the men reported enhanced feelings of well-being compared to a 10% improvement in the placebo group.[7] In a recent study of postmenopausal women, researchers reported that women who received DHEA supplements experienced a restoration of impaired neuroendocrine feedback functions. Adequate supplementation of DHEA is, therefore, one of the ways to reverse hypothalamic castration. The researchers concluded that "DHEA could play a role in the psychological and physical well-being of postmenopausal women..."[8]

Restores Gonadal Hormones

In the scheme of sex hormones (see Figure 10-1), DHEA holds a very important place because it metabolizes itself into estrogen in women and testosterone in men. As you have seen in the patient stories I presented in Chapter 11, DHEA supplementation is a very important component of a comprehensive hormonal intervention. It relieves perimenopausal symptoms and halts the progression of hypothalamic castration by counteracting cortisol damage. It has an important place in the treatment of menopausal symptoms. Canadian researchers, who conducted a recent study of the impact of daily DHEA cream application on healthy postmenopausal women, reported that it improved vaginal tone, increased bone mineral density[9]* and enhanced feelings of well-being.[10]

Cancer Protective

DHEA also plays an important protective role in sex-related cancers.[11] Men with prostatic cancer have DHEA levels that are significantly lower than healthy men of the same age.[12] Women with both benign and malignant breast disease have been shown to have lower DHEA levels than their healthy peers.[13] Researchers who conducted a large epidemiological study in England reported that women with low DHEA levels (less than 10% of that expected for their age group) developed and died from breast cancer.[14]

If the conjugation pathways in the liver are well functioning and the cell receptors are clean, DHEA becomes estrogen in women and testosterone in men.[15]* These hormones bind to the sex organ cell receptors, preempting cancer-inducing substances from taking their place. They have the same beneficial effect as phytoestrogens have in relation to xenoestrogens.

Enhances Immunity

DHEA plays an important role in immune function. It promotes the restoration of cytokines – immune system messengers. In doing so, DHEA facilitates proper immune activity and reduces inflammation.[16, 17] Researchers have recently noted that individuals with inflammatory bowel disease (ulcerative colitis and Crohn's disease) have lower DHEA levels than do normal individuals.[18]

DHEA modulates the synthesis of antibodies. Excessive antibodies in our tissues are the underlying cause of the destructive process in lupus and other autoimmune diseases. In a recent clinical trial at Stanford University in which lupus patients were treated with DHEA, researchers reported that those who received the hormone fared better than placebo-treated patients.[19] DHEA reduces the immune suppressive action of cortisol and other adrenocorticoid hormones.[20] It also improves the activity of the thymus and lymphatic tissues, enhancing cellular immunity. The presence of adequate amounts of DHEA protects against cancer and viral-induced diseases, such as AIDS and CFIDS. Dr. William Regelson of the Medical College of Virginia, a world-renowned authority on DHEA, reported that people with HIV do not develop full-blown AIDS until their adrenal output of DHEA drops.[21]

Prevents Obesity

DHEA, like the hormones secreted by the thyroid gland, prevents obesity when the levels are adequate. In fact, DHEA supports thyroid activity by increasing the biologically active form of the hormone. DHEA also inhibits the production of the glucose-6 phosphate dehydrogenase enzyme, an action that limits the conversion of carbohydrates to fat. Some researchers have concluded that the weight loss effect of DHEA may be due to improved mitochondrial respiration.[22] DHEA's antiobesity action is multifaceted. It does not simply inhibit fat synthesis and deposition, but as we have seen, works through a number of pathways.[23] DHEA has also been shown to improve insulin resistance,[24, 25] and holds promise for a role in the prevention and treatment of diabetes.

DHEA is very interactive with the master anti-aging hormone of the pituitary gland – GH. While GH itself enhances fat metabolism, the administration of this hormone also increases the level of DHEA. This is why I always do hormonal mapping when I administer either DHEA or GH.

Protects the Heart

DHEA decreases the thickness of platelets, the blood particles that when clumped together can cause heart attacks and strokes.[26] It has been shown to lower cholesterol levels in obese postmenopausal women.[27] It has been established that DHEA is inversely associated with death from cardiovascular disease in men, and a recent Japanese epidemiological study found that DHEA increases protective HDL and reduces damaging LDL in both sexes. The authors concluded that "high levels of…DHEA may have an inhibitory effect on the development of atherosclerosis and have an important role in its etiology and prevention."[28]

DHEA and the Brain

One of the most interesting new findings about DHEA is that the brain has the capacity to make the hormone from cholesterol through pregnenolone. This cerebral production through a convoluted biochemical pathway leads to high levels of free radicals. These free radicals will damage the brain unless this important organ is rich in buffering antioxidants.

During my long career as a physician, I have noticed that any system that is willing to take the risk of damage for the production of a substance that ordinarily is produced by other organs will do so only if that substance is absolutely necessary for the survival of that organ. Researchers, in fact, have found that DHEA has cerebral protective actions,[29] and that there is an inverse relationship between DHEA and cognitive impairment and decline.[30] DHEA also improves sleep quality, especially the restorative REM sleep, during which memory storage is enhanced. These facts justify giving adequate and well-controlled amounts of exogenous DHEA to supply the brain with the end product, rather than forcing it to do exhaustive cellular work that causes dangerous levels of cerebral free radicals.

DHEA Supplementation

Although DHEA is now readily available in the marketplace, it is a powerful hormone and should not be self-administered, even in the smallest quantities, without first measuring your current level through saliva, tissue or blood tests.[31*, 32*] The best DHEA supplementation results are obtained using creams, gels or sublingual forms. These delivery forms are almost as powerful as intramuscular (IM) or intravenous (IV) administration. The tablet form delivers only approximately 25% of the ingested quantity. DHEA is poorly absorbed in the gastrointestinal tract, with very little making it past the liver's circulation system.[33]

DHEA is too powerful and too important to be taken lightly. When we include DHEA as one of our hormonal interventions, we do so only after mapping DHEA and all other related hormones, and reviewing clinical symptoms. To bring levels to that of a healthy 30-year-old, I've prescribed as much as 50 and 100 milligrams a day for women, and 100 and 300 milligrams for men, alternating between the lower and higher doses. Our goals are to obtain youthful levels and increase immune system competency, energy and libido, while enhancing feelings of well-being.

After 2 or 3 months, we re-evaluate DHEA levels and the hormones they turn into (estrogen and testosterone in women and testosterone and dihydrotestosterone in men). Based on test results and clinical symptoms, a maintenance pulsated (on and off) daily dose is established, with a biochemical follow-up scheduled every 3 to 6 months.

While DHEA supplementation is helpful in preventing cancer, it is not advisable once the disease has established itself. Since DHEA can convert to estrogen, women with established breast or endometrial cancer, endometriosis or fibroids are usually not good candidates for supplementation. Men, with prostatic cancer, similarly, are not viable candidates, since one of the metabolites of testosterone, dihydrotestosterone, will stimulate cell proliferation in the prostate gland.

DHEA has been used in Europe for decades to modulate the stress response. During my medical school years in Italy, we experienced much success using an injectable form of DHEA called Astenile. Adequate levels of DHEA prevent cellular decay, accelerated aging, obesity and chronic degenerative diseases, such as cancer and heart disease.

Melatonin

The pineal, embedded in the brain behind and above the pituitary gland, is an extremely important gland. Often called the "third eye," it was recognized by ancient yogis as the link between the individual and the cosmos. We now know that the pineal gland can perceive subtle energies, such as extremely low frequency (ELF) radiation, and transform them into physiological signals that influence the nervous, endocrine and immune systems.

The pineal gland's primary hormone, melatonin, has wide-ranging effects on the entire body. It is produced from the neurotransmitter, serotonin, which is derived from the amino acid tryptophan. Melatonin synthesis is regulated by light/dark cycles, with its production beginning to rise at nightfall and peaking between midnight and 3:00 a.m. By sunrise, it returns to baseline levels.

The hormone reaches its peak level in adolescence and remains fairly stable in healthy adults. As aging proceeds, the level decreases. This is due mostly to a decline in the enzyme, n-acetyl-transferase, which is necessary for the transformation of serotonin into melatonin. Inadequate levels of dietary tryptophan can also hinder melatonin levels.

With age, the gland tends to become calcified and less functional. In women, melatonin levels decrease more slowly than in men until menopause, when its decline accelerates exponentially, stabilizing after age 60. In advanced age, melatonin levels are barely detectable. At any age, decreased melatonin secretion is associated with acceleration of the aging process. Melatonin production is disrupted when the circadian cycle (24-hour biological clock) is disturbed by frequent changes in work shifts or long-distance air travel. It has received much attention in recent years as a remedy for jet lag.

Impacts Female Cycle

As you may recall from Chapter 10, hypothalamic gonadotropin-releasing hormone (GnRH) promotes the secretion of the pituitary follicle-stimulating hormone (FSH), which stimulates ovarian estrogen production. Too much estrogen inhibits the pituitary production of luteinizing hormone (LH). Low levels of LH make ovulation and production of progesterone difficult and, at times, impossible (anovulatory cycles).

Female Hormone Pathway

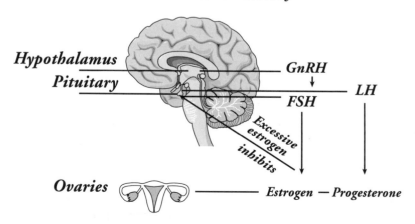

Figure 12-1

Melatonin modulates the secretion of GnRH. It, therefore, has antiestrogenic properties[34] and its use can be one way to reduce overwhelming estrogen dominance, such as found in severe PMS. Integrative physicians in Italy use large amounts of melatonin as a component of breast cancer treatment.

Effective for Insomnia

Melatonin is the link between the light/dark cycles and many aspects of human physiology. It improves the quality of sleep and reduces the time needed to fall asleep. Researchers, therefore, have found it to be effective in treating chronic insomnia as well as delayed sleep syndromes.[35, 36] Melatonin, in fact, not only induces the physiological response that promotes prompt sleep, but also increases the beneficial, deeply restorative REM stage.[37]*

I consider melatonin to be one of the most effective remedies for perimenopausal and postmenopausal insomnia. Since melatonin is synergistic with DHEA, when we use both, less of both hormones are required once the body has reached a level of physiological equilibrium. In my experience, it takes between 3 to 6 months to reach this desirable state, a which point a gradual reduction is attempted.

Improves Immune Function

Like DHEA, melatonin plays an important role in immune function. Melatonin stimulates T-helper lymphocytes to release cytokines, and a number of animal studies have documented its ability to counteract the immune-suppressive effects of corticosteroids.[38, 39]

As you may recall from Chapter 6, a number of researchers have found an association between breast cancer, low melatonin levels and ELF fields. ELF exposure is known to suppress melatonin, something very harmful for women with breast cancer, who already have diminished melatonin levels compared to healthy women.[40] Low DHEA levels also predispose women to breast cancer. It stands to reason that a combination of low

DHEA and low melatonin increases the risk for breast cancer even more. In a number of animal studies, researchers have reported increased growth of experimentally implanted tumors when the animals' pineal glands, which make melatonin, were removed.[41, 42, 43] These and other studies provide ample evidence that, among its many beneficial properties, melatonin is an effective cancer protective substance.

Anti-Aging Actions

According to renowned aging and endocrinology researcher, Dr. Vladimir Dilman,[44] melatonin, like DHEA, is another substance that can restore hypothalamic sensitivity to feedback regulation – the failure of which is one of the major causes of aging. Both DHEA and melatonin have long been important tools in my patients' rejuvenation and the reversal of hypothalamic castration.

Melatonin, like DHEA, opposes the damaging effects of corticosteroids. In doing so, it prevents suppression of immune functions, excessive tissue wasting and blood glucose metabolism problems – all symptoms of high cortisol and aging. Melatonin is also a powerful antioxidant. It has the capacity to effectively neutralize hydroxy radicals – the most damaging of all free radicals, especially to fat-rich tissues, such as the brain.

Melatonin Supplementation

Although some researchers, such as Dr. Russel J. Reiter,[45] believe that melatonin can be taken continually after menopause, I prefer skipping a few nights here and there (pulsating), as I do for DHEA. I always recommend the sublingual form, as it is totally and rapidly absorbed. For postmenopausal women and perimenopausal women with insomnia, I generally recommend alternating between 3 and 6 milligrams sublingually, 15 to 30 minutes before bedtime, 5 days a week. If sleep difficulties occur during the "off days," I recommend taking Stabilium 200 and/or GABA (2 or 3 pills). To counteract estrogen dominance in PMS, I recommend 3 to 6 milligrams from ovulation to menstruation, when the estrogen dominance is significant. Very often, women with PMS also experience sleep disturbance, and melatonin is a necessary therapeutic agent.

Melatonin works well for people who experience changes in circadian rhythms, due to such factors as air travel to different time zones or variable work shifts. For air travel, I suggest taking 1 to 3 milligrams at bedtime at least 1 week prior to departure. Upon arrival, I recommend staying awake in the new location until what would be your normal bedtime. Then take 3 milligrams of melatonin 15 to 30 minutes before your desired sleep time. To restore proper sleep upon returning home, I recommend continuing to take the amount that has obtained the best results for you for at least 1 week. This maneuver generally switches your sleeping clock back to your home time. People who have variable work shifts should use the same strategy.

Growth Hormone

The anti-aging field, every so often, buzzes with newly discovered panaceas. Growth hormone (GH), the third interactive rejuvenation hormone, is the one that has been touted as the "end all" in some anti-aging circles. GH, also called somatotropin, is produced by the pituitary in response to stimulation by hypothalamic growth releasing hormone (GHRH). The hypothalamus, faithful to its counter-regulatory function, also produces an antagonist of GH called somatostatin, which decreases the production of GH.

Growth Hormone Pathway

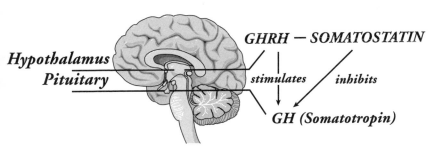

Figure 12-2

GH is the most abundant pituitary hormone, just as DHEA is the most abundant hormone produced by the adrenal cortex. GH is high during youth, begins to decline around ages 25 to 30 and then continues to decrease as we age. GH reaches the liver through the general circulation, where it is transformed (metabolized) into a hormone with similar properties called insulin-like growth factor-1 (IGF-1), also known as somatomedin. To establish the body's level of GH we, in fact measure IGF-1.

Age-related diminution of GH and IGF-1 is so striking that IGF-1, like DHEA, is used as a biomarker of aging.[46]★ Once released by the pituitary, free GH only stays in the blood for 5 to 20 minutes. It binds quickly to albumin, its transporting vehicle, while it goes to the liver to become IGF-1. It is, therefore, more practical to measure IGF-1, this stable metabolite, than the ephemeral GH. Scientists are split on the issue of whether the pituitary actually diminishes production of GH as we age or whether the albumin-bound GH has difficulty being released. Liver toxicity and inefficient enzymatic systems might be two major reasons the hormone does not get released.

GH has many functions. During childhood it stimulates growth. At menarche and thereafter, it takes on many other important roles. It burns fat for energy production, just like the thyroid hormone. GH, in fact, stimulates thyroxine secretion. It increases protein synthesis. Most importantly, it improves immune functions. According to a recent review article by a British endocrinologist, "Growth hormone deficiency in adult life is associated with a number of adverse biological changes, which include osteopenia (bone thinning), reduced exercise capacity, altered body composition, deleterious alterations in the lipid profile and insulin status, and reduced quality of life. Most of these changes can be reversed by growth hormone replacement therapy."[47] As you have probably observed, most of GH's properties are shared by DHEA and some by thyroxine.

Enhances Immune Function

The immune-enhancing properties of GH are one of the newest and most reassuring benefits of GH supplementation. Chronic stress, with its tremendous production of cortisol, leads to the atrophy of the master regulator of the immune system – the thymus gland. GH improves immune efficiency by protecting the thymus from atrophy. At the same time, GH increases the production of lymphocytes (defending white cells) by the bone marrow. Another important immune-boosting property of GH is its ability to stimulate the maturation of a special family of lymphocytes called natural killer (NK) cells. NK are the lymphocytes that attack and destroy viruses and cancer cells.[48, 49★, 50★]

Facilitates Weight Loss and Increases Lean Muscle Mass

GH mobilizes fat from adipose tissues and uses fat rather than protein for energy production. This muscle-sparing action decreases fat concentration and increases lean muscle mass. Incidentally, this is just the opposite of what cortisol does. Results of recent studies on older men have verified this beneficial effect on muscles.[51, 52, 53]

Similar results have been noted for postmenopausal women. Stanford University researchers recently conducted a study of moderately obese postmenopausal women, who were given GH and its more stable metabolite, IGF-1, in conjunction with a prescribed diet and exercise regime. The authors concluded that "…a sound diet and exercise program will result in a significant loss of weight and body fat in obese postmenopausal women, and that GH and IGF-1 may play an 'important adjunctive role' in the process."[54]

Prevents Osteoporosis

It has been well documented that people deficient in GH have reduced bone density. Recent research has found that GH supplementation both increases bone density and stimulates bone turnover.[55] Italian researchers, who used the lowest dose of GH yet administered, concluded from their recent study that low doses normalized bone metabolism and improved bone density without causing adverse effects.[56]

Increases Insulin Sensitivity

One of my concerns regarding GH supplementation has been the fact that it raises the level of glucose. Recently, researchers have reported that the increase in glucose is counterbalanced by increased insulin sensitivity.[57] Since Type 2 diabetes is brought about by decreased insulin sensitivity (increased resistance), GH, in combination with a judicious diet and moderate exercise, can be an effective therapy for this all too common disease.

Other Benefits

The results of two recent studies indicate that GH improves heart function.[58, 59] It has also been proven to increase skin thickness by stimulating the synthesis of collagen.[60] GH improves antibody production, another immune-protective mechanism. It also promotes the transport of most amino acids across cell membranes, which facilitates protein synthesis within cells. These two capacities speed the ability of the body to heal injuries. Like DHEA, GH has been reported to increase energy and exercise tolerance, and to enhance feelings of well-being.

GH Supplementation

For years, I have recommended GH secretagogues – substances that stimulate hormone secretion – when my patients' IGF-1 levels were below normal. The amino acid arginine has been one of the most studied GH secretagogues. It seems to act by antagonizing somatostatin, the hormone that puts the brake on the production and release of GH by the pituitary.[61] Many other substances, such as ornithine, lysine, tryptophan and niacin have been proven to increase GH and to promote its beneficial effects.[62, 63, 64, 65]

My experience is that, in most cases, a health-promoting lifestyle (including exercise)[66] and supportive nutrients can increase GH levels. The use of a combination of interventions can reduce the quantity of secretagogues needed for maximum benefit. Many of my patients have significantly benefited from using **CC Fat Burner Plus** and **CC Appestat** (see Appendix A).

I had been on the fence for many years regarding the use of GH itself. In addition to concern about increased glucose, I was also afraid that it might trigger the growth of yet unidentified cancers. The new research on GH immune-enhancing properties and improvement of insulin resistance has allayed my fears. My change in position has also been influenced by discussions with many of my colleagues who have been using GH for many years. I am now integrating it, when appropriate, into my patient interventions.

Side effects from GH supplementation include water retention, myalgia and some "pins and needles" in the extremities. These problems appear to be dose-related, as they disappear when the dosage is reduced.[67] From my own personal experience, I have found 200 to 300 milligrams of vitamin B_6 and its active metabolite, pyridoxl-5-phosphate, (both natural diuretics) combined with at least an equal amount of magnesium reduce many of these side effects.

Rather than injections, which are very costly and somewhat impractical, I have chosen to use a bioavailable, sublingual form of the hormone that is derived from plant organisms.[68] The dosage is 1:500 to 1:1,000 less than the injectable form. This lower-dose form is much less costly and has fewer side effects. Depending on the IGF-1 level, I recommend from 1 puff, 2 times a day, up to 2 puffs, 3 times a day. After 1 month of use, I remeasure IGF-1 and adjust the dosage accordingly.

Synergistic Rejuvenation Strategies

I consider DHEA, melatonin and GH supplementation essential tools in the field of anti-aging medicine. Some researchers are providing evidence that they restore hypothalamic sensitivity to hormonal feedback. *I am a firm believer that, once the hypothalamic sensitivity to hormonal feedback stimuli is gone (hypothalamic castration), the war on aging is lost. Conversely, once hypothalamic sensitivity is re-established, small amounts of all hormones (gonadal and others) are capable of reducing the misery of menopause and reversing the aging process.*

As all hormones are interactive and synergistic, and often metabolize one into the other, they need to be assessed together. The correct orchestration of these divine instruments requires humility and superb expertise. This is best accomplished by integrative physicians experienced in neuroendocrinology, and the science and art of anti-aging medicine.

13 *When Self-Care is Not Enough*

Sometimes you need additional support.

Professional Help

*M*y goal in this book is to empower you with knowledge and provide you with tools you can utilize on your own to optimize your health, maximize your lifespan, and retain the vitality and zest of youth for as long as you live. By this time, I trust you have an organic understanding of the Loading Theory, and how multiple factors contribute to disease and aging. Hopefully, you have come to appreciate how my self-care longevity strategies can assist you in unloading toxic burdens and rejuvenating your vital organs and glands.

You have undoubtedly noticed that my patient transformation stories usually include some interventions that you cannot do on your own. People often seek us out because the natural approaches they have tried on their own brought them only to a certain point in the healing process. To achieve total wellness, they required expert professional assistance. We also frequently see chronically ill patients, who come to us seeking the answers that only functional medicine can provide.

You may be perimenopausal or postmenopausal, and

despite the natural interventions you have undertaken, everything seems to be falling apart. Or you may be a young woman, who is just more tired all the time than you should be. Perhaps you have cleansed and healed your bowel and liver, and implemented a number of other longevity strategies, but you still don't feel well. In all these situations, it would be wise to seek assistance from a healthcare provider who practices functional medicine. Unbeknown to you, you may have subtle genetic glitches, subclinical nutritional deficiencies, complex hormonal imbalances, toxic metal accumulation – or a combination of several factors.

Functional Medicine

Practitioners of functional medicine engage in more complex evaluation processes and healing strategies than do mainstream physicians. *Rather than solely assessing organ pathology, they focus on organ function. By identifying early signs of organ malfunction on a cellular level, subtle imbalances can be remedied before they result in serious disease.*

Functional medicine practitioners use sophisticated assessment tools, not currently employed for the most part in mainstream medicine, to examine how the body is performing its digestive, detoxification, immunological, hormonal and cardiovascular tasks. Tests are minimally invasive and typically involve the sampling of blood, urine, saliva, stool and hair. When further analysis is warranted, more sophisticated assessments may be ordered, such as tests that "challenge" organs to see how they respond to extra work. This allows for the correct evaluation of how organs function under stress. The Glucose Tolerance Test and the Cortosyn Test are diagnostic tools used both in mainstream and functional medicine.

Unlike mainstream medicine, functional medicine emphasizes the biochemical uniqueness of each patient. You and your friend, for example, may have identical levels of B vitamins in your blood, but the actual amounts inside your cells may vary substantially. Such differences, as well as the over-all relationship of your body, mind and spirit, are taken into consideration when a functional medicine practitioner diagnoses and designs a treatment plan. *Treatment is based on natural healing modalities and remedies that focus on improving cellular functions. This ultimately restores the whole body to wellness.*

Functional Medicine Practitioners

If you live in a large urban area, you may have a wide range of choices in heathcare providers who practice functional medicine. During the last 25 years, some conventionally-trained medical doctors (MDs), such as myself, have pursued training in functional medicine. Doctors of osteopathy (DOs) complete the same training as medical doctors and, in addition, learn how to heal through spinal manipulations. Some DOs have also pursued natural healing training. Since these doctors are knowledgeable in both conventional and natural approaches, they are often referred to as integrative physicians. Naturopathic doctors (NDs), currently licensed as primary care providers in about a dozen states, are trained specifically in functional medicine.

Some doctors of chiropractic medicine (DCs), although primarily trained to restore the body's inherent recuperative power through musculoskeletal manipulation, have also taken additional training in nutrition and functional medicine. Practitioners, trained in traditional Chinese medicine (TCM) and licensed as acupuncturists, focus on restoring organ function through balancing energy flow, using acupuncture and herbs. A growing number of American-trained acupuncturists have pursued additional studies in other natural healing modalities, including nutrition, homeopathy and functional medicine.

While the scope of practice and licensing requirements vary from profession to profession and from state to state, all of these healthcare providers offer natural approaches to restoring and maintaining wellness, and can usually order an array of functional-diagnostic laboratory tests. MDs, DOs, and NDs in some states, are the only healthcare practitioners licensed to prescribe drugs, including injectable intramuscular (IM) and infusable intravenous (IV) nutrients, and the individualized hormonal prescriptions prepared by compounding pharmacists.

If you currently have a serious health problem and are taking medications, you would be best served by an experienced MD, DO or ND, who has the knowledge to skillfully interface conventional drugs with natural remedies. In a recent article, published in the *Journal of the American Medical Association,* the authors underscore this point.[1] The Harvard researchers, led by Dr. David Eisenberg, reported that one in five individuals taking prescription medications were also taking high-dose vitamins, herbs or both, often without medical guidance. As the authors noted, "Adverse interactions...including alterations of drug bioavailability or efficacy, are known to occur and are more likely among individuals with chronic medical illness, especially those with liver or kidney abnormalities."

Since functional medicine is based on biochemical individuality and a blending of healing therapies, no two practitioners will approach and treat a problem in exactly the same way. What should be consistent, however, is the goal of enhancing the patients' inner healing ability and educating them so that, once healed, health can be maintained by self-care.

Competence, Experience and Communication

Whomever you choose to work with, be it a physician or a nonphysician provider, make sure that the practitioner is competent and has been involved in the field for a while. In healthcare, like any other profession, expertise comes not only from books but also from years of experience. Each profession has licensing and certifying organizations that can verify a practitioner's training and can also assist you in finding a competent practitioner in your area.[2]

Make sure that the provider you choose is also willing to listen and is a communicative healing partner. As Hippocrates said, "Some patients, though their condition is perilous, recover through their contentment with the goodness of the physician." We now know that this is not magical thinking, but actually a positive immunological response that occurs when people have a sense of trust and feel loved.

Communication, of course, is a two-way street. Even though more and more people are using alternative medicine, (42.1% in 1997 as compared to 33.8% in 1990), according to the Eisenberg study, less than 40% of patients (in both 1990 and 1997) told their mainstream physicians that they were using alternative therapies. All physicians and patients need to communicate with each other. Physicians need to ask and patients need to tell. Mainstream physicians also need to communicate with their integrative medicine colleagues. Positive and supportive interaction among physicians is essential for assuring optimal patient care.

Insurance Reimbursement: A Thorny Issue

The other discouraging fact the Eisenberg study confirmed is that nearly 60% of people using alternative therapies are paying entirely out-of-pocket. The shift in this country towards a more holistic healing paradigm has been and continues to be consumer-driven. We all need to keep pressing the insurance industry to cover legitimate natural therapies.

Even when insurers do offer some limited coverage, they continue to apply the conventional medical paradigm to functional medicine. For example, an insurance company may pay for a limited number of acupuncture treatments to relieve pain, but they will not pay at all for improving digestive or immune function. They might pay for an office visit with an integrative physician, but they will not pay for an IM vitamin injection or an IV nutrient infusion to give the body the boost it needs to recover from chronic fatigue or subclinical nutritional deficiencies.

In my opinion, many insurance companies fear that supporting functional medicine will have a negative impact on their investments in the pharmaceutical industry. Therefore, even though they may realize that these preventive and early-intervention approaches will ultimately save them money, they are resistant to change. In addition to pressuring the insurance companies, we need to work with our legislators, many of whom are sympathetic to a paradigm shift, to initiate laws supportive of the practice and reimbursement of functional medicine.

Integrating with Mainstream Treatment

Throughout this book, I have presented natural healing approaches that, hopefully, will keep your need for more aggressive mainstream interventions to a minimum. Sometimes, despite our best efforts, we may become severely ill or be impacted by an unexpected trauma, such as a car accident. In such situations, mainstream approaches can literally be life-saving. It is wise, however, to complement these interventions with natural therapies since they can minimize many of the toxic side effects of pharmaceutical and surgical interventions, and speed recovery. If you need to take antibiotics, for example, taking probiotics will counterbalance the negative effect of antibiotics on your protective intestinal flora.

Surgery

Although modern surgery can produce life-saving and life-altering results, the procedure and the accompanying anesthesia are among the most toxic and aging events of life. The explosion of cortisol that occurs with any trauma and the obliteration of consciousness produced by anesthesia are both very damaging to the body. Anesthetics are mostly stored in the brain, liver and other fatty organs, and are released for weeks and sometimes longer after surgery. These toxins strain both Phase 1 and Phase 2 liver detoxification processes and slow down the body's natural healing processes.

Over the years, I have prepared many of my patients to handle the side effects of anesthesia and to optimize healing after surgery. With appropriate preparation and after-care, surgical results are far superior and recovery is greatly speeded. A patient of mine recently underwent a 12-hour mastectomy coupled with a reconstructive procedure. The surgeons and nurses were astounded by her ability to "bounce back." My pre-surgery preparation for this patient and many others involves thorough attention to bowel health, liver detoxification and adequate administration and storage of protective antioxidants, such as glutathione and taurine. This is done both orally and by injections or infusions. I dream of the day when such interventions are routinely administered weeks before surgery, at the hospital and immediately after the procedure.[3] Until then, if you can, find a knowledgeable integrative physician who will know how to appropriately prepare you. Many of my patients have benefited from the strategies we use at our Centers.

Corsello Surgery Preparation Strategies

1. Complete the Bowel Healing Program (Steps 1-3), if possible, at least a week before the surgical procedure.
2. If not already doing so, make sure you eat nutritionally-balanced meals for at least a couple of weeks before surgery. If possible, add freshly-pressed vegetable juices to your diet for at least 2 days prior to the procedure.
3. Cut down gradually on any omega-3 EFAs (flaxseed, fish oil, etc.) you are currently taking, as they may increase bleeding. You should be completely off EFAs 3 days prior to surgery.
4. Vitamin E can be continued until the day before the procedure, providing you don't exceed 400 international units.
5. If you are taking large amounts of vitamin C and will be unable to continue while hospitalized, start to diminish the dosage gradually so that your body will not undergo the

shock of sudden deprivation. You should wean yourself down so that you are taking no more than 500 milligrams the day before surgery. To maintain the vigilance of your immune system, add echinacea (1 capsule or 15 to 30 drops of extract, three times a day) or astralagus (400 milligrams, two times a day) for a week prior to the surgery.

6. A week before the procedure, if you are not already doing so, start taking the powerful antioxidants contained in **CC Antioxidant Formula** (2 capsules, 2 times a day) and in **CC GlutaPath** (2 capsules a day), alpha-lipoic acid (100 milligrams 3 times a day) and Co-Q10 (at least 50 milligrams a day). Not only is Co-Q10 a phenomenal antioxidant, but it also strengthens the heart's pumping ability. Since antioxidants work in concert with each other, this combination is necessary to facilitate the body's ability to cope with the biochemical threat of anesthesia and the trauma of surgery.

7. To replace the anti-inflammatory EFAs, I recommend Wobenzym N[4], a combination of natural enzymes, which has powerful anti-inflammatory properties. During trauma, excessive inflammation not only can hinder healing, but it can also produce the formation of excessive scar tissue known as keloids. This is an over-reaction of the body's natural response to localized trauma. Not only are keloids aesthetically unappealing, they can be functionally harmful. I have found Wobenzym N to be very helpful in avoiding them. Many plastic surgeons are now recommending their use. I suggest taking 5 to 10 tablets 3 times a day between meals, beginning when you start to wean off EFAs and continuing after surgery until the scars are healed.

8. Have a positive attitude about the success of the procedure. Prepare yourself by meditation, affirmations, prayer or other faith-building techniques, and try to surround yourself with supportive people.

Dental Surgery

Dental surgery is very stressful to the whole body. The removal of impacted wisdom teeth is perhaps the most painful of all dental procedures. Often, impacted teeth harbor subclinical infections, and the removal always causes severe gum inflammation, temporary nerve damage and severe pain.

I have prepared myself and many of my patients for dental surgery and have found that there is a significant reduction in discomfort and accelerated recovery. Recently, a patient came to see me because she was facing the removal of two remaining impacted wisdom teeth. She was very fearful since the removal of the first two had her bedridden and in extreme pain for a week. Following my recommendations, she was back at work two days later. Adhering to the detoxification routine I had recommended was the major reason for such fast results, as toxins increase inflammation, and inflammation increases pain.

Corsello Dental Surgery Strategies

1. Complete the Bowel Healing Program (Steps 1-3), if possible, at least a week before the procedure.
2. Detoxify by consuming only protein shakes and freshly pressed vegetable juices for 2 days prior to the procedure.
3. Maintain a positive attitude.
4. Utilize the dental surgery remedies (see below).
5. If you are unable to chew for a few days after the procedure, continue to nourish yourself with protein shakes and fresh-pressed vegetable juices.

Corsello Dental Surgery Remedies

The following remedies are recommended prior to and following dental surgery. When using homeopathic products, they must be taken in an "empty mouth," with no food, gum, toothpaste, etc., for 15 minutes prior to and after ingestion of the remedy.

- **CC Infection Nutrients Pack:** Take one pack with each meal, 3 days prior to procedure. Continue after surgery until pain and/or swelling is relieved. The zinc lozenges are particularly effective for disinfecting the oral cavity and upgrading general immunity.

- **Oscillococcinum:** A homeopathic anti-viral remedy, oscilloccinum is packaged three tubes to a box. Use one tube every 2 hours, up to four times per day, starting 2 days prior to the procedure and continue after surgery for at least 24 hours or until you feel well.

- **Arnica (30C):** This well-known homeopathic trauma remedy is especially helpful in reducing pain and swelling. Take 3 pellets one-half hour before surgery. Take 3 pellets as soon as possible after surgery and continue the remedy 4 times a day until the pain and/or swelling is relieved.

- **Rescue Remedy:** This Bach Flower Remedy is also good for trauma and stress. For 24 hours prior to the procedure, swish and swallow 3 drops every 8 hours. Immediately, after the procedure, place 4 drops under the tongue every 3 to 5 minutes and swallow until you feel calm and in control. A few doses should do.

- **Phosphorus (30C):** This homeopathic remedy helps to control bleeding. Take one dose of this remedy 10 minutes prior to your appointment if you anticipate that bleeding will be a problem.

- **Hypericum (30C):** If you have nerve root pain, take 3 pellets of this homeopathic remedy every half-hour until the pain abates. Hypericum not only reduces nerve damage, but it is also an antiviral and a mood stabilizer.

14 *Wellness & Rejuvenation*

Unlimited vitality is possible.

Aging Factors

As we have reached the last chapter, I am certain that you well realize that *the factors that age us are synergistically interactive and cumulative* – and that they can affect our wellness in a variety of ways. It has been my clinical experience that bowel and liver toxicity play a very significant role in the aging process. In addition, other forms of toxicities and imbalances pile up, eventually leading to cellular damage, impaired organ function and loss of vitality.

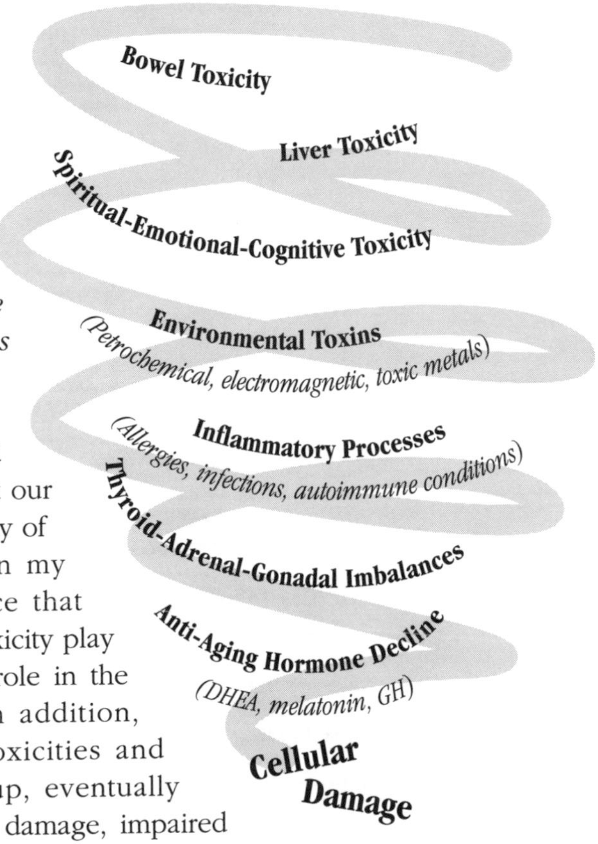

Bowel Toxicity

Liver Toxicity

Spiritual-Emotional-Cognitive Toxicity

Environmental Toxins
(Petrochemical, electromagnetic, toxic metals)

Inflammatory Processes
(Allergies, infections, autoimmune conditions)

Thyroid-Adrenal-Gonadal Imbalances

Anti-Aging Hormone Decline
(DHEA, melatonin, GH)

Cellular Damage

Aging Spiral
Figure 14-1

Rejuvenating Therapies

At our Centers, we always start the journey of decelerating and reversing the aging process with the Bowel Healing Program and nutritionally supporting the liver detoxification functions. Attention to absorption of nutrients is vital, for it is not only what we take in but mostly what we absorb that counts. Depending on the individual, a variety of therapies may be implemented to address absorption problems – from large quantities of oral digestive enzymes to IV infusions of nutrients. The next steps are dependent on what has caused the imbalances and the severity of the dis-ease. Some of the most common interventions, such as liver detoxification, stress management, allergy desensitization and hormonal balancing have been described in earlier chapters. We often use intravenous nutrient therapy to repair deficient enzymatic systems. When the cellular architecture has been permanently damaged by toxic metals, toxic metal chelation therapy is frequently very effective in reversing the downward spiral. After the entire cellular machinery has been finely tuned, if we still need a powerful rejuvenation push, we refer patients for live cell therapy – a technique that brings new life to aging organs.

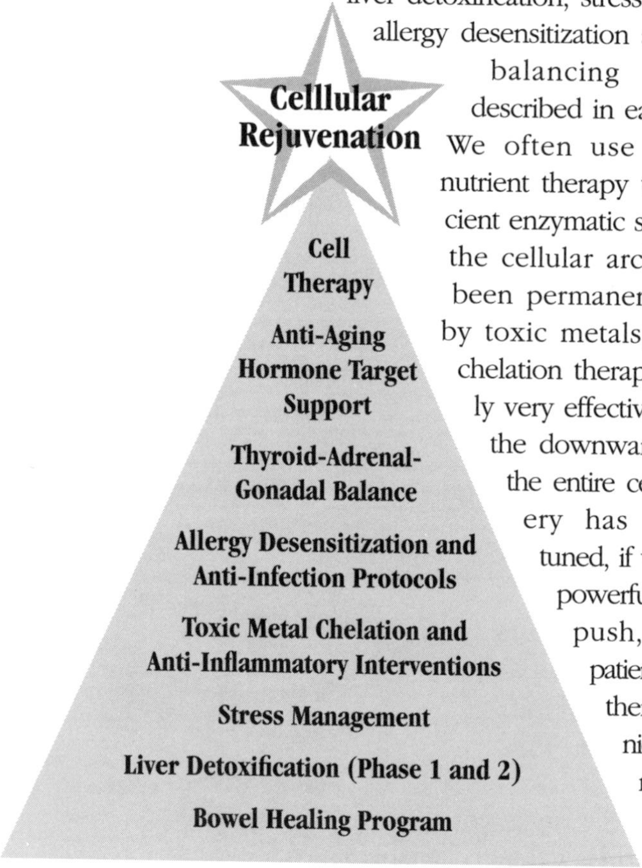

Celllular Rejuvenation

Cell Therapy

Anti-Aging Hormone Target Support

Thyroid-Adrenal-Gonadal Balance

Allergy Desensitization and Anti-Infection Protocols

Toxic Metal Chelation and Anti-Inflammatory Interventions

Stress Management

Liver Detoxification (Phase 1 and 2)

Bowel Healing Program

Healing Pyramid
Figure 14-2

Knowledge and Patience are Essential

In many mass-market health books, the reader is often given the impression that serious illnesses can be reversed "in no time." This is not the case, even in the hands of an experienced practitioner. The time it takes to unravel and treat complex conditions very much depends upon the number of years it took to develop them and how many systems have been damaged in the process. When a seriously ill patient is totally compliant, it can take as long as 6 to 12 months to achieve wellness. When patients slow their journey up the Healing Pyramid for personal or financial reasons, resolution of the condition can take even longer. The healing process, of course, is always greatly hindered when people hold onto negative attitudes.

Once wellness is attained, periodic tune-ups once or twice a year are advisable to assure that there is no backsliding. As long as patients continue to apply what they have learned during their time with us, they sustain remarkable resilience and youthfulness. Occasionally, patients return with a new problem. Invariably, when the layers of toxic burden have been adequately removed, and the organs and glands sufficiently revitalized, it takes very little to restore balance and wellness.

Intracellular Nutrient Therapy

As I have said *ad nauseum*, we always start from the foundation of the Healing Pyramid – healing the bowel and liver. Often, people have severe dysbiosis, which hinders the capacity of the intestines to absorb oral nutrients. When such absorption problems exist, they are best treated by large quantities of nutrients administered via IM injections or IV infusions. This type of therapy is an effective way to repair enzymatic systems and "jump-start" deficient cells by flooding them, via the bloodstream, with what they need.

What particular nutrients are given depends on the patient's needs. Therapy usually includes adequate amounts of B vitamins and sophisticated antioxidants. Most patients, whose symptoms are being aggravated by a poorly functioning liver, almost immediately benefit from injections of antioxidants, such as glutathione and taurine, and other liver protective substances.

Remember Peter, from Chapter 4, who had chronic diarrhea and anxiety? Four weeks of vitamin B injections and large quantities of digestive enzymes began to heal his system to the point where his diarrhea stopped, he was able to start absorbing nutrients from his food and he began to feel less anxious. When dysbiosis is severe, such as it was with Peter, not only are oral nutrients not well absorbed but, some of them – such as B vitamins – further stimulate the growth of pathogenic organisms. Bypassing the digestive system is a way to initiate an effective course of healing, while keeping a bad situation from becoming even worse. In patients who are very sick, we often use IV infusions. Judith's story will give you an idea of the power of such an intervention.

Judith's Transformation

Judith, a professional in her mid-30s, had come to us with severe diarrhea and nausea that precluded adequate food intake. Our evaluation indicated that both her uric acid and cholesterol "third-line antioxidant defenses" were extremely low. (It has been my clinical experience that when third line defenses are being utilized, the body has depleted first and second line defenses, such as vitamin C, bioflavonoids, B vitamins, glutathione, taurine and, most likely, Phase 1 and 2 liver detoxification enzymes.) To address such serious free radical pathology, we immediately started Judith on antioxidant infusions and liver protective substances.

The day after her first infusion, Judith called to report that she was feeling less nauseous (her nausea was due to liver toxicity and other malabsorption problems) and that she felt "something profound was happening." We gave her two more antioxidant infusions that week, and the nausea disappeared and the diarrhea became manageable. Three infusions took care of the acute problem. Now, we could begin to deal with serious, underlying healing impediments, such as high levels of toxic metals, a compromised immune system, parasites and a whole host of hormonal problems. We continued the infusions on a weekly basis as we moved her steadily and progressively, without healing crises, through the various steps of the Healing Pyramid. Judith is now on her way to a level of wellness she never thought possible.

Chronic Metal Toxicity

As you may recall from Chapter 6, we are all exposed to persistent low levels of toxic substances and metals. Symptoms may not appear for years as the body hides these toxic substances in various tissues. Bones and fatty deposits are favorite sites. Symptoms of chronic metal toxicity are, therefore, insidious and nonspecific, such as fatigue, malaise or increased susceptibility to infections.

One reason symptoms of chronic toxicity are so vague and wide-ranging is because the metals interfere with so many cellular functions.[1] They destroy the architecture of cell membranes, disrupt the activity of enzymes and damage the mitochondria – the energy factories of our cells. This translates into aged tissues, unable to exert the functions designated by nature. Brain cells might lose their capacity to think, while liver cells might not be able to complete detoxification processes or may lose their ability to transform precursor hormones into gender-specific hormones. Researchers, who studied nearly 20,000 pairs of twins, recently reported in the *Journal of the American Medical Association* that in people diagnosed with Parkinson's disease after age 50, the most common cause is environmental factors, including exposure to toxins. [2]

When the tissues are in such a state of disarray, the efficacy of all therapeutic interventions is severely hampered. Do you remember Jack and Tina from Chapter 6, the siblings with healthy lifestyles, who both ended up very sick – he with cardiovascular problems and she with severe peri-menopausal symptoms? We discovered that the source of their problems was the consumption of the organic produce they grew in the garden of their shared house. Ironically, the food that was supposed to keep them well was making them ill – it was being poisoned by the lead-laden fumes emitted by nearby trains in transit. The large quantities of oral supplements they were taking had no effect because their cellular architecture and enzymatic systems had been severely damaged. It was only after we treated the siblings with chelation therapy that their supplement regime became effective.

While acute metal toxicity, such as the constant ingestion of leaded paint chips by children (pica), can be detected by a blood test, chronic toxicity seldom can be identified by this means. Children with pica have large skeletal deposits, but they are also constantly ingesting and adding lead to their systems. For this reason, high levels of lead frequently show up in their blood.

The presence of lead and other toxic metals in the blood that bathes vital organs is a serious threat to survival. Nature, in her infinite wisdom, promptly removes them from the circulation and places them in less vital components of our bodies – bones and fatty deposits. These toxic stores are slowly brought back into circulation as the fat melts and the bones remodel themselves. Our cellular and enzymatic systems are poisoned very gradually by these released toxins. Hair, a secretory tissue, both accumulates toxic metals and eliminates excessive amounts. Hair analysis, therefore, is one way to take a look at chronic toxic metal load (accumulation-excretion). (See Chapter 6, Note 19.)

Chelation Therapy

The word chelation is derived from the Greek *chela*, which means "claw." Chelating agents grab or bind substances and transport them to where they belong. They also bring toxic substances to elimination organs. Chelating agents are usually amino acids, capable of incorporating minerals and metals. One example in nature is hemoglobin, consisting of iron-containing heme linked to globin, a protein (composed of amino acids). Hemoglobin's function as an oxygen transporter is well known. The only biochemical difference, incidentally, between our hemoglobin and chlorophyll ("plant blood") is that magnesium rather than iron is the chelated substance in chlorophyll. During World War I, I am told, the Germans infused chlorophyll into their soldiers in the battlefield when they ran out of blood.

There are many types of therapeutic chelating agents used in medicine, both oral and intravenous. When I speak of chelation therapy in this book, I am referring to intravenous treatment using the amino acid, ethylenediaminetetraacetic acid (EDTA). Modern EDTA chelation therapy has been practiced since World War II, but the origination of the chelation process goes way back to 1893, when Alfred Werner, a French-Swiss chemist, developed the theories that later became the foundation of chelation therapy. Werner was awarded the Nobel Prize in 1913 for his work. A different type of chelation therapy was originally used during World War I to deal with the metal contaminants of poison gas warfare. By the mid-1950s, EDTA chelation therapy had become the preferred treatment for lead poisoning, and to date it has been safely used on more than 500,000 patients for that purpose. It is also the treatment of choice for digitalis toxicity.

Multi-Purpose Therapy

The chelating agent EDTA, developed by chemist Frederick Bersworth in 1933 and brought to Clark University in Massachusetts, is still being used today. *Like many great synchronicities in medicine, in the course of using EDTA for the treatment of lead poisoning, it was discovered that EDTA also reversed cardiovascular disorders, relieved impotency and reduced the incidence of cancer.* A large landmark retrospective study, conducted by Drs. Edward Olszewer and

James Carter, documenting such results, was published in 1988.[3] Other researchers have confirmed those findings.[4, 5, 6]

Protects Bones

Since chelation also binds and removes calcium, concern has been raised that the procedure might accelerate osteoporosis. In fact, it has quite the opposite effect. EDTA pulls calcium out of where it doesn't belong – the small arterial capillaries, arthritic joints, traumatized tendons, strained ligaments and calcium oxalate kidney stones, and deposits it where it does belong – in the bones. The sudden drop of calcium in the blood produced by EDTA stimulates the parathyroid gland to mobilize calcium reserves. The first source to be mobilized is the newly-deposited calcium in the vast array of capillaries. This EDTA-bound calcium, on its way to elimination, mostly through the kidneys, passes through various parts of the body. The bone-building osteoblasts, hungry for calcium, break the EDTA-calcium bonds and grab the calcium for deposition in the bones.

EDTA therapy eventually also reduces lead in the bones, which also improves calcium binding. These biochemical mechanisms, documented experimentally, have been corroborated by the clinical experience of many chelating physicians performing thousands of chelation treatments. Contrary to concerns about losing calcium from the bones, chelation therapy actually helps both in the prevention and reduction of osteoporosis.[7]

Powerful Rejuvenator

Chelation therapy has far-reaching benefits and is one of the best rejuvenating therapies available. As British researchers have noted, concentrations of aluminum, lead, mercury, cadmium and arsenic increase as we age.[8] When we remove toxic metals that have accumulated over the years, we, in essence, are restoring our cells and enzymatic systems to a younger and healthier state. By removing calcium from the walls of the vast capillary bed, we reduce the rigidity of the vessels and create a larger capillary pathway. This enhanced capillary circulation brings nutrient-rich blood to the most distant of our body's cells, and carries away waste and carbon dioxide.

Heart Protective

EDTA provides many benefits for the heart as well. It is a powerful antioxidant that binds and removes harmful oxidized cholesterol (LDL). It also reduces the tendency of the platelets to stick together. This property of EDTA prevents inappropriate clotting that can lead to heart attacks and strokes.

Many Diseases Responsive

Because of its complex mechanisms of action, chelation therapy has been effective in promoting the healing of a wide variety of seemingly unrelated ailments, such as cardiovascular disease, osteoporosis, arthritis, scleroderma, Alzheimer's disease, Parkinson's disease, impotence and multiple sclerosis. According to chelation experts, Dr. Elmer M. Cranton and Dr. James P. Frackelton, "EDTA chelation therapy combined with supplemental antioxidants and moderation of health-destroying habits act to prevent and partially reverse many common age-associated diseases, which cause disability and death through a common pathway of free radical pathology."[9]

Toxic metals play a large role in many diseases and their removal alleviates many disparate symptoms. Chelation therapy reduces free radicals and restores immune functions of patients with chronic fatigue and cancer. In an 18-year retrospective study conducted in a Swiss city adjacent to a heavily traveled highway, Dr. Cranton and Dr. Walter Blumer found that patients who were treated with calcium EDTA for lead toxicity had 90% less incidence of cancer compared to untreated city residents, who constituted the control group.[10]

An Effective Healing Tool

Although EDTA chelation therapy is approved by the Federal Drug Administration (FDA) for lead and digitalis toxicity, it has remained controversial because of its other "off-label" uses. The reality is, and the American Medical Association admits so, that up to 60% of all prescriptions written by mainstream physicians are for other than approved uses. Another often heard criticism is that the therapy has not undergone double-blind controlled studies. In reality, such a study was attempted, but funding was withdrawn by a pharmaceutical company after the initial offer. Although this company stood to financially benefit from the research, the industry at large would have lost significant revenues from products sold for the treatment of cardiovascular disease, cancer and other ailments.

Interestingly enough, according to a report released by the federal government's Office of Technology Assessment, only 10% to 20% of the treatments used by mainstream physicians have been evaluated in controlled clinical studies.[11] Chelation therapy suffers from the same dilemma as do many other successful alternative treatments – the lack of adequate funding to document its clinical success. Chelation therapy is currently being used effectively by more than 1,000 physicians in the United States and has helped hundreds of thousands of people. The best way to find a physician who has been properly trained (board certified) in chelation therapy is to contact the American College for Advancement in Medicine (see Chapter 13, Note 2).

Part of a Comprehensive Approach

At our Centers, we make certain that patients start bowel and liver healing interventions, and adopt a health-promoting lifestyle as we initiate chelation therapy. The worst scenario is that in which patients continue to poison themselves while under the illusion that chelation will "cure it all." This is detrimental not only for the patient but also for the reputation of the therapy.

The number of treatments required varies from patient to patient, depending on history, toxic burden, clinical evaluation and symptoms. Generally, IV infusions for removal of the toxic burden (toxic metal chelation) include EDTA, calcium, magnesium, potassium, heparin (an anti-inflammatory), procaine (a cardioprotective, rejuvenating substance), B vitamins and liver protective substances. It is important to understand that EDTA binds and removes not only unwanted substances, but also some very important nutrients, such as chromium, potassium, magnesium, zinc and vitamin B_6. When the primary goal is removal of calcium from the vast network of small capillaries, calcium is omitted from the formula.

An individualized nutrient plan to balance cellular deficiencies, compensate for nutrient depletion and support the adrenal glands is a necessary component of all chelation therapy interventions. We also make sure to saturate the cells with antioxidants prior to chelation, as toxic metals in transit for excretion can cause free radical damage. Progress is carefully monitored through creatinine clearance, analysis of both hair and urine,[12] and periodic, comprehensive metabolic screenings (blood tests).

Impotence and Chelation Therapy

Many of my male patients have found that chelation therapy also reverses impotence. John, a 51-year-old executive, came to our Center because his physician had recommended that he undergo coronary artery bypass graft (CABG) to resolve his angina, shortness of breath and other cardiovascular problems. Resolved to try a less invasive approach, he came to our Center for chelation therapy. Lab tests revealed that John also had low DHEA, testosterone and GH levels. We walked him rapidly up the Healing Pyramid step-by-step, including restoring his hormones to a normal level. After 20 chelation treatments, John told our nurse that he had regained his full erectile capacity and was "better than ever."

Impotence and various forms of erectile dysfunctions are

becoming a much too frequent problem among men in this country. Unfortunately, many men blame themselves or their partners for a physiological problem. Serious atherosclerosis of the vast capillary bed of the penis, cardiovascular disease and the medications used to reduce symptoms often lead to impotence. In contrast, chelation therapy unplugs all small vessels, including those of the genitourinary organs. This leads to improved blood flow, necessary for a sustainable erection. Restoration of the male hormones and reduction of the cardiovascular drugs does the rest.

Preventive Anti-Aging Therapy

Because toxic metals, poor circulation and the production of free radials are such major culprits in aging, many people are now coming to us for brief courses of toxic metal chelation therapy as a prophylactic anti-aging intervention. We use hair and urine analysis to gauge the extent of the toxic load and to determine when the "mission is accomplished." Even a brief course of 10 to 15 treatments, which might not remove the entire toxic burden, does provide substantial benefits. I also recommend periodic infusions every 1 to 3 months, depending upon the circumstances, to assure removal of newly-acquired toxins. City dwellers, in particular, are constantly exposed to high levels of pollutants and toxic byproducts that undermine even the best health-promoting lifestyle.

Cell Rejuvenation Therapies

Stem Cells

You may recall the exciting news about how two groups of scientists, funded by a biotechnology company, have recently succeeded in cultivating human embryonic stem cells.[13] Stem cells are very early stage embryonic cells that have not yet differentiated into specialized functions or specific organs. These cells are called "pluripotent" because they are capable of growing new tissue of any kind. When injected into a patient, they go on a "search and repair mission" to wherever they are needed.

Stem cells are now being used for sophisticated medical treatments, such as the correction of genetic disorders in-utero and in children. The first formal clinical study of in-utero stem cell transplantation in the United States is currently underway at the Fetal Treatment Center at the University of California, San Francisco, under the direction of Dr. Michael Harrison. The goal of the trial is to correct inherited immunodeficiency diseases in developing fetuses so that the diseases are cured before the babies are born. At Duke University, Dr. Rick Howrey and his associates recently reported their success with correcting genetic disorders in children by transplantation of stem cells from umbilical cord blood.[14]

Stem cells also have the capacity to provide the best support after radiation and chemotherapy. They are used as one solitary infusion in place of a bone marrow transplant. Since these cells have no antigenic properties, a search for a compatible donor is unnecessary; and the infusion, in contrast a bone marrow transplant, is not painful.

Stem cell transplants are gaining great momentum both in Europe and the United States. Because stem cells go to wherever they are needed in the body, they are also the best rejuvenation strategy for those who can afford its price. Because the FDA has not yet approved this therapy, people currently need to go to Europe or the Bahamas to obtain this treatment. The potential of this therapy is spectacular, both in curing illness and in promoting wellness.

Cell Therapy

Although the ability to culture and transplant human stem cells is new, the transplantation of other human cells, such as whole blood (transfusions) or its components (white cells, red cells or platelets) has been a common practice worldwide for eons. Using young cells to rejuvenate organs is also an ancient practice. The Egyptian Eber Papyrus refers to the use of animal organs in medicinal preparations in 1550 B.C., while the Chinese prescribed human placenta as a tonic centuries ago.

It is Dr. Paul Niehans, the renowned Swiss physician, however, who is considered the father of modern live cell therapy. Niehans' method was instituted in Europe in 1937 and has since been used by many of the rich and powerful, including Pope Pius XII, Winston Churchill and Charlie Chaplin, and by many others desirous of remaining young and vital. Neihans' method of cell therapy – the injection of fresh embryo cells of specific animal organs to revitalize the same organ in a human patient – is still in use today in Europe and Mexico.[15]

Although we don't yet know everything about cell therapy, we do have some understanding about how it works. European researchers have shown, through radioactive tagging studies, that injections of specific cellular groups from animal embryos find their way through the blood to the counterpart tissue in the recipient – liver goes to liver, pancreas finds pancreas, brain finds brain, etc. While the cells are organ specific, they are not species specific, which allows for the successful transplantation of animal cells into humans.[16] We also know that embryo cells are immunologically immature and, therefore, are not recognized by the recipient as foreign cells. It is this same immunological immaturity that allows women to keep their fetuses in their wombs.

A couple of major theories exist regarding the ability of cell therapy to rejuvenate aged organs. In one theory, it is proposed that the fresh DNA from embryo cells replaces the defective genetic material of the "old" cells. Revitalized, the cells are then able to function correctly once again. In the other theory, it is posited that the young, fresh cells produce cytokines (stimulating substances) that promote the production of new and vibrant cells or help diseased cells to get back on track. The effects can be quite dramatic, but they are not immediate. Positive results are noticeable usually 2 to 6 months after treatment, as it takes a little time for cells to regenerate and for organ function to improve.

I recommend cell therapy when we have been unable to achieve the desired results with our most comprehensive and intensive healing interventions, or when people want or need to function at a much higher level of proficiency than their chronological age allows. I have personally used cell therapy in the past, and I intend to soon repeat it. With the appropriate preparation of antioxidant infusions and toxic metal chelation therapy, the results can be astounding, as Bob's and Claire's experience demonstrates.

Bob's Transformation

Bob is a 54-year-old executive who needs to function at the level of his much younger colleagues and, being their leader, he wants to surpass their performance. When he came to our Center, he felt he was beginning to lose ground and could no longer handle his extensive travel schedule. He was increasingly feeling the effects of jet lag and was unable to arrive rested and ready to spring into action.

For him, time was of the essence. Since he was an out-of-towner, we asked him to give us a full week, during which we compressed all the interventions of the Healing Pyramid, having done all the preliminary testing 2 weeks before. My whole team worked on Bob. We adjusted his gonadal and adrenal hormones, prescribed melatonin and GH and, most importantly, did continuous infusions of antioxidants, alternating with toxic metal chelation for 6 hours every day. Then, we referred him for appropriate cell therapy.[17] Within 2 or 3 months, Bob's transformation was clearly visible to everyone around him and, most importantly, to himself. He had, in essence, turned back the hands of his biological clock so fast that he could now be in full command of his abilities and lead by example.

Claire's Transformation

Claire is currently 63-years-old and a world traveler. I first met her when, in her mid-40s, she asked me to help her heal. She had been diagnosed with multiple sclerosis (MS), had progressed from a cane to a walker, and was deteriorating very fast into total reliance on a wheelchair.

I found Claire to have one of the highest levels of lead I had ever seen. I subsequently learned that she had begun using a lead-laden, toxic dark hair dye in her late 20s. Over the years, the lead had been absorbed into her system, and in my opinion, had created neurotoxic damage, which contributed to the destruction of the protective myelin sheath surrounding her nerves. She was also a smoker, overweight and did not have the healthiest eating habits.

We began walking up the Healing Pyramid, and Claire followed my instructions very diligently. She changed her hair-coloring product, improved her diet and engaged in our smoking cessation program. We instituted a program of antioxidant infusions, alternating with toxic metal chelation. As her lifestyle changed, her metabolism improved and the toxic load diminished. The fat she had accumulated began to melt away effortlessly, and she emerged as a trim and stunning woman. She was soon able to replace her walker with a cane, and then progressed to walking unassisted, straight and steady.

As I knew that Claire's tissues had been severely damaged and were in need of repair, I referred her for cell therapy. She had her first set of injections and then returned to us for further "cleaning and tuning-up." Claire then went back for two more cycles of cell therapy during the following 12 months. She felt and looked so young and was so grateful that she became the most outspoken proponent of our comprehensive healing approach.

Claire is wise enough to know that she has a chronic autoimmune disease that can flare-up if her body and mind are not kept in a state of harmonious balance. A tangible reminder of this reality was her regression when her mother died a few years ago. The stress of the event immediately forced her back to using a cane for 3 or 4 days. She resumed her meditative practice, her bovine myelin pills, and specialized nutrients and antioxidants. Within a week, she was walking normally again.

Today, Claire travels all over the world (her favorite pastime) and has resumed playing tennis. She has remained a staunch defender of the innovative therapies that have allowed her to regain her health and revitalize her beyond everyone's expectations.

Bringing It All Together

I trust that you have now gained an awareness of the complexity of the process we call "aging" and the strategies needed to slow and reverse it. Stress, toxic substances, infections, allergies and a host of health-depleting habits, such as poor diet, lack of exercise, inadequate sleep, smoking and excessive partying, all play a role. Each one wreaks its own damage, depleting organ reserves and increasing free radical production. It is, however, the accumulated impact and synergistic interaction of many of the above factors that age us fast and furiously. When our natural state of balance is disrupted, biological systems begin to break down, often far earlier than they should – and aging accelerates.

As you have journeyed with me into each petal of the rejuvenating flower, you have learned many strategies you can implement to take control of your own destiny, increase your lifespan and maximize your vitality. Hopefully, you have come to understand how each longevity strategy contributes to the integrity of each petal and how they all work together synergistically to promote youthfulness (see Appendix B: Self-Care Longevity Strategies).

Stress, in particular, affects all three templates – energetic, chemical and physical. Reducing and managing stress has a profound anti-aging effect. When our bowels and livers are clean and strong, our immune systems are more effective. A health-promoting lifestyle that includes exercise, a nutrient-rich, balanced diet, and adequate and diversified antioxidants will go a long way in staving off the degenerative diseases that age us. When we stay connected with the universe and each other, miracles occur. You are also now aware, that should you need professional assistance, good integrative healthcare practitioners have many powerful healing tools at their disposal to help you regain balance and youthfulness.

My dear readers, as I part from you, I hope I have enticed you to take charge of your health and to chose the path of a long, fruitful, full and engaged life. I hope you will join me as an *Ageless Woman* and live, like I do, in the joyful realm of optimal wellness and sustainable vitality.

Nutritional Supplements

Corsello Center Formulas

As I noted in the text, the quality of nutrients determines their efficacy. Like other integrative healthcare providers, I purchase the best available products from reputable companies for my patients. When I am unable to find a high quality, synergistic product to meet specific needs, I develop my own formulations, which I call the Corsello Center (CC) Formulas. Described below are the CC Formulas I have mentioned in the book. Since nutrients have varied and multiple functions, I only include the actions that most closely relate to the overall purpose of each formula.

To Order

The CC Formulas described below are only a small portion of what is available from our dispensary. To order any CC Formula or other high quality products mentioned in the book, such as specialized protein powders produced by Metagenics, call Global Nutrition at 888-461-0949 or visit the Corsello Centers' website @http//www.corsello.com.

Product Descriptions

AdrenoMax
Purpose: To balance the functions of the adrenal glands, which are terribly overworked during any stressful event, such as allergies, infections and, of course, emotional upsets.

Therapeutic Actions: The raw adrenal concentrate enhances the body's ability to handle physical and emotional stress. Well-functioning adrenals lead to heightened resistance. It is the synergistic action of the nutrients contained in the formulation that accounts for its therapeutic properties.

Contents per Capsule:
Raw adrenal concentrate: 200 mgs.
Vitamin C: 50 mgs.
Vitamin B$_5$: 125 mgs.

Recommended Dosage: 1 to 2 capsules at breakfast and again at lunch, or as recommended by your integrative healthcare provider.

AdrenoSupport
Purpose: To provide the nutrients necessary for the support of optimal adrenal function. This product is designed for people whose belief system or allergies preclude the use of raw adrenal concentrate. The synergistic action of the vitamins reduces adrenal insufficiency.

Therapeutic Actions:
Vitamin C, under normal circumstances, is concentrated in the largest amounts in the adrenal glands.
Vitamin B6 (Pyridoxine) is critical in the formation of all enzymes and in the metabolism of corticoadrenal hormones.
Vitamin B5 (Pantothenic Acid), like Vitamin C, is concentrated in the largest quantities in the adrenals.

Contents per Capsule:
Vitamin C: 50 mgs.
Vitamin B6: 12.5 mgs.
Vitamin B5: 125 mgs.

Recommended Dosage: 1 to 2 capsules with breakfast and again at lunch, or as directed by your integrative healthcare provider.

Aller-1
Purpose: This combination of herbs is known to diminish the allergic response, both from airborne contact and gastrointestinal reactions.

Therapeutic Actions:
Nettles is an antiarthirtic and expectorant, useful in treating skin allergic conditions as well as allergic gastritis, rhinitis and hay fever. It is rich in chlorophyll, formic acid, magnesium, silicon, potassium, sulfur, tannins, as well as Vitamins A and C.
Horehound is an herb that is used for asthma, allergies,

coughs, colds, sore throats and intestinal gas. As an expectorant, it thins mucous in the bronchial tree and, therefore, aids in increasing its expulsion. It is rich in B vitamins as well as Vitamins A, C and E.

Fenugreek is a well-known herb that has been used for many medicinal purposes, including as an expectorant and a gastrointestinal tonic. It is useful in asthma, allergies and sinus problems. It can also help to lower fever and lubricate the intestinal tract. It is rich in biotin, choline, inositol, iron, lecithin, mucilage, PABA (para-aminobenzoic acid) and is a good source of B vitamins.

Slippery Elm is an herbal remedy effective in the treatment of mucous membrane inflammation. It is excellent in cases of allergy, asthma, and upper respiratory infections, as well as for bowel and urinary tract problems. It is rich in calcium, phosphorous, tannins and mucilage.

White Willow Bark is derived from the bark of the common willow tree. This very old remedy has been used to reduce both fever and pain. The principle active ingredient, salicin, was ultimately used to develop aspirin. Salicin becomes a potent anti-inflammatory through a conversion process in the liver. Side effects of white willow bark are far less than that of aspirin. This herb is rich in calcium, cobalt, iron, phosphorous, sulfur and vitamin B_{12}.

Mullein is an herbal remedy known for its soothing effects on respiratory tract inflammation. It aids in shortness of breath related to pulmonary diseases, asthma and hay fever. It is rich in PABA, choline, aucubin, sulfur, vitamins B_2, B_5, B_{12} and vitamin D.

Thyme is an herb that provides excellent relief from sinus, nasal and pulmonary congestion. It can also reduce fever, headaches and intestinal gas. This herb is rich in trace minerals, essential oils, tannins, vitamin B complex, vitamins C and D.

Contents per Capsule:
Nettles: 230 mgs.
Horehound: 67 mgs.
Fenugreek: 67 mgs.
Slippery Elm: 76 mgs.
White Willow Bark: 44 mgs.
Mullein: 22 mgs.
Thyme: 22 mgs.

Recommended Dosage: 2 to 3 capsules between meals, 2 to 3 times a day; one dose preferably at bedtime, or as directed by your integrative healthcare provider.

Appestat
Purpose: To help curb the appetite, stabilize mood, and facilitate both the breakdown of fat and the increase of muscle mass.

Therapeutic Actions:
L-Ornithine, an amino acid, is a powerful booster of growth hormone (GH).

DL-Phenylalanine is also a stimulator of GH.

CitriMax (Hydroxycitric Acid) is a well-researched natural appetite suppressant made from the pulp of an exotic Indian fruit.

Choline is an essential nutrient that facilitates the clearance of fats through the liver.

Inositol rebalances the neurotransmitters and works synergistically with choline to transport fat from the liver.

Tyrosine is the amino acid component of thyroid hormone, which, among its many functions, regulates glucose metabolism, and the breakdown of fat for energy production. Thyroid and GH are intimately related.

Glutamine has many beneficial effects, including that of facilitating the release of GH.

Methionine is an amino acid that works synergistically with inositol and choline to transport fat from the liver.

Contents per Capsule:
L-Ornithine: 16.7 mgs.
DL-Phenylalanine: 16.7 mgs.
CitriMax: 333 mgs.
Choline: 67 mgs.
Inositol: 67 mgs.
Tyrosine: 67 mgs.
Glutamine: 15 mgs.
Methionine: 10 mgs.

Bone Plus

Purpose: This product contains a combination of bone supportive nutrients, each of which has been independently proven to prevent or reduce osteoporosis. Their synergistic action makes them even more effective.

Therapeutic Actions: Microcrystalline hydroxyapatite has been found to be the best bone-building calcium. Boron increases calcium binding to the bone cells, acting somewhat like estrogen, while vitamin D also increases calcium binding. Calcium citrate, vitamin K and the other substances in this formula work synergistically to provide important additional bone support.

> ### *Contents per Capsule:*
> Elemental Calcium: 125 mgs. (mostly from hydroyapatite)
> Phosphorus: 64 mgs.
> Vitamin D-3: 66 IUs.
> Vitamin K: 10 mcgs.
> Boron: 1 mg.
> L-Cysteine: 33 mgs.
> Shave Grass, containing trace minerals: 66 mgs.
> Total Protein Content: 115 mgs.

Recommended Dosage: 3 to 6 capsules in 2 divided doses, preferably between lunch and dinner, and at bedtime, or as directed by your integrative healthcare provider.

C Minerals Powder

Purpose: This powder is a combination of vitamin C and some of the antioxidant minerals that are depleted by chronic stress and infection. We use it to raise the blood levels of ascorbic acid, antioxidants and heart-supportive minerals, such as magnesium and potassium. It is also an essential component in our Bowel Health Program.

Therapeutic Actions: This combination formula is a potent antioxidant that enhances immunity and promotes bowel elimination.

Content per Teaspoon:
Vitamin C: 3,300 mgs.
Magnesium: 200 mgs.
Potassium: 99 mgs.
Zinc: 15 mgs.
Selenium: 50 mcgs.
Manganese: 5 mgs.

Recommended Dosage: 1 to 3 teaspoons daily, depending upon bowel tolerance, or as directed by your integrative healthcare provider.

CV (Cardiovascular) Antioxidant Formula
Purpose: This combination has been designed to provide a sophisticated antioxidant delivery system that supports the heart, brain and other vital organs.

Therapeutic Actions:
Taurine is a sulfur-containing amino acid found in a high concentration in the heart muscle. It protects this fast, hardworking organ from free radical damage. It is also contained in the bile, promoting its fluidity and reducing the chance of gallstones. It diminishes brain excitability and has been used in large quantities as an anti-epileptic. It is highly concentrated in the eyes, where it exerts protective action against excessive ultraviolet damage. It is an all-around, powerful antioxidant.

Co-Q10 is an essential global co-enzyme in the adenosine triphosphate production (ATP) cellular energy cycle. It is found in all of the body's cells, but is highly concentrated in the heart. It protects the heart and brain from oxygen deprivation, even when blood supply is limited. It increases the heart's pumping ability like digitalis, but without its side effects. It is very useful in prevention of cardiomyopathy and reduces carcinogenesis.

Dimethylglycine is an amino acid important in muscle energy production. It lends further assistance to the heart's pumping action. In large doses, it assists in the release of GH.

L-Carnitine is needed for the transport of essential fatty acids (EFAs) as well as nonessential fatty acids into the mitochondria (the cells' batteries) to be utilized for energy production. It helps prevent heart disease by keeping cholesterol in check as well as through its antioxidant properties.

Niacinamide is a liver-friendly form of niacin (Vitamin B₃) that aids in the metabolism of carbohydrates, fats and proteins.

Vitamin B₆ (Pyridoxine) helps to prevent atherosclerosis by reducing homocysteine. It also helps to maintain suppleness of the vascular lining and diminishes platelet aggregation. It is necessary for the proper metabolism of all proteins, including those of the myocardial muscle. It is also a natural diuretic. This vitamin is rapidly depleted by stress.

Magnesium is the most important mineral for the heart. Among its numerous functions is that of a vasodilator (vessel relaxer), which reduces hypertension. It also regulates the electrical activity of the heart, reducing arrhythmias. Because it is a bronchodilator, it is helpful for asthmatic conditions. This mineral is also necessary for proper carbohydrate and essential fatty acid (EFA) metabolism.

Potassium is another mineral that, in conjunction with magnesium, assures proper heart pumping strength and the reduction of blood pressure. All tissues require potassium for the proper release of toxic byproducts.

Selenium is a trace mineral that has its own antioxidant properties. It is also part of one of the most important endogenous antioxidants, glutathione peroxidase – the most overused liver detoxification enzyme. Selenium offers protection against heart disease and stroke through its general antioxidant actions as well as its ability to enhance a favorable cholesterol ratio.

Contents per Capsule:

Niacinamide: 25mgs.

Vitamin B₆. 15 mgs.

Magnesium: 50 mgs.

Selenium: 12 mcgs.

Potassium: 50 mgs.

Co-Q10 (Ubiquinone): 15 mgs.

Dimethylglycine: 10 mgs.

L-Carnitine: 50 mgs.

Taurine: 20 mgs.

Recommended Dosage: 4 capsules per day, preferably 2 with breakfast and 2 with dinner, or as directed by your integrative healthcare provider.

Fat Burner Plus
Purpose: When used in conjunction with Appestat, this product has all the natural ingredients to control appetite, stimulate GH production and release, burn fat and increase muscle mass.

Therapeutic Actions:
Italian L-Carnitine (the most effective form of carnitine) stimulates energy production by burning fats in the mitochondria. (For more information, see **CV Antioxidant**.)

L-Arginine, an amino acid, enhances the production of GH, which increases muscle and decreases fat.

Chromium Picolinate is very efficacious in the proper metabolism of cholesterol and important in cholesterol and glucose metabolism. It aids in insulin transport action.

Zinc works synergistically with other nutrients and, among its many other properties, assists in EFA metabolism and the adequate production of the protective endogenous antioxidant superoxide dismutase (SOD).

Contents per Capsule:
Italian L-Carnitine: 100 mgs.
L-Arginine: 170 mgs.
Chromium Picolinate: 18 mcgs.
Zinc: 25 mgs.

Recommended Dosage: 2 capsules, 3 times a day, between meals, or as directed by your integrative healthcare provider. Taking it 20 to 30 minutes before exercise enhances its fat burning ability.

Female Supplemental Pack
Purpose: This self-contained packet of different nutrients provides a combination of diuretic herbs, minerals, EFAs and vitamins designed to not only reduce the symptoms of PMS but to also treat some of its causes.

Therapeutic Actions:

Magnesium is the most used of all intracellular minerals. Magnesium facilitates EFA metabolism (faulty EFA metabolism is one of the major factors in PMS). It regulates sugar metabolism and ensures proper distribution of nutrients throughout the body. Since magnesium relaxes all muscles, it reduces menstrual cramps. Asparatate is one of the better forms for the facilitation of intracellular transport.

Vitamin B6 (Pyridoxine) is depleted by stress, oral contraceptives and other prescription drugs. Many women are deficient in this important nutrient. Vitamin B6 reduces water retention, which is responsible for the increased moodiness and weight gain that often accompany PMS.

Wild Yam (*Dioscorea*) is one of the most important female phytochemicals (plant chemicals). As a progesterone promoter, wild yam can inhibit and prevent menstrual cramps as well as uterine discomfort. It reduces estrogen dominance, typical of PMS.

Agnus Castus **(Vitex)**, also known as chaste berry, is capable of stimulating the release of luteinizing hormone (LH), which is necessary for ovulation and consequently the formation of the corpus luteum and its production of progesterone. The herb itself has progestenic properties and, therefore, reduces symptoms of depression, cramps, water retention and weight gain – all symptoms associated with inadequate progesterone.

Borage Oil is an important EFA of the omega-3 family, which reduces the predominance of the arachidonic cascade responsible for uterine inflammation and dysmenorrhea (painful menstruation). It also has mild phytoestrogenic properties. Like other EFAs, borage oil is essential for the health of all organs and for proper immune and nerve function.

Zinc is an extremely important trace mineral, which like Vitamin B6, is depleted by stress. It is necessary for EFA metabolism and many other life-sustaining biological processes. It is part of the antioxidant SOD and is necessary for many immunological functions. The picolinate form is one of the best zinc transport systems.

Ox Bile Extract is necessary for the breakdown of fats and their absorption. It facilitates the digestion and absorption of the borage oil in this formula.

Juniper, Buchu, Uva-Ursi, Bear Berry and Cubeb are natural diuretic herbs, which work well when combined, even in small doses. Water retention is a common PMS symptom.

Contents per Packet:
Magnesium: 200 mgs.
Vitamin B₆: 250 mgs.
Wild Yam: 25 mgs.
Agnus Castus (Vitex): 400 mgs.
Borage Oil: 1,200 mgs.
Zinc: 50 mgs.
Quantities of other described nutrients are too small to cite.

Recommended Dosage: 1 packet with breakfast or lunch, or as directed by your integrative healthcare provider.

FiberMax
Purpose: This blend of insoluble and soluble dietary fibers is designed to trap toxic gut byproducts, lower oxidized LDL cholesterol and optimize bowel elimination. Because it also contains 6% essential fatty acids (EFAs) of the omega-3 family, it also reduces inflammation.

Therapeutic Actions: The soluble fiber binds to the toxic intestinal debris, while the insoluble scrubs them out. The lignans, contained in the flaxseed meal powder, have beneficial mild phytoestrogenic properties. The EFAs, by reducing inflammation, support the immunological integrity of the gut. The formula also contains dandelion, which protects the liver while the toxic debris is being removed.

Contents per Teaspoon:
Flaxseed Meal Powder: 80%
Apple Pectin: 20%
Dandelion: Not measured

Recommended Dosage: 1 to 3 teaspoons daily (see Chapter 7) or as directed by your integrative healthcare provider.

GlutaPath

Purpose: This complex antioxidant formulation is designed for general organ protection. It is particularly important for protecting the liver while using conventional drug therapy, and during weight reduction diets or any form of detoxification, since there is inevitably an increase in the load of toxic byproducts dumped into the bloodstream and then into the liver for further processing and elimination.

Therapeutic Actions:

Reduced Glutathione is a powerful antioxidant that aids in the detoxification of chemicals, toxic metals and radiation, supporting one of the body's most important enzymes – glutathione peroxidase of the Phase 2 liver detoxification pathway.

N-acetyl L-cysteine, a precursor of glutathione, is one of the most sophisticated and highly researched antioxidants. It is particularly important in any neurological disorder and promotes the buildup of glutathione peroxidase.

Inositol is a nonessential amino acid that stimulates adenosine triphosphate (ATP) energy release and increases muscle endurance.

Taurine is a nonessential amino acid, since it can be made from cysteine and methionine. However, it is considered a "conditionally essential" amino acid because of its extensive utilization in the body and the inability of our diets to provide adequate amounts of either taurine or its precursors. Therefore, supplementation of taurine is important. Taurine is part of the liver's Phase 2 detoxification system. It also impedes bile condensation and, thus, reduces the potential for gallstones. Taurine also renders the central nervous system less susceptible to excessive stimuli.

Selenium: See **CV Antioxidant**.

Manganese, a trace mineral, is part of the very important and ubiquitous endogenous antioxidant system called superoxide dismutase (SOD), which reduces oxidative stress and inflammation.

Zinc is a trace mineral, found in many body systems, and most notably as a component of SOD. The highest concentration of this mineral is in the prostate gland, where it exerts immune protective functions. It is necessary for the proper functioning of the senses of taste, smell and vision. Zinc enhances both immune and sexual functions, and is the mineral part of the insulin molecule.

Copper is also part of SOD and is an essential trace mineral found in high concentrations in the brain and liver. It aids in the proper balance of cholesterol, as well as in the control of anemia and arthritis.

Vitamin B₂ (Riboflavin) is one of the most important components of the mitochondrial Krebs Cycle in the energy production chain. It is the antioxidant part of the B complex.

Contents per Capsule:
Reduced Glutathione: 50 mgs.
N-Acetyl L-Cysteine: 100 mgs.
Taurine: 50 mgs.
Inosine: 50 mgs.
Selenium: 25 mgs.
Manganese: 1 mg.
Zinc: 2.5 mgs.
Copper: 0.25 mgs.
Vitamin B₂: 7.5 mgs.

Recommended Dosage: 1 to 2 capsules, 2 times a day with meals, or as directed by your integrative healthcare provider.

Hormonal Balance Natural Body Cream
Purpose: This cream has been designed to provide an adequate amount of natural progesterone to reduce female hormonal imbalances.

Therapeutic Actions: This body cream, contains three essential hormones (progesterone and small amounts of pregnenolone and DHEA). In appropriate quantities, it assists in harmonizing the body's own internal balance of these substances. The small amount of DHEA included in the formula modulates the shunting of progesterone into testosterone. Both pregnenolone and DHEA, even in small amounts, protect brain integrity.

Contents:
Progesterone, Pregnenolone and DHEA in a base of aloe vera gel, natural vitamin E and mixed tocopherols, and grapeseed extract.

Recommended Dosage: As a general balancing cream, 1 teaspoon per day, applied topically, varying sites of application. For more specific use, follow recommendations pertaining to specific conditions (see Chapters 10 and 11).

Infection Nutrients Pack

Purpose: This multi-products packet provides everything needed to fight any infection. Because it contains antiviral, antibacterial, antiyeast, antiparasitic and immune-stimulating substances, it prevents the "domino effect", in which frequent viral infections open the door to bacterial infections and make us more vulnerable to parasites and yeast overgrowth. The Infection Nutrients Pack, which contains standardized herbal remedies and high quality vitamins and minerals, has the capacity to deal with all pathogens at once. It is all my patients use during most acute infections.

Therapeutic Actions:
Multi-vitamin mineral botanical complex provides all of the B vitamins and antioxidants (A, C, E) needed for protection from the damage of the infective cascade. Also included in these tablets are botanicals that protect the liver and combat viral infections.
Malic Acid is necessary for the removal of the toxic load that distracts the immune system from inhibiting infections.
Magnesium is a bronchodilator as well as an important mineral involved in multiple cellular enzymatic functions, such as that of EFA metabolism and sugar regulation.
Standardized Echinacea is an immune-stimulating herb.
Standardized Goldenseal is an herb that reduces inflammation of the mucous membranes and has anti-infective properties. The alkaloid in goldenseal works synergistically with echinacea. *Do not use if you are pregnant.*
Standardized Ginger is an herb that not only helps in maintaining the integrity of the gastrointestinal tract (which can be

damaged during infection) but also has anti-inflammatory and antinausea properties.

Bromelain, an enzyme derived from the pineapple stem, has two major properties: anti-inflammatory and pancreatic support. Inflammation that leads to tissue damage often occurs during infections.

Acidophilus is a probiotic that supports the intestinal system, a significant site of our immune defenses, and prevents yeast overgrowth.

Zinc Lozenge: Sucking the lozenges supports the overall immune response as well as disinfects the oral cavity – the site where most airborne infections enter.

Contents per Capsule
Malic Acid: 500 mgs.
Magnesium: 161 mgs.
Standardized Echinacea: 250 mgs.
Standardized Goldenseal: 125 mgs.
Standardized Ginger: 250 mgs.
Bromelain: 5,000 mcus.
Acidophilus: 2 Billion CFUs.
Zinc Lozenge: 20 mgs.
Each packet also contains Vitamin C: 325 mgs., Vitamin D-3: 12.5 IUs., Vitamin E: 50 IUs, Vitamin B_1 (Thiamine): 12.5 mgs., Vitamin B_2 (Riboflavin): 6 mgs., Vitamin B_3 (Niacin/Niacinamide): 30 mgs., Vitamin B_6 (Pyridoxine): 6 mgs., Folate: 200 mcgs., B_{12}: 25 mcgs., Biotin 75 mcgs., Vitamin B_5 (Pantothenic Acid): 37.5 mgs., Calcium: 75 mgs., Selenium: 50 mcgs., Copper: 0.5 mgs., Manganese: 4 mgs., Chromium: 50 mcgs., Molybendum: 12.5 mcgs., Potassium: 19 mgs.

Recommended Dosage: During acute infections, take 1 packet, 3 to 4 times a day with meals, or as directed by your integrative healthcare provider. Do not take longer than 2 weeks since *echinacea's* efficacy diminishes with long-term use. ***Do not use if you are pregnant, since the packet includes goldenseal.***

Meno-Pack

Purpose: This packet contains a combination of phytoestrogens and phytoprogesterones, EFAs, minerals and vitamins, in a base of digestive enzymes. It is very effective in reducing hot flashes, sleep disturbance, mood swings, poor concentration and other symptoms associated with menopause. The best results are obtained in the early stages of the menopausal transition when symptoms are mild.

Therapeutic Actions:

Magnesium is a very important mineral necessary for bone nourishment, promoting proper alkaline blood balance (see Chapter 11: Osteoporosis) and for protecting the electrical system of the heart.

Vitamin E is a general antioxidant necessary for cardiovascular health. It has estrogenic properties, and clinical studies have demonstrated its effectiveness in reducing the severity of hot flashes.

Marine Lipid, a concentrate that includes omega 3 and omega 6 EFAs, reduces cholesterol, and keeps skin, hair and nails healthy. EFAs have beneficial phytoestrogenic properties.

Borage Oil has been used for centuries as a rich source of EFAs and is effective in reducing hot flash severity.

Pancreas Enzymes, from organically-fed cows, provide enzymatic support for digesting and absorbing the oil-based products (Vitamin E, Marine Lipid and Borage Oil).

Agnus Castus (Vitex), also known as chaste berry, stimulates LH and has progesterone-like properties. It relieves hormonal imbalance symptoms, such as depression, cramps, water retention and weight gain.

Dong Quai, a phytoestrogenic Chinese herb, relieves menopausal symptoms and promotes blood circulation.

Licorice Root is an herb known for its ability to support the adrenals. It, too, is has mild phytoestrogenic properties.

Ginseng (Siberian) enhances energy and stamina, and stabilizes moods. Ginseng also has phytoestrogenic properties and helps in the management of hot flashes.

Black Cohosh has mild phytoestrogenic properties. It is a pain reliever and also lessens the nervous system upheaval that can accompany the menopausal transition.

Wild Yam (Dioscorea) has phytoprogestenic properties. It diminishes cramps and uterine discomfort, and indirectly helps nourish bones.

Contents per Packet:
Magnesium: 100 mgs.
Vitamin E (mixed tocopherols): 400 IUs.
Marine Lipid Concentrate: 333 mgs.
Borage Oil: 62.5 mgs.
Pancreas Enzymes: 350 mgs.
Agnus Castus (Vitex): 400 mgs.
Dong Quai: 200 mgs.
Licorice Root: 500 mgs.
Siberian Ginseng: 150 mgs.
Black Cohosh: 100 mgs.
Wild Yam: 100 mgs.
Gamma Linoleic Acid: 15 mgs.
Bromelain: 100 mgs.
Passion Flower: 25 mgs.

Recommended Dosage: Depending upon the severity of symptoms, 1 to 2 packets daily with meals, or as directed by your integrative healthcare provider.

ProBiotic Plus
Purpose: This product is designed to provide the ultimate intestinal bacterial balance, boost the immune response and improve digestion and absorption of nutrients.

Therapeutic Actions: Probiotics are friendly bacteria that are destroyed by lifestyle habits, stress and antibiotics. Probiotics maintain a healthy balance in intestinal flora, and activate both local and generalized immune defenses. Designed by Dr. Corsello in conjunction with renowned probiology researcher, Dr. Kim Shahani, ProBiotic Plus, is a unique product, which combines a variety of the highest quality bacterial cultures (with the fructo-oligosaccharides (FOS) that further boosts their growth) with digestive enzymes and colostrum. The digestive enzymes improve digestion and reduce fermentation. Colostrum is a very important additional immune boosting ingredient.

Content per One-Quarter Teaspoon:
Probiotic Blend: 2 Billion CFS

DDS-TM L. Acidophilus: 40%
L. Bulgaris: 15%
L. Casei: 10%
B. Bifidum: 15%
S. Faechum: 15%
S. Thermphilus: 10%

Enzyme Blend

Protease: 8,000 HUTs.
Amylase: 2,880 Dus.
Lipase: 29 Lus.

Colostrum: 160 mgs.
FOS: 184 mgs.

Recommended Dosage: 1 to 3 teaspoons daily with any meal, or as directed by your integrative healthcare provider.

Vege-Zyme
Purpose: This vegetable-based product includes the complete array of enzymes needed for the efficient digestion of all types of food.

Therapeutic Actions: Stress impairs digestion, and causes the fermentation and accumulation of undigested toxic debris in the intestinal tract. As we age and our glands become less efficient, we often lack adequate digestive enzymes. Vege-Zyme assists in the breakdown of fats, proteins, starches and cellulose. It ensures absorption of their beneficial components while reducing unhealthy gut fermentation.

Contents per Two Capsules:
Protease: 10,500 units
Amylase: 10,500 units
Lipase: 3,000 units
Cellulase: 3,000 units
Lactase: 1,000 units
Bromelain: 1,000 mcus.
Pancreatin: 125 mgs.
Ox Bile Extract: 125 mgs.
Papain: 65 mgs.
All of the above are contained in a base of *Lactobacillus Acidophilus/Bifidus*.

Recommended Dosage: 1 to 3 capsules with every meal, or as directed by your integrative healthcare provider.

Self-Care Longevity Strategies

Petal 1: **Minimized Genetic Impact** (Chapter 3)

∞ Know your family history and compensate for it.

Petal 2: **Positivity & Spirituality** (Chapter 4)

∞ Commune with nature.

∞ Listen to elevating and relaxing music.

∞ Meditate.

∞ Pray.

∞ Affirm the positive.

∞ Stay mentally active.

∞ Stay connected with people.

∞ Find sources of happiness.

∞ Take yourself lightly.

Petal 3: **Healthful Lifestyle** (Chapter 5)

∞ Minimize and manage stress.

∞ Eat less, but eat the best.

∞ Add high quality nutritional supplements to a well-balanced diet.

∞ Keep on moving.

Petal 4: Minimized Toxins (Chapter 6)

- ∾ Purify your water.
- ∾ Purify your air.
- ∾ Consume the least toxic produce.
- ∾ Cleanse your produce.
- ∾ Consume the least toxic animal foods.
- ∾ Avoid and protect yourself from toxic metals.
- ∾ Limit X-ray exposure.
- ∾ Protect yourself from the sun.
- ∾ Limit exposure to ELF electromagnetic fields.

Petal 5: Vitalized Detox Organs (Chapter 7)

- ∾ Eat a high fiber diet.
- ∾ Tune-up your bowel.
- ∾ Nurture and protect your liver.
- ∾ Cleanse and support your kidneys.
- ∾ Sweat.
- ∾ Breathe deeply.

Petal 6: Enhanced Immunity (Chapter 8)

- ∾ Maintain a well-defended and vigilant immune system.
- ∾ Identify and desensitize allergies.
- ∾ Take quick action and fight infections naturally.

Petal 7: Balanced Hormones (Chapters 9 – 12)

- ∾ Maintain thyroid health.
- ∾ Maintain adrenal health.
- ∾ Use natural remedies to treat hormonal imbalance conditions.
- ∾ Manage perimenopause naturally.
- ∾ Maintain yourself naturally during postmenopause.

Notes

Prologue

[1] Toffler, A. (1991).
[2] For further information, contact HealthComm International, Inc. (telephone: 800-843-9660).

Chapter 1: The Ticking Clock

[1] Dilman, V. and Dean W. (in press).
[2] Dean,W. (1997).
[3] Redelmier, D.A., et al. (1998).
[4] Steinbrook, R. (1998).
[5] Harman, D. (1981).
[6] The Wear and Tear Theory was introduced in 1882 by Dr. August Weismann, a German biologist. He proposed that our cells and organs were damaged over time by overuse and abuse.
[7] Dean, W. (1988). p.24
[8] Hayflick, L. (1996).
[9] Vita, A.J., et al. (1998).
[10] Rowe, J.W. and Kahn R. (1998).

Chapter 2: Overloading Our System

[1] Seeman,T.E. (1997).
[2] Ornish, D. (1990).
[3] Rowe, J.W. and Kahn, R.L. (1998).

Chapter 3: Express the Best

[1] Bland, J.S. (1998).
[2] Abrosome, C.B., et al (1996).
[3] Nordin, C., et al. (1997).

[4] Montalescot, G, et al. (1997).

[5] Grahm, I.M. (1997).

[6] McCully, K.S. (1997).

[7] Bigaouette, J. (1997).

[8] McFadden, S.A. (1996).

[9] Steventon, G.B. (1989).

[10] Steventon, G.B. (1990).

[11] Wei, Y.H. and Dao, S.H. (1996).

[12] Mecocci, P., et al. (1994).

Chapter 4: *Stay Uplifted & Connected*

[1] Hixson, K. et. al (1998).

[2] Oman, D. and Reed, D. (1998).

[3] Berkman, L.F. and Syme, S.L. (1979).

[4] Campbell, D.G. (1997).

[5] To learn more about Steven Halpern's music, contact Steven Halpern's Inner Peace Music (telephone: 800-876-8637).

[6] Tompkins, P. and Bird, C. (1989).

[7] Updike, P. (1990).

[8] Cook, J.D. (1986).

[9] Rider, M.S. (1985).

[10] Miluk-Kolasa, B. (1994).

[11] Belli, R.(1994).

[12] For more information about Rhythm for Life, contact REMO, Inc. (telephone: 805-294-5600.).

[13] Orne-Johnson, D. (1973).

[14] Kiecolt-Glaser, J. et. al. (1986).

[15] Kiecolt-Glaser, J. et. al. (1985).

[16] Kaplan, K.H., et. al. (1993).

[17] WNET (1993).

[18] Shelly, M.W. (1972).

[19] Kabat-Zinn, J. (1992).

[20] Chopra, D. (1993), pp. 164-167.

[21] See 20.

[22] See 20.

[23] Adapted from Kahn, S. (1996). *The Nurse's Meditative Journal* provides guidance on a variety of meditation and journaling techniques, and on how to combine the two practices. It includes a 52-week journal to chronicle your journey of self-discovery.

[24] I first met Dr. Larry Dossey and his wife, Barbara, in 1992 while working on the formation of the Office of Alternative Medicine (OAM).

[25] Dossey, L. (1996).

[26] Rowe, J.W. and Kahn, R.L. (1998). See pps. 125-142.

[27] Cohen, S. et. al. (1997)

[28] Borysenko, J. (1993).

[29] Rowe, J.W. and Kahn, R.L. (1998). See pps.152-166.

[30] ReutersHealth/MedNews. (1997).

[31] ReutersHealth/MedNews. (1998).

[32] Luks, A. and Payne, P. (1991).

[33] Cousins, N. (1979).

Chapter 5: *Take Charge*

[1] This is the nutrient distribution proposed by nutritionist Dr. Barry Sears. For more information, refer to Sears, B. and Lawren, B. (1995).

[2] At our Centers, we use various protein powder combinations from the Metagenics product line. All Metagenics protein blends are thoroughly researched and medically tested for suitability in various applications. The two products we use most frequently for our patients are UltraClear PLUS, which contains nutritional support for Phase 1 and Phase 2 detoxification pathways, and UltraiInflamX, which contains nutritional and herbal anti-inflammatory support for chronic inflammatory conditions. Both products are based on rice protein concentrate, have a low allergy potential, and are nutritionally fortified. They may be obtained from licensed healthcare practitioners. We also frequently use UltraMeal, a soy-based product providing 17 milligrams of soy isoflavones

per serving, which we have found to be helpful in modulating some menopausal symptoms. UtraMeal is available from healthcare practitioners and can also be found in pharmacies, labeled as MetaPharma Protein and Nutrient Complex. Unipro's Perfect Protein, another Metagenics quality protein powder, is available in many health food stores and is sold directly to consumers by Ethical Nutrients (telephone: 800-877-1704).

3 To learn more about this complicated and evolving science, I recommend that you review Foster-Powell, I and Miller, J.B. (1995).

4 If you cannot locate stevia in your local area, contact Body Ecology Products (telephone: 800-982-7431.)

5 D'Adamo, P. (1997).

6 Ornish, D. (1990).

7 For the last couple of years, I have been using NutriCheck, a self-administered questionnaire that alerts us to potential nutritional deficiencies and subclinical maladies, such as hypoglycemia or dysbiosis. This tool is the result of many years of research by nutritionist and medical researcher, Eleanor Barrager, who is currently an invaluable assistant to Dr. Jeffrey Bland. The colorful graph and reader-friendly explanations have been very useful to my patients as well. For more information, contact NutriCheck USA (telephone: 800-771-7926).

7 I recently observed a low uric acid level in a patient of mine who had high levels of antimitochondrial antibodies, and who subsequently developed breast cancer.

9 Diplock, A.T. (1991).

10 Mayer-Davis, E.J. (1998).

11 Goodyear, L.J. and Kahn, B.B. (1998)

12 Sherrill, D.L., et al. (1998).

13 Gregg, E.W., et al. (1998).

14 Kujala, U., et al. (1998).

15 Pollock, M., et al. (1998)

Chapter 6: *Protect Yourself*

[1] Newton, .J and Maugh II, T. (1998).

[2] National Institutes of Health/National Cancer Institute (1997).

[3] Padungtod, C., et al. (1998).

[4] For more information, contact the National Sanitation Foundation (NSF) International (telephone: 313-769-8010.

[5] Rylander, R, et.al. (1991).

[6] Marier, J.R. (1978).

[7] Murray, M. (1996), pp. 159-175.

[8] United States Environmental Protection Agency, Office of Air & Radiation, Office of Air Quality Planning & Standards (1997).

[9] Speiser, R. (1998).

[10] Buckalew, L.W. and Rizuto, A. (1982).

[11] Morton, L.L. and Kershner, J.R. (1987).

[12] Morton. L.L. and Kershner, J.R. (1984).

[13] Krueger, A.P. and Reed, E.J. (1976).

[14] Terman, M. and Terman, J.S. (1995).

[15] Wein Products, Inc. (telephone: 213-749-6049).

[16] Smith, B.L. (1993).

[17] A liquid grapefruit seed extract is manufactured by NutriBiotic, which is commonly available in health food stores. A powdered capsusle form, ParaMicrocidin, which has been clinically demonstrated to be an effective ingested antimicrobial agent, is available from Allergy Research Group (telephone: 800-782-4274).

[18] Takabe, K., et al. (1998).

[19] Stohs, S.J. and Bagchi, D. (1995).

[20] Hair is a excretory tissue that accumulates and eliminates excessive toxins in the blood. Toxic metals are not necessarily in circulation unless challenged by chelation therapy. The continuous consumption of chelating foods and strong support of the Phase 2 hepatic detoxification process promotes removal of toxic byproducts of all sorts. At our

Centers, we use hair analysis as one initial diagnostic indication of excessive metal toxins, and to monitor the excretion of toxic metals during the course of chelation therapy and other intensive detoxification programs. Hair level of toxins initially increases and then eventually begins to go down as the body eliminates metals and other toxic substances.

[21] Lindgren, K., et al. (1999).

[22] ReutersHealth/MedNews.(1998, July 10).

[23] Supplementing pregnant women with large amounts of calcium (not from animal sources, which have a higher risk of contamination) will diminish the maternal osteoblastic activity. This, in turn, reduces the release of endogenous toxic reserves.

[24] Goyer, R.A. (1996).

[25] Centers for Disease Control. (1998).

[26] Charbonneau, J.E. (1997).

[27] Abercrombie, D.E. and Fowler, R.C. (1997).

[28] Brotons, J.A., et al. (1995).

[29] Sandborgh-Englund, G. (1998).

[30] Drasch, G., et al. (1998).

[31] After the Versonate challenge (see Chapter 14, note 10).

[32] Eberlein-Konig, B., et al. (1998)

[33] Sunscreens greater than 8 block the ultraviolet light that convert precursors of vitamin D into the form the body needs. If you use a sunscreen with a higher SPF, be sure to take 400 international units of vitamin D.

[34] Personal conversation, August 15, 1998. For additional information, contact the Marie Badin Institute (telephone: 516-427-6484).

[35] Becker, R.O. and Selden, G. (1985).

[36] Feychting, M and Ahlbom, A. (1995).

[37] Coogan, P. (1996).

[38] Liburdy, R.P., et al. (1993).

[39] National Institute of Health/National Cancer Institute. (1997).

[40] Second World Congress for Electricity and Magnetism in Biology and Medicine. (1997).

[41] ReutersHealth/MedNews. (1998, May 19).

[42] Braune, S., et al. (1998).

Chapter 7: *Tune-Up Your Detox Organs*

[1] Gebbers, J.O. and Laissue, J.A. (1989).

[2] Katz, J.P., et al. (1998).

[3] Nakla,M.L., et al. (1998).

[4] Doig, C.J., et al. (1998).

[5] See Kamen, B. (1997) for a user-friendly discussion of fiber.

[6] Cara, L, et al (1992)

[7] Anderson, J., et al. (1994).

[8] Crook, W.G. (1997).

[9] We need both omega-3 and omega-6 EFAs in our diet in a healthy balance. The typical Western diet (high in animal fat) has an overabundance of omega-6 and inadequate omega-3. Omega-6 can become arachidonic acid, which is a precursor of pro-inflammatory prostaglandins (PG2s), while omega-3 is a precursor of anti-inflammatory prostaglandins (PG1s and PG3s). Prostaglandins are hormone-like substances involved in a variety of physiological functions. A healthy ratio of anti-inflammatory omega-3 to pro-inflammatory omega-6 is 6:4.

[10] Thompson, L. U. (1991).

[11] Murray, M. (1996), pp. 245-268.

[12] Aviram, M. and Elias, K. (1993).

[13] Visioli, F., et al. (1998)

[14] La Vecchia, C. (1995).

[15] Trichopoulou, A., et al. (1995).

[16] Components of garlic are known to inhibit cholesterol 7 alpha hydroxylase, which is a rate-limiting enzyme in cholesterol synthesis. Garlic can enhance fibrinolytic activity, act as an anticoagulant, and has antioxidant effects.

[17] Bernet-Camard, M.F., et al. (1997).

[18] Binita, R. and Khetarpaul, N. (1997).

[19] Mital, B.K. and Garg, S.K. (1995).

[20] Rangavajhyala, N., et al. (1997).

[21] Schiffrin, E.J., et al. (1995).

[22] Bengmark, S. (1998).

[23] Nitsch, A. and Nitsch, F.P. (1998).

[24] Clements, M.L., et al. (1983).

[25] Melillo, K.D. (1998).

[26] Bragg Liquid Aminos is a concentrated amino acid product derived from vegetable sources. It is stocked by most health food stores.

[27] FitzGerald, G.A. (1998).

[28] Both the brain and the skin come from the same embryonic tissue, the ectoderm. Many stressors that affect the brain also manifest signs and symptoms in the skin, such as lipofuscin and liver spots. Eczema, a multifactorial skin disease, is, in my clinical experience, always aggravated by emotional stress.

[29] Packer, L. (1995).

[30] Conducted by Yankelovich Partners for the Nutrition Information Center at the New York Hospital-Cornell Medical Center and the International Bottled Water Association, June 1998.

[31] Rodale Press. (1991).

[32] The Marie Badin Institute (telephone: 516-427-6484).

[34] Cheng, S. (1989).

Chapter 8: *Defend Yourself*

[1] Weinberg, K. and Parkman, R. (1995).

[2] Hechter, O., et al. (1997).

[3] Wyatt, J., et al. (1993).

[4] Lapcevic, J. (1997).

[5] Developed by Dr. Joseph B. Miller of Mobile, AL, this technique uses the maximum tolerated intradermal concentration of allergens, in contrast to mainstream allergy skin testing, which provides no information concerning the precise dosage needed for each individual allergen. Unlike mainstream procedures, optimal-dose injections provide protec-

tion from and relief of the patient's actual symptoms. Typically, improvement occurs within 1 to 3 weeks with optimal-dose immunotherapy.

[6] Wall Street Journal Interactive. (1998, May 14).

[7] Mattman, L. (1993).

[8] Willatts, P., et al. (1998).

[9] Available from Klabin Marketing (telephone: 800-933-9440).

[10] See note 4.

[11] Allison, M.C. (1992).

[12] Witsell, D.L., et al. (1995).

Chapter 9: *The Hormonal Symphony*

[1] Rozenberg, S, et al. (1988).

[2] Cleare, A.J., et al. (1995).

[3] Hechter, O. (1997).

[4] Hauser, P., et al. (1998).

[5] Baker, J.R. (1997).

[6] Baker, J.R. (1997).

[7] Murray, M., p. 411

[8] Fleet, J.C. and Mayer, J. (1997).

[9] Stohs, S.J. and Bagchi, D. (1995).

[10] Gaitan, E, et al. (1967).

[11] Brouwer, A., et al. (1998).

[12] The blood-brain (bb) barrier is an innate system of defense that protects the brain from toxic substances and infections. The bb barrier, however, can be penetrated on occasion, such as when it is damaged by inflammatory processes caused by infective agents (viruses, bacteria, etc.). It can also be penetrated by disguised toxins bound to a normally acceptable substance. This is what happens when pentachlorophenol piggybacks on thyroid hormone.

[13] Brouwer, A., et al. (1998).

[14] Hauser, P., et al. (1998).

[15] Lemcke, D.P. and Pattison, J. (1995), p. 149.

[16] Lee, J. R.(1996), pp. 98,145-149.

[17] Martin, R. (1997), pp. 66-67.

[18] The test for TRH, the hypothalamic hormone that stimulates the pituitary to produce TSH, which, in turn, elicits the production of thyroid hormones, is a far better laboratory measure of thyroid function than the TSH Test. It is still the lab test of choice of endocrinologists, but as it is a "challenge" test that takes more time, skill and costs more, it is seldom used. The patient's TSH level is initially measured and then an injection of synthetic TRH is given. The TSH level is again measured 25 minutes later. Unlike the standard tests, the TRH Test is able to determine how well the pathway from the hypothalamus to the pituitary gland is functioning. However, even this more sophisticated test can fail to identify early thyroid malfunctions because the problem might be at the tissue level, where conversion of T_4 into T_3 and binding takes place.

[19] Murray, M. (1996), p. 441.

[20] The biochemistry of the stress response involves four fundamental hormones: CRH from the hypothalamus, adrenaline (norepinephrine [NE] from the locus ceruleus in the pons and epinephrine [EP] from the adrenal medulla), ACTH from the pituitary gland, and the corticoadrenal hormones. As various stimuli reach the hypothalamus from the five senses, CRH is released and goes both to the locus ceruleus for NE production and to the pituitary for ACTH production. The CRH-NE feedback is a circular one in which the release of NE keeps on stimulating more CRH production to perpetuate the "fight or flight" response. At the same time, through the splanchnic nerve, the adrenal medulla EP secretion is activated. The ACTH stimulation will continue as long as the CRH secretion is activated, and the three layers of the adrenal cortex will continue to be stimulated. Failure to terminate the feedback between the locus ceruleus and hypothalamic CRH secretion is responsible for the chronic stress response. Hypercortosolism is the most damaging end product.

[21] Born, J. et al. (1999).

[22] Chronic stress and high levels of cortisol ultimately damage the hippocampal cortisol receptors. These receptors are, in essence, a mid-station designed to keep high levels of cortisol in check. When the hippocampal receptors are damaged, the ability of the hypothalamus to counteract and counter-regulate the effect of chronic stress is diminished.

[23] Oelkers, W. (1996).

[24] Dilman, V. and Ward, D. (in press).

[25] Tintera, J.W. (1955).

[26] *1999 Physician's Desk Reference* (1998), p.1498.

Chapter10: *Strictly Female*

[1] The level of estrogen needed to trigger this response varies from woman to woman. Too little will not do and too much, such as the ingestion of large amounts of xenoestrogens (estrogens foreign to the body), can inhibit LH secretion.

[2] Lee, J.R. (1996), p. 100.

[3] Wright, J.V. and Morgenthaler, J. (1997).

[4] Lee, J.R. (1996).

[5] Dalton, K. (1977).

[6] Lee, J.R. (1993).

[7] See also Kamen, B. (1997) for a user-friendly discussion of progesterone, estrogen, hormone replacement therapy and other strategies for dealing with PMS, menopause and osteoporosis.

[8] Brotons, J.A., et al. (1995)

[9] Nagel, S.C., et al. (1997).

[10] Shekhar, P.V., et al. (1997).

[11] Lee, J.R. (1996), p. 59.

[12] Barrinton, L.A., et al. (1992).

[13] Peeters, P.H., et al. (1995).

[14] Vihko, R. and Apter, D. (1984).

[15] Progestins lead to signs and symptoms of unopposed estro-

gen because of their inability to effectively bind to cell receptors. When they are given in conjunction with pharmaceutical estrogen they are incapable of opposing its proliferative effect on endometrial and breast tissues. This is responsible for the high incidence of cancer in women treated with conventional hormonal replacement therapy.

[15] I have received exceptional service from Wellness Health & Pharmaceuticals (telephone: 800-227-2627).

[16] Smith, S. and Schiff, I. (1989).

[17] Brush, M.G., et al. (1984).

[17] Budoff, P.W. (1983).

[19] There are three essential fatty acid (EFA) families. They are essential to our survival, yet our bodies cannot produce them and must obtain them from external food sources. The three essential EFA families are linoleic, linolenic and arachidonic. EFAs, such as those found in flaxseed and fish oils, are precursors of the anti-inflammatory prostaglandins – PG3s. The PG3 series are direct antagonists of the PG2 series and harmonize their effect. The body needs both types of prostaglandins. The average American diet, however, contains an overabundance of PG2 precursors (arachidonic acids), found not only in animal fats but also in some other foods, including peanuts, walnuts and corn oil.

[20] Massaging the cream into the breasts can sometimes increase breast tenderness.

[21] GABA is a neuroregulator that diminishes neuronal firing and is used as an antiepileptic under various pharmaceutical proprietary names. I prescribe 500 milligrams to be taken during the day to reduce aggressive behavior and 1,000 to 1,500 milligrams at night to facilitate sleep. GABA stimulates the deepest stage of sleep and doubles the amount of growth hormone released by the body. Neuroactive amino acids, such as GABA, require a little insulin to penetrate the brain barrier. They are more effective with a concomitant ingestion of an acceptable carbohydrate, such as a small apple. As GABA cannot compete with

other amino acids for neuronal binding, it needs to be taken separately from others.

[22] DeMarco, C. (1994).

[23] Telephone and fax communication with Dr. Carolyn DeMarco, February 19, 1999. See also DeMarco, C. (1994).

[24] Ghent, W.R., et al. (1993).

[25] MacFarlane, J.K. (1993).

[26] Sea-Adine, derived from seaweed, is a quality tri-iodine. It is available from Heritage Products (telephone: 800-726-2232).

[27] Wobenzyme N contains pancreatin, trypsin, chymotrypsin, bromelain, papain and rutosid. It is available in many health food stores and from Marlyn Healthcare Group (telephone: 800-4-MARLYN).

[28] During my many years of experience with desperate cases, I have invariably found endometriosis patients to have estrogen dominance and a severely dysbiotic gut. They typically have a whole host of hormonal imbalances, including very low DHEA. Most early stage hormones, such as pregnenolone and also DHEA, turn into estrogen and aggravate the condition. This "preferential estrogenic shunt" might be due to an acquired or inborn defect in the hepatic conjugation process, more specifically in the sulfation pathway. I always check the prolactin level in these patients, as it is usually elevated. In my clinical experience, mildly elevated prolactin is seldom a sign of pituitary adenoma. Researchers have recently confirmed it as a sign of a challenged immune system (Kelly, K.W., et al.,1992). Patients with severe endometriosis do best with prompt attention to the dysbiosis, which, untreated, increases estrogen dominance. Treatment with progesterone and testosterone – both antiestrogenic in their actions, is also beneficial. In some cases, I have had to resort to progesterone rectal suppositories, at times combined with testosterone. I routinely recommend nightly sublingual melatonin for its antiestrogenic and immune-enhancing properties.

Chapter 11: *Beyond Babies*

[1] A little progesterone is found in well-working adrenal glands.

[2] Rako, S. (1996).

[3] Rexrode, K.M., et al. (1998).

[4] Lee, J.R. (1996), pp. 45-147.

[5] Lemcke, D.P., et al. (1995), p. 149.

[6] Hunt, C.M., et al. (1992).

[7] Kuiper, G.G., et al. (1998).

[8] Lock, M. (1995).

[9] Anderson, J.W., et al. (1995).

[10] Messina, M.J., et. al. (1994).

[11] Wang, D. and Kurzer, M.S. (1996).

[12] Erdman, J.W., Jr. (1995).

[13] Seraino, S. (1992).

[14] Bierenbaum, M.L. (1993).

[15] Messina, J.J. (1996).

[16] Baum, J.A., et al. (1998).

[17] Seidl, M.M. and Stewart, D.E. (1998).

[18] Love, S. (1997), p. 200.

[19] They rob the body of magnesium, a vascular stabilizer, to use for their metabolism into glucose-6-phosphate, an obligatory metabolic stop on their way to energy degradation.

[20] Notelovitz, M. and Tonnessen, D. (1993).

[21] Bravo, G. (1996).

[22] Murray, M. (1996), pp. 356-357.

[23] Carper, J. (1997), p. 66.

[24] Murray, M. (1996), p. 357.

[25] Carper, J. (1997), pp. 62-63.

[26] Stabilium 200 may be ordered from the Allergy Research Group (telephone: 800-782-4274).

[27] Popper, C.W. (1993).

[28] Dorman, T., et al. (1995).

[29] Klatz, R. M. (1999).

[30] While estrogen promotes proliferation of breast tissue and

the endometrial lining, progesterone modulates this process. Uncontrolled proliferation of breast tissue and the endometrium creates the environment for cancer. Women given only Premarin (estrogen) for menopausal management have an increased incidence of breast and endometrial cancer. Nature has created a wonderful system of checks and balances (estrogen and progesterone) to protect us. When we tamper with the wisdom of this design, we create problems for ourselves.

[31] Raskin, M.A., et al. (1994).

[32] Barrett-Connor, E. and Goodman-Gruen, D. (1995).

[33] Colditz, G.A. (1990).

[34] Grady, D., et al. (1995).

[35] Tall, thin light-skinned women have a genetically programmed higher propensity for osteoporosis. Diabetics, both men and women, also have a higher osteoporosis risk.

[36] Morter M.T. and Panfili, A. (1998).

[37] Heany, R.P. (1993).

[38] Like all other conditions, osteoporosis is not just a calcium deficiency sysndrome. I once read a study that reported that traditional women from India had no signs of osteoporosis with a 350 milligram calcium intake, solely from food.

[39] Epstein, O., et al. (1982).

[40] Feskanich, D., et al. (1999).

[41] Civitelli, M., et al. (1992).

[42] In contrast to the generalized action of isoflavones, Ipriflavone binds specifically to bones.

[43] Agnusdei, D., et. al (1997).

[44] Agnusdei, D. and Bufalino, L. (1997).

[45] Lee, J. R. (1996).

[46] Raisz, L. and Prestwood, K. (1998).

[47] Prior, J.C. (1990).

[48] Wright, J.V. and Morgenthaler, J. (1997)

[49] Lee, J. (1996), pp. 159-167.

[50] To be effective, natural progesterone creams need to contain 400 milligrams to 600 milligrams of progesterone per

ounce. Companies which produce creams in the correct concentration include Transitions for Health (telephone: 800-648-8211), Broadmoor Labs, Inc. (telephone: 800-822-3712) and HM Enterprises (telephone: 800-742-4773). For a more detailed list, see Lee, J. R. (1996), pp. 334-335. The CC Hormonal Balance Natural Body Cream I have developed contains the appropriate concentration of progesterone. The small amount of DHEA included in the formula modulates the shunting of progesterone into testosterone, while both that hormone. and the small amount of included pregnenolone protect brain integrity. Personally, I apply it to my face and neck 3 days a week and to other parts of my body the remaining days.

Chapter 12: *The Magical Anti-Aging Hormones*

[1] McCraty, R., et al. (1998).

[2] Straub, R.H., et al. (1998).

[3] Bellino, F.L., et al, eds. (1995).

[4] Chopra, D. (1993), pp. 164-167.

[5] Morales, A.J., et al. (1994).

[6] Labrie, F. (1997).

[7] Bellino, F.L., et al, eds. (1995).

[8] Rubino, S., et al. (1998).

[9] The effect on the bones is due mostly to the androgens, while the effect on the vagina is due to the transformation of DHEA into estrogen in the vaginal mucosa.

[10] Labrie, F. (1997).

[11] Couillard, S., et al. (1998).

[12] Stahl, F., et al. (1992).

[13] Ivanovic, S., et al. (1990).

[14] Kalimi, M. and Regelson, W., (1990).

[15] Both sexes, however, have small amounts of nongender-related hormones.

[16] Casson, P.K., et al (1993).

[17] Whiteside, T.L. and Herberman, R.B. (1993).

[18] Straub, R.H., et al. (1998).

[19] ReutersHealth/MedNews. (1996).

[20] Hechter, O., et al. (1997).

[21] Kalimi, M. and Regelson, W. (1990).

[22] Cleary, M.P. (1991).

[23] Berdanier, C.D., et al. (1993).

[24] Buffington, C.a., et al. (1993).

[25] Svec F, et al. (1995).

[26] Jesse, R.L., et al. (1995).

[27] Morrola, J.F. and Yen, S.S.C. (1990).

[28] Okamoto, K. (1998).

[29] Herbert, J. (1998).

[30] Kalmijn, S., et al. (1998).

[31] Saliva tests are a good way of measuring free, active forms of hormones, especially gonadal and adrenal hormones. In New York, as of now, we are prohibited by law from utilizing saliva and urinary tests for hormones and must rely solely on blood measurements.

[32] DHEA is secreted by the adrenal cortex as DHEA Sulfate (DHEA-S). To be biologically active, it needs to be enzymatically desulfated, since the sulfated form is unable to cross the cell membrane. Once inside the cell, it again takes on the sulfated form. To get a complete picture of the body's DHEA status and its enzymatic conversion ability, both DHEA-S and total DHEA should be measured.

[33] Svec, F. and Porter, J.R. (1998).

[34] MacIntosh, A. (1996).

[35] Regestein, Q.R. and Pavola, M. (1995).

[36] Garfinkel, D., et al. (1995).

[37] A high level of circulating melatonin promotes the urge to sleep on cloudy days and is associated with Seasonal Affective Disorder (SAD).

[38] Pierpaoli, W. and Maestroni, G. (1987).

[39] Maestroni, G., et al. (1988).

[40] Tamarkin, L., et al. (1982).

[41] El-Domeiri, A. and Das Gupta, T.K. (1973).

[42] Das Gupta, T.K. and Terz, J. (1967).

[43] Das Gupta, T.K. (1968).

[44] Dilman, V. and Dean, W. (in press).

[45] Reiter, R.J. (1996).

[46] In most cases, the level of IGF-1 parallels the level of GH. In approximately 20% of the population, this is not the case. I think we need to develop more precise testing to account for these variables.

[47] Shalet, S.M. (1998).

[48] Kelley, K.W., et al. (1992).

[49] Researchers have noted that during stressful periods both GH and prolactin secretion increases. Prolactin, the hormone responsible for milk production, and GH both have immune-modulating properties. During chronic stress, both hormones are produced by circulating lymphocytes, although their primary production site is the pituitary gland. Their levels are increased, the researchers claim, to counteract the immune suppressive effect of glucocorticoids. See Kelley, K.W., et al. (1992).

[50] Researchers have reported that IGF-1 is capable of reducing tumor metastases by stimulating NK defenses (see Kelley, K.W., et al. [1992]). Until further research is available, I would not use GH to reduce tumor metastases, even if the primary lesion has been surgically removed. Most cancer patients have depleted systems, and the lymphocyte stimulation by GH might be insufficient to oppose metastatic growth.

[51] Rudman, D., et al. (1990).

[52] Baum, H.B., et al. (1996).

[53] Papadakis, M.A., et al (1996).

[54] Thompson, J.L., et al (1998).

[55] Baum, H.B., et al. (1996).

[56] Amato, G., et al. (1996).

[57] Moses, A.C., et al. (1996).

[58] Fazio, S., et al. (1996).

[59] Yang, R. et al. (1995).

[60] Kann, P. (1996).

[61] Alba-Roth, J., et al. (1988).

[62] Isidor, A., et al. (1981).

[63] Harp, J.B., et al. (1991)

[64] Cynober, L. (1994).

[65] Murray, R., et al. (1995).

[66] Roemnich, J.N. and Rogol, A.D. (1997).

[67] Holmes, S. and Shalet, S. (1995).

[68] The product I have been using is LifeSpan1. More information can be obtained from Robert Dimple (telephone: 518-383-5410).

Chapter 13: *When Self-Care Is Not Enough*

[1] Eisenberg, D.M., et al. (1998).

[2] American Academy of Anti-Aging Medicine
1341 W. Fullerton, Suite 111
Chicago, IL 60614
773-528-4333

American Academy of Medical Acupuncture
5820 Wilshire Blvd., Ste. 500
Los Angeles, CA 90036
323-937-5514

American Association of Naturopathic Physicians
2366 Eastlake Ave., Ste. 322
Seattle, WA 98102
206-328-8510

American Chiropractic Association
1701 Clarendon Blvd.
Arlington, VA 22201
703-276-8800

American College for Advancement in Medicine
23121 Verdugo Dr., Ste 204
Laguna Hills, CA 92653
800-532-3688

American Foundation for Alternative Health Care
25 Landfield Ave.
Monticello, NY 12701
914-794-8181

American Holistic Health Association
P.O. Box 17400
Anaheim, CA 92817
714-779-6152

American Osteopathic Association
142 E. Ontario St.
Chicago, IL 60611-2864
312-380-5800

Foundation for the Advancement of Innovative Medicine
100 Airport Executive Park, Ste. 105
Nanuet, NY 10954
914-371-3246

[3] I also dream of the day when antioxidant infusions are administered at the site of an accident to avoid a rapid cascade of free radicals, and when a patient is in coma. Reperfusion damage occurs during intensive administration of oxygen or when a patient comes out of coma. Coma is nature's way of shutting down brain metabolism as much as possible to diminish lipid peroxidation. While oxygen can be helpful, one also needs to simultaneously administer antioxidants and other protective substances to stop the progression of the free radical cascade. If this was done, comas would be much shorter and the consequences of

free radical pathology much more limited. This knowledge is available in journals, such as *Free Radical Pathology Magazine*. Why this practice has not been routinely instituted in hospitals escapes me.

[4] Wobenzym N is available in many health food stores and can be ordered directly from Marlyn Health Care Group (telephone) 800-4MARLYN.

Chapter 14: *Wellness & Rejuvenation*

[1] Stohs, S.J. and Bagchi, D. (1995).
[2] Tanner, C.M., et al. (1999).
[3] Olszewer, E., et al. (1988).
[4] Rudolph, C.J. (1991).
[5] Chappell, L.T. and Stahl, J.P. (1993).
[6] Hancke, C. and Flytlie, K. (1993).
[7] Rudolph, C.J., et al. (1988).
[8] Baron, P., et al. (1989).
[9] Cranton, E.M. and Frackelton, J.P. (1998).
[10] Blumer, W. and Cranton, E.M. (1989).
[11] Carper, J. (1998), pp. 26-27.
[12] Toxic metals are generally tightly bound to storing sites. To dislodge them, we use a 3-hour infusion, called Versonate, which contains EDTA, calcium and many antioxidants. The bladder is emptied before the infusion and urine is collected for exactly 24 hours. Analysis of the urine by a specialized laboratory gives the levels of the most common stored toxic metals. We compare this acute challenge with chronic accumulation of toxic metals that are identifiable in the hair. Very often, the hair toxic load goes up, while the collected urine shows a decrease of toxic burden. The decrease varies with subsequent Versonates, since new dislodged metals might appear in the blood and promptly be bound and removed by the EDTA. For example, the first Versonate might show a high level of aluminum, in my clinical experience, the most ubiquitous of all toxic metals. A few months

later, the patient may show unexpectedly high levels of cadmium, mercury, lead or other metals. When we treat patients with high levels of toxic metals, we might run three to four Versonates, one every ten chelation treatments, to evaluate toxic metal burden removal.

[13] Wade, N. (1998).

[14] ReutersHealth/MedNews. (1998).

[15] Bradford, R.W., et al. (1986).

[16] Bradford, R.W., et al. (1986).

[17] I refer patients to American Biologic Institute, 1180 Walnut Avenue, Chula Vista, CA (telephone: 800-227-4458) and to The Four Seasons Medical Center and Clinic, P.O. Box 244, 83700 Rottach-Egern, Germany (telephone: 011-49-8022-24041).

Bibliography

1999 Physician's Desk Reference. (53rd ed.). (1998).   Montvale, NJ: Medical Economics.

Abercrombie, D.E. and Fowler, R.C. (1997). "Possible Aluminum Content of Canned Drinks." *Toxicology and Individual Health,* 13(5), 649-654.

Abrosome C.B., et al. (1996). "Cigarette Smoking, N-Acetyltransferase 2 Genetic Polymorphisms, and Breast Cancer Risk. *Journal of the American Medical Association,* 276(18), 1494-1501.

Agnusdei, D. and Bufalino, L. (1997). "Efficacy of Ipriflavone in Established Osteoporosis and Long-Term Safety." *Calcified Tissue International,* 61, Suppl 1, S23-27.

Agnusdei, D., et al. (1997). "A Double Blind, Placebo-Controlled Trial of Ipriflavone for Prevention of Postmenopausal Spinal Bone Loss." *Calcified Tissue International,* 2,142-147.

Alba-Roth, J., et al. (1988). "Arginine Stimulates Growth Hormone Secretion by Suppressing Endogenous Somatostatin Secretion." *Journal of Clinical Endocrinology and Metabolism,* 67(6), 1186-1189.

Allison, MC et al. (1992). "Gastrointestinal Damage Associated with the Use of Nonsteroidal Anti-Inflammatory Drugs." *New England Journal of Medicine,* 327 (11), 794.

Amato, G., et al. (1996). "Low Dose Recombinant Human Growth Hormone Normalizes Bone Metabolism and Cortical Bone Density and Improves Trabecular Bone Density in Growth Hormone Deficient Adults without Causing Adverse Effects." *Clinical Endocrinology,* 45(1), 27-32.

Anderson, J., et al. (1994) "Health Benefits and Practical Aspects of High-Fiber Diets." *American Journal of Clinical Nutrition,* 59(Suppl.), 124S-127S.

Anderson, J.W. et al. (1995). "Meta Analysis of the Effects of Soy Protein Intake on Serum Lipids." *New England Journal of Medicine,* 333, 276-282.

Avriam, M. and Elias, K. (1993). "Dietary Olive Oil Reduces Low-Density Lipoprotein Uptake by Macrophages and Decreases the Susceptibility of the Lipoprotein to Undergo Lipid Peroxidation." *Annals of Nutrition Metabolism,* 37, 75-84.

Baker, J. R. (1997)."Autoimmune Endocrine Disease." *Journal of the American Medical Association*, 278(22), 1931-1937.

Baron, P., et al. (1989). "A Literature Review of Concentrations of Arsenic, Lead, Cadmium and Mercury in Body Fluids and Tissues for Establishing Normal Values and Detection of Body Burden: Lead – Summary of Average Values for As, Cd, Hg and Literature References." *Zentralblatt fur Hygiene and Umweltmedizin*, 3-4, 195-239.

Barrett-Connor, E. and Goodman-Gruen, D. (1995). "Prospective Study of Endogenous Sex Hormones and Fatal Cardiovascular Disease in Postmenopausal Women." *British Medical Journal*, 311,1193-1196.

Barrinton L.A., et al. (1992). "Reproductive, Menstrual and Medical Risk Factors for Endometrial Cancer: Results From a Case-Control Study." *American Journal of Obstetrics and Gynecology*, 167(5), 1317-1325.

Baum, J.A., et al. (1998). "Long-Term Intake of Soy Protein Improves Blood Lipid Profiles and Increases Mononuclear Cell Low-Density-Lipoprotein Receptor Messenger RNA in Hypercholesterolemic, Postmenopausal Women." *American Journal of Clinical Nutrition*, 68, 545-551.

Baum, H.B., et al. (1996). "Effects of Physiologic Growth Hormone Therapy on Bone Density and Body Composition in Patients with Adult-Onset Growth Hormone Deficiency: A Randomized, Placebo-Controlled Trial." *Annals of Internal Medicine*, 125(11), 883-890.

Becker, R.O. and Selden, G. (1985). *The Body Electric: Electromagnetism and the Foundation of Life*. New York: William Morrow and Company.

Belli, R. (1994, July). "The Expanding Market for Percussion Products." *Think Drums*, Valencia, CA: REMO, Inc.

Bellino, F.L., et al. (Eds.). (1995). "Dehydroepiandrosterone (DHEA) and Aging." *Annals of the New York Academy of Sciences*, 774, 1-350.

Bengmark, S. (1998). "Probiotic Bacteria and the Gastrointestinal Tract." *Clinical Pearl News*, 8(10),160-163.

Berdanier, C.D. (1993). "Is Dehydroepidandrosterone an Antiobesity Agent?" *Federation of American Societies for Experimental*

Biology Journal, 7(5), 414-419.

Berkman, L.F. and Syme, S.L. (1979). "Social Networks, Host Resistance and Mortality: A Nine Year Follow-Up Study of Alameda County Residents. *American Journal of Epidemiology*. 115(5), 684-694.

Berndanier, D.D., et al. (1993). "Is Dehydroepiandrosterone an Antiobesity Agent?" *Federation of American Societies for Experimental Biology*, 7(5), 414-419.

Bernet-Camard, M.F., et al. (1997). "The Human Lactobacillus Acidophilus Strain LA1 Secretes a Nonbacteriocin Antibacterial Substance(s) Active in Vitro and in Vivo." *Applied Environmental Microbiology*, 63(7), 2727-2753.

Bierenbaum, M.L. (1993). "Reducing Atherogenic Risk in Hyperlipemic Humans with Flaxseed Supplementation: A Preliminary Report." *Journal of the American College of Nutrition*, 12(5), 501-504.

Bigaouette H.V. (1997). "Call for Endorsement of a Petition to the Food and Drug Administration to Always Add Vitamin B-12 to Any Folate Fortification or Supplement. *American Journal of Clinical Nutrition*, 277(10), 818-821.

Binita, R. and Khetarpaul, N. (1997). "Probiotic Fermentation: Effect on Antinutrients and Digestibility of Starch and Protein of Indigenously Developed Food Mixture." *Nutritional Health*, 11(3), 139-147.

Bland, J.S. (1998). "The Use of Complementary Medicine for Healthy Aging." *Alternative Therapies*, 4(4).

Blumer, W. and Cranton, E.M. (1989). "Ninety Percent Reduction in Cancer Mortality After Chelation Therapy with EDTA." *Journal of Advancement in Medicine*, 2(1-2), 183-188. Available from the American College for Advancement in Medicine (see Chapter 13, Note 2).

Born, J., et al. (1999). "Timing the End of Nocturnal Sleep." *Nature*, 397(6714), 29-30.

Borysenko, J. (1993). *Fire in the Soul: A New Psychology of Spiritual Optimism*. New York: Warner.

Bradford, R.W., et al. (1986). *Biochemical Basis of Live Cell Therapy*. Chula Vista, CA: Bradford Foundation.

Braune, S., et al. (1998). "Resting Blood Pressure Increases During Exposure to a Radio-Frequency Electromagnetic Field." *Lancet,* 351,1857-1858.

Bravo, G. (1996). "Physical Exercise Benefits Postmenopausal Women." *Journal of the American Geriatric Society*, 44, 756-762.

Brotons, J.A., et al. (1995). "Xenoestrogens Released from Lacquer Coatings in Food Cans. *Environmental Health Perspectives,* 103(6), 608-612.

Brouwer, A., et al. (1998). "Interactions of Persistent Environmental Organohalogens with the Thyroid Hormone System: Mechanisms and Possible Consequences for Animal and Human Health." *Toxicology and Industrial Health*, 14(1-2), 59-84.

Brush, M.G., et al. (1984). "Abnormal Essential Fatty Acid Levels in Plasma of Women with Premenstrual Syndrome." *American Journal of Obstetrics and Gynecology,* 150, 363-366.

Buckalew, L.W. and Rizuto, A. (1982). "Subjective Response to Negative Air Ion Exposure." *Aviation Space and Environmental Medicine*, 53(8), 822-823.

Budoff, P.W. (1983). "The Use of Prostaglandin Inhibitors for the Premenstrual Syndrome." *Journal of Reproductive Medicine*, 28, 469-478.

Buffington, C.A., et al. (1993). "Case Report: Amelioration of Insulin Resistance in Diabetes with Dehydroepiandrosterone." *American Journal of Medical Science,* 306, 320-324.

Campbell, D.G. (1997). *The Mozart Effect: Tapping the Power of Music to Heal the Body, Strengthen the Mind and Unlock the Creative Spirit.* New York: Avon.

Cara, L., et al. (1992). "Effects of Oat Bran, Rice Bran, Wheat Fiber, and Wheat Germ on Postprandial Lipemia in Healthy Adults." *American Journal of Clinical Nutrition*, 55(1), 81-88.

Carper, J. (1998). *Miracle Cures.* New York: HarperPerennial.

Casson, P.K., et al. (1993) "Oral Dehydroepiandrosterone in Physiological Doses Modulates Immune Function in Postmenopausal Women. *American Journal of Obstetrics and Gynecology.* 169,1536-1546.

Centers for Disease Control. (1998). *Morbidity and Mortality Weekly Report,* 47,1041-1043.

Chappell, L.T. and Stahl, J.P. (1993). "The Correlation Between EDTA Chelation Therapy and Improvement in Cardiovascular Function: A Meta-Analysis." *Journal of Advancement in Medicine*, 6(3), 139-160. Available from the American College for Advancement in Medicine (see Chapter 13, Note 2).

Charbonneau, J.E. (1997). "Recent Case Histories of Food Product-Metal Container Interactions Using Scanning Electron Microscopy-X-ray Microanalysis." *Scanning*, 19(7), 512-518.

Cheng, S. (1989). *The Tao of Voice*. New York: Destiny Books.

Chopra, D. (1993). *Ageless Body, Timeless Mind*. New York: Crown Publishers, Inc.

Cleare, A.J., et al. (1995). "Contrasting Neuroendocrine Responses in Depression and Chronic Fatigue Syndrome." *Journal of Affective Disorders*, 35, 283-289.

Civitelli, M., et al. (1992). "Dietary L-Lysine and Calcium Metabolism in Humans." *Nutrition*, 8(6), 100-105.

Cleary, M.P. (1991). "The Antiobesity Effect of Dehyroepi-androsterone in Rats." *Proceedings of the Society for Experimental Biology and Medicine*, 196, 8-16.

Clements, M.L., et al. (1983). "Exogenous Lactobacilli Fed to Man: Their Fate and Ability to Prevent Diarrheal Disease." *Progressive Education in Nutritional Science*, 7, 29-37.

Cohen, S., et al. (1997). "Social Ties and Susceptibility to the Common Cold", *Journal of the American Medical Association*, 277, 1940-1944.

Colditz, G.A. (1990). "The Nurses' Health Study: Findings During 10 Years of Follow-up of a Cohort of U.S. Women." *Current Problems in Obstetrics and Gynecology Fertility*, 13, 129-174.

Conteras, V. (1995). "Natural Method for Boosting Human Growth Hormone." *Journal of Longevity Research*, 1(8), 38-39.

Coogan, P., et al. (1996). "Occupational Exposure to 50-Hertz Magnetic Fields and Risk of Breast Cancer in Women." *Epidemiology*, 7, 459-464.

Cook, J.D. (1986). "Music as an Intervention in the Oncology Setting." *Cancer Nursing*, 9(1), 23-28.

Couillard, S., et al. (1998). "Effect of Dehydroepiandrosterone and the Antiestrogen EM-800 on Growth of Human ZR-75-1 Breast

Cancer Xenografts." *Journal of the National Cancer Institute,* 90, 772-777.

Cousins, N. (1979). *Anatomy of an Illness.* New York: W.W. Norton & Co.

Cranton, E.M. and Frackelton, J.P. (1998). "Free Oxygen Radical Pathology and EDTA Chelation Therapy: Mechanisms of Action." *Journal of Advancement in Medicine,* 11(4), 277-309. Available from the American College for Advancement in Medicine (see Chapter 13, Note 2).

Crook, W.G. (1997). *The Yeast Connection and the Woman.* Jackson, TN: Professional Books, Inc.

Cynober, L. (1994). "Can Arginine and Ornithine Support Gut Function?" *Gut,* 35(1Suppl), S42-45.

D'Adamo, P. (1997). *Eat Right 4 Your Type: The Individualized Diet Solution to Staying Healthy, Living Longer & Achieving Your Ideal Weight.* New York: Putman Publishing Group.

Dalton, K. (1977). *The Premenstrual Syndrome and Progesterone Therapy.* Chicago, IL: Year Book Medical Publishers, Inc.

Das Gupta, T.K. (1968). "Influence of the Pineal Gland on the Growth and Spread of Malignant Tumors." *Surgical Forum,* 19, 83-84.

Das Gupta, T.K. and Terz, J. (1967). "Influence of the Pineal Gland on the Growth and Spread of Malignant Tumors." *Surgical Forum,* 27, 1306-1311.

Dean, W. (1988). *Biological Aging Measurement: Clinical Applications.* Los Angeles: Center for Biogerontology.

Dean, W. (1997, November). "History of Anti-Aging Medicine," presented at Longevity Workshop, Fall American College for the Advancement of Medicine (ACAM) Meeting, Anaheim, CA.

DeMarco, C. (1997). *Take Charge of Your Body.* Winlaw, British Columbia, Canada: The Well Woman Press. Available from: 800-387-4761.

Dilman, V. and Dean, W. (in press). *The Neuroendocrine Theory of Aging and Degenerative Disease.* Pensacola, FL.: The Center for Bio-Gerontology.

Diplock, A.T. (1991). "Antioxidant Nutrients and Disease Prevention: An Overview." *American Journal of Clinical Nutrition,* 53,189s-193s.

Doig, C.J., et al. (1998). "Increased Intestinal Permeability is Associated with the Development of Multiple Organ Dysfunction Syndrome in Critically Ill Patients." *American Journal of Respiratory and Critical Care Medicine*, 158, 444-451.

Dorman, T., et al. (1995). "The Effectiveness of Stabilium 200 on Reducing Anxiety in College Students." *Journal of Advancement in Medicine*, 8(3), 193-200. (Available from the American College for Advancement in Medicine. See Chapter 13, Note 2.)

Dossey, L. (1996). *Prayer is Good Medicine: How to Reap the Healing Benefits of Prayer.* San Francisco: Harper San Francisco.

Drasch, G., et al. (1998). "Mercury in Human Colostrum and Early Breast Milk: Its Dependence on Dental Amalgam and Other Factors." *Journal of Trace Elements in Medicine and Biology*, 12, 23-27.

Eberlein-Konig, B., et al. (1998). "Protective Effect Against Sunburn of Combined Systemic Ascorbic Acid (Vitamin C) and D-Alpha Tocopherol (Vitamin E). *Journal of American Academy of Dermatology*, 38, 45-48.

Eisenberg, D. M., et al. (1998). "Trends in Alternative Medicine Use in the United States, 1990-1997: Results of a Follow-Up National Survey." *Journal of the American Medical Association*, 280,1569-1575.

El-Domeiri, A. and Das Gupta, T.K. (1973). "Reversal by Melatonin of the Effect of Pinealectomy on Tumor Growth." *Cancer Research*, 33, 2830-2833.

Epstein, O., et al. (1982). 'Vitamin D, Hydroxyapatite and Calcium Gluconate in Treatment of Cortical Bone Thinning in Postmenopausal Women with Primary Biliary Cirrhosis." *American Journal of Clinical Nutrition*, 36, 426-430.

Erdman, J.W., Jr. (1995). "Control of Serum Lipids with Soy Protein." *New England Journal of Medicine*, 333, 313-314.

Fazio, S., et al. (1996). "A Preliminary Study of Growth Hormone in the Treatment of Dilated Cardiomyopathy." *New England Journal of Medicine*, 334(13), 809-814.

Feychting, M. and Ahlbom, A. (1995). "Childhood Leukemia and Residential Exposure to Weak Extremely Low Frequency

Magnetic Fields." *Environmental Health Perspectives,* 103(Suppl. 2), 59-62.

Feskanich, D., et al. (1999). "Vitamin K Intake and Hip Fractures in Women: A Prospective Study." *American Journal of Clinical Nutrition,* 69, 74-79.

FitzGerald, G.A. (1998). "Increased F₂-Isoprostanes in Alzheimer's Disease: Evidence for Enhanced Lipid Peroxidation in Vivo. *"Federation of American Societies for Experimental Biology Journal,* 12, 1777-1783.

Fleet, J.C. and Mayer, J. (1997). "Dietary Selenium Repletion May Reduce Cancer Incidence in People at High Risk Who Live in Areas with Low Level Selenium." *Nutrition Reviews,* 55(7), 277-279.

Foster-Powell, I. And Miller, J.B. (1995). "International Tables of Glycemic Index." *American Journal of Clinical Nutrition,* 62(4), 871s-890s.

Gaitan, E., et al. (1967). "Identification of a Naturally Occurring Goitrogen in Water." *Transactions of the Association of the American Physicians,* 132, 141-152.

Garfinkel, D., et al. (1995). "Improvement of Sleep Quality in Elderly People by Controlled-Release Melatonin." *Lancet,* 346(8974), 541-544.

Gebbers, J.O. and Laissue, J.A..(1989). "Immunologic Structures and Functions of the Gut." *Schweiz Arch Tierheilk,* 131, 221-238.

Ghent, W.R., et al. (1993). "Iodine Replacement in Fibrocystic Disease of the Breast." *Canadian Journal of Surgery,* 35(5), 456-459.

Goodyear, L.J. and Kahn, B.B. (1998) "Exercise, Glucose Transport, and Insulin Sensitivity." *Annual Review of Medicine, 49, 235-261.*

Goyer, R.A. (1996). "Results of Lead Research: Prenatal Exposure and Neurological Consequences." *Environmental Health Perspectives,* 104(10),1050-1054.

Grady, D., et al. (1995). "Hormone Replacement Therapy and Endometrial Cancer Risk: A Meta-Analysis." *Obstetrics and Gynecology,* 85(2), 304-313.

Grahm, I.M., et al. (1997). "Plasma Homocysteine as a Risk Factor for Vascular Disease: The European Concerted Action Project." *Journal of the American Medical Association,* 227,1775-1781.

Gregg, E.W., et al. (1998). "Physical Activity and Osteoporotic Fracture Risk in Older Women." *Annals of Internal Medicine,* 129(2), 81-88.

Hancke, C. and Flytlie, K. (1993). "Benefits of EDTA Chelation Therapy in Arteriosclerosis: A Retrospective Study of 470 Patients." *Journal of Advancement in Medicine,* 6(3), 161-172. Available from the American College for Advancement in Medicine (see Chapter 13, Note 2).

Harman, D. (1981). "The Aging Process." *Proceedings of the National Academy of Science,* 78, 7124-7128.

Harp, J.B., et al. (1991). "Nutrition and Somatomedin. XXIII. Molecular Regulation of IGF-1 by Amino Acid Availability in Cultured Hepatocytes." *Diabetes,* 40(1), 95-101.

Hauser, P., et al. (1998). "Resistance to Thyroid Hormone: Implications for Neurodevelopment Research on the Effects of Thyroid Hormone Disruptors." *Toxicology and Industrial Health,* 14(1-2), 85-101.

Hayflick, L. and Butler, R.N. (1996). *How and Why We Age.* New York: Ballantine Books.

Heany, R. P. (1993). "Thinking Straight About Calcium." *New England Journal of Medicine,* 328(7), 503-505.

Hechter, O., et al. (1997). "Relationship of Dehydroepiandrosterone and Cortisol in Disease." *Medical Hypotheses,* 49, 85-91.

Herbert, J. (1998). "Neurosteroids, Brain Damage and Mental Illness." *Experimental Gerontology,* 7-8, 713-727.

Hixson, K., et. al. (1998). "The Relation Between Religiosity, Selected Health Behaviors and Blood Pressure." *Preventive Medicine,* 27, 545-552.

Holmes S. and Shalet, S. (1995). "Which Adults Develop Side-Effects of Growth Hormone Replacement?" *Clinical Endocrinology,* 43,143-149.

Hunt, C.M., et. al. (1992). "Effect of Age and Gender on the Activity of Human Hepatic CYP3A." *Biochemical Pharmacology,* 44, 275-283.

Isidori, A., et al. (1981). "A Study of Growth Hormone Release in Man After Oral Administration of Amino Acids." *Current Medical Research and Opinion*, 7(7), 475-481.

Ivanovic, S., et al. (1990). "The Urinary Dehydroepiandrosterone, Androsterone and Etiocholanolone Excretion of Healthy Women and Women with Benign and Malignant Breast Disease." *Journal of Clinical Pharmacy and Therapeutics*, 15(3), 213-219.

Jesse, R.L., et al. (1995). "Dehyroepiandrosterone Inhibits Human Platlet Aggregation In Vitro and In Vivo." *Annals of the New York Academy of Sciences*, 774, 281-290.

Kabat-Zinn, J. et. al. (1992). "Effectiveness of a Meditation-Based Stress Reduction Program in the Treatment of Anxiety Disorders." *American Journal of Psychiatry*, 149(7), 936-943.

Kahn, S. (1996). *The Nurse's Meditative Journal*. Albany, NY: Delmar Publishers. Available from: 800-347-7707.

Kalimi, M. and Regelson, W., (Eds.). (1990). *The Biologic Role of Dehydroepiandrosterone (DHEA)*. New York: Walter de Gruyter.

Kalmijn, S., et al. (1998). "A Prospective Study on Cortisol, Dehydroepiandrosterone Sulfate, and Cognitive Function in the Elderly." *Journal of Clinical Endocrinology and Metabolism*, 83(10), 3487-3492.

Kamen, B. (1997). *Hormone Replacement Therapy: Yes or No?: How to Make an Informed Decision about Estrogen, Progesterone, & Other Strategies for Dealing with PMS, Menopause & Osteoporosis*. Novato, CA: Nutrition Encounter. Available from: 415-883-5154.

Kamen, B. (1997). *New Facts About Fiber*. Novato, CA: Nutrition Encounter. Available from: 415-883-5154.

Kann, P. (1996). "Growth Hormone Substitution in Growth Hormone-Deficient Adults: Effects on Collagen Type 1 Synthesis and Skin Thickness." *Experiments in Clinical Endocrinology and Diabetes*, 104(4), 327-333.

Kaplan, K.H. et. al. (1993). "The Impact of Meditation-Based Stress Reduction Program on Fibromyalgia." *General Hospital Psychiatry*, 15(5) 284-289.

Katz, J.P., et al. (1998). "Rheumatologic Manifestations of Gastrointestinal Diseases." *Gastroenterology Clinics of North America*, 27(3), 533-562.

Kelley, K.W. (1992). "Growth Hormone, Prolactin and Insulin-Like Growth Factors: New Jobs for Old Players." *Brain, Behavior and Immunity*, 6, 317-326.

Kiecolt-Glaser, J. et. al. (1985). "Psychosocial Enhancement of Immunocompetence in a Geriatric Population." *Health Psychology*, 4, 24-41.

Kiecolt-Glaser, J., et. al. (1986). "Modulation of Cellular Immunity in Medical Students." *Journal of Behavioral Medicine*, 9, 5-21.

Klatz, R.M. (1999). *Hormones of Youth*. Chicago, IL: Sports Tech Labs, Inc.

Krueger, A.P. and Reed, E.J. (1976). "Biological Impact of Small Air Ions." *Science*, 193(4259), 1209-1213.

Kuiper, G.G., et al. (1988). "Interaction of Estrogenic Chemicals and Phytoestrogens with Estrogen Receptor Beta." *Endocrinology*, 129 (10), 4252-4263.

Kujala, U., et al. (1998). "Relationship of Leisure-Time Physical Activity and Mortality. *Journal of the American Medical Association*, 279, 440-444.

La Vecchia, C., et al. (1995). "Olive Oil, Other Dietary Fats, and the Risk of Breast Cancer." *Cancer Causes Control*, 6(6), 545-550.

Labrie, F. (1997). "Effect of 12-Month Dehydroepiandrosterone Replacement Therapy on Bone, Vagina and Endometrium in Postmenopausal Women." *Journal of Clinical Endocrinology and Metabolism*, 82, 3498-3505.

Lapcevic, J. (1997). "A New Biologically Active Thymic Protein to Stimulate Cell-Mediated Immunity." *Townsend Letter for Doctors & Patients, February-March*.

Lee, J.R. (1993). *Natural Progesterone: The Multiple Roles of a Remarkable Hormone*. Sebastopol, CA: BLL Publishing.

Lee, J.R. (1996). *What Your Doctor May Not Tell You About Menopause*. New York: Warner Books.

Lemcke, D.P., et al. (Eds.). (1995). *Primary Care of Women*. East Norwalk, CT: Appelton & Lange.

Liburdy, R.P., et al. (1993). "ELF Magnetic Fields, Breast Cancer, and Melatonin: 60 Hz Fields Block Melatonin's Oncostatic Action on ER+ Breast Cancer Cell Proliferation." *Journal of Pineal Research*, 14(2):89-97.

Lindgren, K. et al. (1999). "The Factor Structure of the Profile of Mood States (POMS) and its Relationship to Occupational Lead Exposure." *Journal of Occupational and Environmental Medicine*, 41, 3-10.

Lock, M. (1995). "Menopause: Lessons from Anthropology." Paper presented at the Annual Meeting of the North American Menopause Society, San Francisco, CA, September 21-23.

Love, S. (1997). *Dr. Susan Love's Hormone Book*. New York: Random House.

Luks A. and Payne P. (1991) *Healing Power of Doing Good: The Health and Spiritual Benefits of Helping Others*. New York: Ballantine.

MacFarlane, J.K. (1993). "Elemental Iodine: Relief for the Painful Breast?" *Canadian Journal of Surgery*, 35(5), 405.

MacIntosh, A. (1996). "Melatonin: Clinical Monograph." *Quarterly Review of Natural Medicine*, Spring, p. 52.

Maestroni, G., et al. (1988). "Role of the Pineal Gland in Immunity. Melatonin Antagonizes the Immuno-Suppressive Effects of Acute Stress Via an Opiatergic Mechanism." *Immunology*, 63, 465-469.

Marier, J.R. (1978). "Cardio-Protective Contribution of Hard Waters to Magnesium Intake. *Review Canadian Biology*, 37(2), 115-125.

Martin, R. (1997). *The Estrogen Alternative*. Rochester, VT: Healing Art Press.

Mattman, L. (1993). *Cell Wall Deficient Forms: Stealth Pathogens*. Boca Raton, FL.: CRC Press.

Mayer-Davis, E.J. (1998). "Intensity and Amount of Physical Activity in Relation to Insulin Sensitivity: The Insulin Resistance Atherosclerosis Study." *Journal of the American Medical Association*, 279, 669-674.

McCraty, R., et al. (1998). "The Impact of a New Emotional Self-Management Program on Stress, Emotions, Heart Rate Variability, DHEA and Cortisol." *Integrative Physiology and Behavioral Science*, 2,151-170.

McCully, K.S. (1997). *The Homocysteine Revolution*. New Canaan, CT.: Keats Publishing, Inc.

McFadden, S.A. (1996). "Phenotypic Variation in Xenobiotic Metabolism and Adverse Environmental Response: Focus on Sulfur-Dependent Detoxification Pathways." *Toxicology*, 111, 43-65.

Mecocci, P., et al. Al. (1994). "Oxidative Damage to Mitochondrial DNA Is Increased in Alzheimer's Disease." *Annals of Neurology*, 36, 747-751.

Melillo, K.D. (1998). "Clostridium Dificile and Older Adults: What Primary Care Providers Should Know."*The Nurse Practitioner*, 25-43.

Messina, J.J. (1996). "Hypothesized Health Benefits of Soybean Isoflavones." *Fundamentals of Applied Toxicology*, 30(1), 87.

Messina, J.J., et al. (1994). "Soy Intake and Cancer Risk: A Review of the In-Vitro and In-Vivo Data." *Nutrition Cancer*, 21,113-131.

Miluk-Kolasa, B., et al. (1994) "Effects of Music Treatment on Salivary Cortisol in Patients Exposed to Pre-Surgical Stress." *Experimental and Clinical Endocrinology*, 102, 118-120.

Mital, B.K and Garg, S.K. (1995). "Anticarcinogenic, Hypo-choesterolemic,and Antagonistic Activities of Lactobacillus Acidophilus." *Critical Review Microbiology*, 21(3):175-214.

Montalescot G, et al. (1997). "Plasma Homocysteine Levels and Mortality in Patients with Coronary Artery Disease." *New England Journal of Medicine*, 337(4), 230-236.

Morales, A.J., et al. (1994). "Effect of Replacement Doses of Dehydroepiandrosterone in Men and Women of Advancing Age." *Journal of Clinical Endocrinology and Metabolism*, 78, 1360-1367.

Morrola, J.F. and Yen, S.S.C. (1990). "The Effect of Oral Dehyroepiandrosterone on Endocrine-Metabolic Parameters in Postmenopausal Women." *Journal of Clinical and Endocrinological Metabolism*, 71, 696-704.

Morter, M.T. and Panfili, A. (1998). "The Body's Negative Response to Excess Dietary Protein Consumption." *The Journal of Orthomolecular Medicine*, 13(2), 89-94.

Morton, L.L. and Kershner, J.R. (1984). "Negative Air Ionizations Improves Memory and Attention in Learning-Disabled and Mentally Retarded Children." *Journal of Abnormal Child Psychology,* 12(2), 353-365.

Morton, L.L. and Kershner, J.R. (1987). "Negative Ion Effects on Hemispheric Processing and Selective Attention in the Mentally Retarded." *Mental Deficiencies Research,* 31(Pt2), 169-180.

Moses, A.C., et al. (1996). "Recombinant Human Insulin-Like Growth Factor I Increases Insulin Sensitivity and Improves Glycemic Control in Type II Diabetes." *Diabetes,* 45, 91-100.

Murray, M. (1996). *Encyclopedia of Nutritional Supplements.* Rocklin, CA. Prima Publishing.

Murray, R., et al. (1995). "Physiological and Performance Responses to Nicotinic-Acid Ingestion During Exercise." *Medical Science Sports Exercise,* 27(2), 1057-1062.

Nagel, S.C., et al. (1997). "Relative Binding Affinity-Serum Modified Access (RBA-SMA) Assay Predicts the Relative In-Vivo Bioactivity of the Xenoestrogens Bisphenol A and Octylphenol." *Environmental Health Perspective,* 105(1), 70-76.

Nakla, M.L., et al. (1998). "Ophthalmologic Effects of Bowel Disease." *Gastroenterology Clinics of North America,* 27(3), 697-711.

National Institutes of Health/National Cancer Institute. (1997). "62991-02 EMF and Breast Cancer." Available from: http://www.epa.gov/edrlupvx/inventory/NCI-018.html.

National Institutes of Health/National Cancer Institute. (1997). "63021-02 Epidemiology of Breast Cancer." Available from: http://www.epa.gov/edrlupvx/inventory/NCI-020.html.

Newton, J. and Maugh II, T. (1998, February 11). "Water Officials Suggest Prudence, Not Panic." *Los Angeles Times,* Home Edition, Part A, Metro Desk, p. 1.

Nitsch, A. and Nitsch, F.P. (1998). "The Clinical Use of Bovine Colostrum." *Journal of Orthomolecular Medicine,* 13(2), 110-118.

Nordin, C., et al. (1997). "Is the Cholesterol-Lowering Effect of Simvatatin Influenced by CYP2D6 Polymorphism?" *Lancet,* 350,29-30.

Notelovitz, M. and Tonnessen, D. (1993). *Menopause and Midlife Health.* New York: St Martin's.

Oelkers, W. (1996). "Adrenal Insufficiency." *New England Journal of Medicine*, 335(16), 1206-1211.

Okamoto, K. (1998). "Distribution of Dehyroepiandrosterone Sulfate and Relationships Between Its Level and Serum Lipid Levels in a Rural Japanese Population." *Journal of Epidemiology,* 8(5), 285-291.

Olszewer, E., et al. (1988). "EDTA Chelation Therapy in Chronic Degenerative Disease." *Medical Hypotheses*, 1, 41-49.

Oman, D. and Reed, D. (1998). "Religion and Mortality Among the Community-Dwelling Elderly." *American Journal of Public Health,* 88, 1469-1475.

Orne-Johnson, D. (1973). "Autonomic Stability and Transcendental Meditation." *Psychosomatic Medicine,* 35 (4): 341-349.

Ornish, D. (1990). *Dr. Dean Ornish's Program for Reversing Heart Disease*. New York: Ballantine.

Packer, L. (1995). "Alpha-Lipoic Acid as a Biological Antioxidant." *Free Radical Biology and Medicine,* 19(2), 227-250.

Padungtod, C., et. al. (1998). "Reproductive Hormone Profile Among Pesticide Factory Workers." *Journal of Occupational and Environmental Medicine,* 40,1038-1047.

Papadakis, M.A., et al. (1996). "Growth Hormone Replacement in Healthy Older Men Improves Body Composition but not Functional Ability." *Annals of Internal Medicine,* 124(8), 708-716.

Peeters, P.H., et al. (1995). "Age at Menarche and Breast Cancer Risk in Nulliparous Women." *Breast Cancer Research and Treatment*, 33 (1), 55-61.

Pierpaoli, W. and Maestroni, G. (1987). "Melatonin: a Principal Neuro-Immunoregulatory and Anti-Stress Hormone: Its Anti-Aging Effect." *Immunology Letters,* 16, 351-362.

Pollock, M., et al. (1998). "The Recommended Quantity and Quality of Exercise for Developing and Maintaining Cardiorespiratory and Muscular Fitness, and Flexibility in Healthy Adults." *Medical Science and Sports Exercise,* 30(6), 992-1008.

Popper, C.W. (1993). "Psychopharmacologic Treatment of Anxiety Ddisorders in Adolescents and Children." *Journal of Clinical Psychiatry*, 54S (52-63).

Prior, J.C. (1990). "Progesterone as a Bone-Trophic Hormone." *Endocrine Reviews,* 11(2), 386-398.

Raisz, L. and Prestwood, K. (1998). "Estrogen and the Risk of Fracture – New Data, New Questions." *New England Journal of Medicine,* 339,767-768.

Rako, S. (1996, September/October). "Testosterone Deficiency and Supplementation for Women: What Do We Need to Know?" *Menopause Management,* 10-15.

Rangavajhyala, N., et al. (1997). "Nonlipopolysaccharide Component(s) of Lactobacillus Acidophilus Stimulate(s) the Production of Interleukin-1Alpha and Tumor Necrosis Factor-Alpha by Murine Macrophages." *Nutrition and Cancer,* 28(2), 130-134.

Raskind, M., et al. (1994). "Hypothalamic-Pituitary-Adrenal Axis Regulation and Human Aging." *Annals of the New York Academy of Science,* 74, 327-335.

Redelmier, D.A., et al. (1998). "The Treatment of Unrelated Disorders in Patients with Chronic Medical Diseases." *New England Journal of Medicine,* 338(21), 1516-1520.

Regestein, Q.R. and Pavola, M. (1995). "Treatment of Delayed Sleep Phase Syndrome." *General Hospital Psychiatry,* 17(5), 335-345.

Reiter, R.J. (1996). *Melatonin.* New York: Bantam Books.

Rexrode, K.M., et al. (1998). "Abdominal Adiposity and Coronary Heart Disease in Women." *Journal of the American Medical Association,* 280, 1843-1848.

ReutersHealth/MedNews. (1998, December 9). "Cord Blood Transplantation an Option for Children with Genetic Disorders." Available from: http://www.reutershealth.com.

ReutersHealth/MedNews. (1996, January 11). "Genelabs Says DHEA Benefits Lupus Patients." Available from: http:www.reuters health.com.

ReutersHealth/MedNews. (1997, December 17). "Holiday Cards Do Spread Cheer." Available from: http://www.reutershealth.com.

ReutersHealth/MedNews. (1998, July 10). "Ignorance About Environmental Toxins Threaten Children's Health." Available from: http//:www.reutershealth/mednews.

ReutersHealth/MedNews. (1998, May 26). "Volunteering Enhances Well-Being of Retirees." Available from: http://www.reuters health.com.

ReutersHealth/MedNews.(1998, May 19). "Mobile Telephone Use May Be Associated With Headaches, Fatigue." Available from: http//:www.reutershealth/mednews.

Rider, M.S. (1985). "The Effect of Music, Imagery, and Relaxation on Adrenal Corticosteroids and the Re-Entrainment of Circadian Rhythms." *Journal of Music Therapy,* 22, 46-58.

Rodale Press (1991). *Prevention Magazines' Giant Book of Health Facts.* Erasmus, PA: Rodale Press.

Roemmich, J.N. and Rogol, A.D. "Exercise and Growth Hormone: Does One Affect the Other?" *Journal of Pediatrics,* 131(1 Pt. 2), S75-80.

Rowe, J.W. and Kahn, R.L. (1998). *Successful Aging.* New York: Pantheon.

Rozenberg, S., et al. (1988). "Serum Levels of Gonadotrophins and Steroid Hormones in the Post-Menopause and Later Life." *Maturitas,* 10(3), 215-224.

Rubino, S., et al. (1998). "Neuroendocrine Effect of a Short-Term Treatment with DHEA in Postmenopausal Women." *Maturitas,* 28(3), 251-257.

Rudman, D., et al. (1990). "Effects of Human Growth Hormone in Men Over 60 Years Old." *New England Journal of Medicine,* 323(1), 1-6.

Rudolph, C.J. (1991). "A Nonsurgical Approach to Obstructive Carotid Stenosis Using EDTA Chelation." *Journal of Advancement in Medicine,* 4(3), 157-166. Available from the American College for Advancement in Medicine (see Chapter 13, Note 2).

Rudolph, C.J., et al. (1988). "The Effect of Intravenous Disodium Ethylenediaminetetraacetic Acid (EDTA) Upon Bone Density Levels." *Journal of Advancement in Medicine,* 1(2), 79-85. Available from the American College for Advancement in Medicine (see Chapter 13, Note 2).

Rylander, R., et al. (1991). "Magnesium and Calcium in Drinking Water and Cardiovascular Mortality." *Scandinavian Journal of Work and Environmental Health,* 17, 91-94.

Sandborgh-Englund, G., et al. (1998). "Mercury in Biological Fluids After Amalgam Removal," *Journal of Dental Research,* 77(4), 615-624.

Schiffrin, E.J., et al. (1995). "Immunomodulation of Human Blood Cells Following the Ingestion of Lactic Acid Bacteria." *Journal of Dairy Science,* 78(3), 491-497.

Sears, B. and Lawren, B. (1995), *The Zone: A Dietary Road Map to Lose Weight Permanently: Reset Your Genetic Code, Prevent Disease, Achieve Maximum Physical Performance.* New York: HarperCollins.

Second World Congress for Electricity and Magnetism in Biology and Medicine. (1997). Available from: http://info-ventures. com/emf/meetings.

Seidl, M.M. and Stewart, D.E. (1988). "Alternative Treatments for Menopausal Symptoms: Systematic Review of Scientific and Lay Literature." *Canadian Family Physician,* 44, 1299-1309.

Seeman,T.E., *et al.* (1997). "Price of Adaptation – Allostatic Load and Its Health Consequences: MacArthur Studies of Successful Aging." *Archives of Internal Medicine,* 157, 2259-2268.

Shalet, S.M. (1998). "Growth Hormone Therapy for Adult Growth Hormone Deficiency." *International Journal of Clinical Practice,* 52(2),108-111.

Shekhar, P.V., et al. (1997). "Environmental Estrogen Stimulation of Growth and Estrogen Receptor Function in Preneoplastic and Cancerous Human Breast Cell Lines." *Journal of the National Cancer Institute,* 89(23), 1743-1744.

Shelly, M.W. (1972). "A Theory of Happiness As It Relates to Transcendental Meditation" (Research paper). Department of Psychology, University of Kansas, Lawrence, KS.

Sherrill, D.L., et al. (1998). "Association of Physical Activity and Human Sleep Disorders," *Archives of Internal Medicine,* 158, 1894-1898.

Seraino, S. (1992). "The Effect of Flaxseed Supplementation on the Initiation and Promotional Stages of Mammary Tumorgenesis." *Nutrition and Cancer,* 17(2),153-159.

Smith, B.L. (1993). "Organic Foods vs. Supermarket Foods: Element Levels. *Journal of Applied Nutrition ,*43,35-39.

Smith, S. and Schiff, I. (1989). "The Premenstrual Syndrome – Diagnosis and Management." *Fertility and Sterility,* 52, 527-543.

Speiser, R. (1998). "The Health Impacts of Environmental Pollution." Presented at the National Environmental Health Association 68th Annual Educational Conference, June 29, 1998.

Stahl, F., et al. (1992). "Dehydroepiandrosterone (DHEA) Levels in Patients with Prostatic Cancer, Heart Diseases and Under Surgery Stress." *Experiments in Clinical Endocrinology and Diabetes,* 99(2), 68-70.

Steinbrook, R. (1998). "Patients With Multiple Chronic Conditions – How Many Medications Are Enough?" *New England Journal of Medicine,* 338(21), 1541-1542.

Steventon, G.B., et al. (1989). "Xenobiotic Metabolism in Parkinson's Disease." *Neurology,* 39, 883-887.

Steventon, G.B., et al. (1990). "Xenobiotic Metabolism in Alzheimer's Disease." *Neurology,* 40, 1095-1098.

Stohs, S.J. and Bagchi, D. (1995). "Oxidative Mechanisms in the Toxicity of Metal Ions." *Free Radical Biology & Medicine,* 18(2), 321-336.

Straub, R.H., et al. (1998)."Association of Humoral Markers of Inflammation and Dehydroepiandrosterone Sulfate or Cortisol Serum Levels in Patients with Chronic Inflammatory Bowel Disease." *American Journal of Gastroenterology,* 11, 2197-2202.

Svec, F. and Porter, J.R. (1998). "The Actions of Exogenous Dehydroepiandrosterone in Experimental Animals and Humans." *Proceedings of the Society for Experimental Biology and Medicine,* 2181, 174-191.

Svec, F., et al. (1995). "The Effect of DHEA Given Chronically in Zucker Rats." *Proceedings of the Society for Experimental Biology and Medicine,* 209, 92-97.

Takabe, K., et al. (1998). "Anisakidosis: A Course of Intestinal Obstruction From Eating Sushi." *American Journal of Gastroenterology,* 93,1172-1173.

Tamarkin, L., et al. (1982). "Decreased Nocturnal Plasma Melatonin Peak in Patients with Estrogen Receptor Positive Breast Cancer." *Science,* 26, 1003-1005.

Tanner, C.M., et al. (1999). "Parkinson's Disease in Twins: An Etiologic Study." *Journal of the American Medical Association,* 281, 341-346.

Terman, M. and Terman, J.S. (1995). "Treatment of Seasonal Affective Disorder with a High-Output Negative Ionizer. *Journal of Alternative and Complementary Medicine,* 1(1), 87-92.

Thompson, J.L., et al. (1998). "Effects of Human Growth Hormone, Insulin-Like Growth Factor 1, and Diet and Exercise on Body Composition of Obese Postmenopausal Women." *Journal of Clinical Endocrinology and Metabolism,* 83, 1477-1484.

Thompson, L.U. (1991). "Mammalian Lignan Production from Various Food." *Nutrition and Cancer,* 16, 43-52.

Tintera, J.W. (1955). "The Hypoadrenal State and Its Management."*New York State Journal of Medicine*, 55, 1-35.

Toffler, A. (1990). *Third Wave.* New York: Bantam Books.

Tompkins, P. and Christopher, B. (1989). *The Secret Life of Plants.* New York: HarperCollins Publishers.

Trichopoulou, A., et al. (1995). "Consumption of Olive Oil and Specific Food Groups in Relation to Breast Cancer Risk in Greece." *Journal of the National Cancer Institute,* 87(2), 110-116.

United States Environmental Protection Agency, Office of Air & Radiation, Office of Air Quality Planning & Standards (1997). "Health and Environmental Effects of Ground-Level Ozone." Available from: http://ttnwww.rtpnc.epa.gov/naaqsfin/o3health.htm.

Updike, P. (1990). "Music Therapy Results for ICU Patients." *Applied Research,* 9(1), 39-45.

Vihko, R. and Apter, D. (1984). "Endocrine Characteristics of Adolescent Menstrual Cycles: Impact of Early Menarche." *Journal of Steroid Biochemistry,* 20(1), 231-236.

Visioli, F., et al. (1998). "Free Radical-Scavenging Properties of Olive Oil Polyphenols." *Biochemical and Biophysical Research Communciation,* 247(1), 60-64.

Vita, A.J., et al. (1998). "Aging, Health Risks, and Cumulative Disability." *New England Journal of Medicine,* 338,1035-1041.

Wade, N. (1998, November 6.) "Scientists Cultivate Cells at Root of Human Life." *New York Times,* p. A1.

Walford, R. (1995). *The Anti-Aging Plan: Strategies and Recipes for Extending Your Healthy Years.* New York: Four Walls Eight Windows.

Wall Street Journal Interactive. (1998, May 14). "Overuse of Antibiotics Threatens World Health, Report Says". Available from http://www.wsj.com.

Wang, D. and Kurzer, M.S. (1996). "Effects of Isoflavones, Flavonoids and Lignans on Proliferation of Estrogen-Dependent and Independent Human Breast Cancer Cells." *Proceedings of the American Association for Cancer Research,* 37, 277.

Wei, Y.H. and Dao, S.H. (1996). "Mitochondrial DNA Mutations and Lipid Peroxidation in Human Aging." In Berdanier, C.D. and Hargrove, J.L. (Eds.) *Nutrients and Gene Expression,* Boca Raton: CRC Press, pp. 165-188.

Weinberg, K. and Parkman, R. (1995). "Age, the Thymus, and T Lymphocytes." *New England Journal of Medicine,* 332, 182-183.

Whiteside, T.L. and Herberman, R.B. (1993). "The Role of Natural Killer Cells in Human Disease." *Journal of Clinical Immunology and Immunopathy,* 53,1-23.

Willatts, P., et al. (1998). "Effect of Long-Chain Polyunsaturated Fatty Acids in Infant Formulas on Problem Solving at 10 Months of Age. *Lancet,* 352 (9129), 688-691.

Witsell, D.L., et al. (1995). "Effect of Lactobacillus Acidophilus on Antibiotic-Associated Gastrointestinal Morbidity: A Prospective Randomized Trial." *Journal of Otolaryngology,* 24 (4), 230-233.

WNET. (1993). *Healing and the Mind* [video] New York. Public Broadcasting Service.

Wright, J.V. and Morgenthaler, J. (1997). *Natural Hormone Replacement For Women Over 45.* Petaluma, CA: Smart Publications.

Wyatt, J., et al. (1993). "Intestinal Permeability and the Prediction of Relapse in Crohn's Disease." *Lancet,* 341, 1437-1439.

Yang R., et al. (1995). "Growth Hormone Improves Cardiac Performance in Experimental Heart Failure." *Circulation,* 92(2), 262-267.

Index

About the
Corsello Centers for Integrative Medicine

Dr. Serafina Corsello oversees a highly-skilled and interactive staff, which includes physicians, nurse practitioners, nutritionists, psychotherapists, biofeedback specialists and other specialized integrative healthcare associates.

Corsello Center: Manhattan
200 W. 57th Street
New York, NY 10019
516-271-0222

Corsello Center: Long Island
175 E. Main Street
Huntington, NY 11743
212-399-0222

Book and Product Orders
Corsello Communications, Inc.
Global Nutrition
175 E. Main Street
Huntington, NY 11743

888-461-0949
Webstite: http//www.corsello.com

The AGELESS WOMAN

Check ❏   AmEx ❏   Discover ❏   MC ❏   Visa ❏

Account No. _____ Exp. _____

Print Your Name _____

Your Signature _____

Address _____

_____

City/State/Zip _____

Daytime Telephone (   ) _____

E-mail _____

Allow 3-4 weeks for delivery (USPS).

Quantity	Amount	S&H	Add
_____	$19.95	$19.95 or less	$4
Subtotal	$_____	$20.00 - $39.99	$7
Shipping & Handling	$_____	$40.00 - $59.99	$10
		$60.00 - $99.99	$15
Sales Tax (NY only) 8.25%	$_____	Add $9 to S&H charges for 2-Day UPS. Call for bulk and foreign orders.	
Total (US funds)	$_____		